Personal Consultancy

Making the case for an integrated approach to the practices of counselling, psychotherapy and coaching, *Personal Consultancy* provides a coherent and systematic framework for working with clients. Nash Popovic and Debra Jinks use their experience in the area of integrative practice to demonstrate how this wider approach can be a more comprehensive way of helping clients than either coaching or counselling alone.

The authors explain how a range of techniques and approaches from various one-to-one practices can be brought together under the framework of Personal Consultancy, creating a method that is systematic, ethical and professional but not limited by any particular theoretical bias or preconception. With chapters by guest authors who discuss their perspectives on the approach and its application across various contexts, *Personal Consultancy* demonstrates that it is possible to combine the reparative work normally associated with counselling with the more proactive, goal-oriented approach of coaching. The result is a method that allows clients to have their counselling and coaching needs met within one relationship and which allows the practitioner more flexibility and freedom.

Personal Consultancy will be essential reading for practising coaches and counsellors, especially those already integrating the two approaches or those looking to do so, as well as for students and those in training.

Nash Popovic is a director of the Personal Well-Being Centre, a senior lecturer at the University of East London and a Personal Consultant in private practice. He runs the Postgraduate Certificate in Integrative Counselling and Coaching, the first programme of its kind in the UK, and has published and presented extensively on Personal Consultancy.

Debra Jinks has a particular interest in the interface between coaching and therapy and is a pioneer in the promotion of integration of the two disciplines. She is a freelance Personal Consultant, trainer and supervisor at Debra Jinks Consulting and the Personal Well-Being Centre, and is the Founding Chair of the Association for Integrative Coach–Therapist Professionals (AICTP).

Personal Consultancy

A model for integrating counselling and coaching

Nash Popovic and Debra Jinks

Routledge
Taylor & Francis Group

LONDON AND NEW YORK

First published 2014
by Routledge
27 Church Road, Hove, East Sussex BN3 2FA

and by Routledge
711 Third Avenue, New York, NY 10017

Routledge is an imprint of the Taylor & Francis Group, an informa business

British Library Cataloguing in Publication Data
A catalogue record for this book is available from the British Library

Library of Congress Cataloging in Publication Data
Popovic, N. (Nash)
Personal consultancy : a model for integrating counselling and
coaching / Nash Popovic and Debra Jinks. -- First Edition.
pages cm
Includes bibliographical references.
1. Counseling. 2. Personal coaching. I. Jinks, Debra. II. Title.
BF636.6.P67 2013
361'.06--dc23
2013017109

ISBN: 978-0-415-83392-9 (hbk)
ISBN: 978-0-415-83393-6 (pbk)
ISBN: 978-1-315-88255-0 (ebk)

Typeset in Times
by Saxon Graphics Ltd, Derby

We are very proud to dedicate this book to our parents Ivanka and Dragoljub Popovic and Pat and Frank Stuart.

Contents

About the contributors

Linda Aspey is a Fellow of BACP, and a psychotherapist–counsellor and executive coach, with over 25 years of experience in personal and professional development working with leaders and leadership teams. She is Managing Director of Coaching for Leaders, was Founding Chair of the BACP Coaching Division and is now Honorary President of the Association of Integrative Coach–Therapist Professionals (AICTP).

Sarah Baker is a PhD research student and teaches coaching psychology at the University of Bedfordshire. Her doctorate research focuses on investigating practitioners' views of the boundary between counselling and coaching. The research aims to identify whether discrete areas of practice for coaching and counselling disciplines can be established. She has also provided research consultancy to the Open University.

Ann Collins has had over 17 years of HR experience within the telecoms, computing and media industries, leaving corporate life as an HR Director. With a BSc (Hons) Psychology degree, she is also a qualified coach and counsellor and has over 15 years of experience working within the private and public sectors, including the probationary service, EAP work, the volunteer sector and her own private practice.

Siobhan Dunleavy is the business manager for a social enterprise organisation that offers coaching, counselling, consultancy and training. She has a degree in psychology and a particular interest in health psychology. In addition she is MBTI qualified.

Jayne Hildreth works as a freelance Personal Consultant, coach and trainer, with a corporate speciality in health and well-being and a particular interest in the area of integration and workplace stress. Jayne is co-director of Integrate Training who offer training in Personal Consultancy and director and founder member of the Association of Integrative Coach–Therapist Professionals (AICTP).

Yannick Jacob has worked with private clients as a coach and Personal Consultant since 2011. He is also a practising mediator, teacher, trainer and devoted academic involved in personal development projects in the UK and Germany as well as being a guest lecturer at the University of East London and the Danish Institute for Study Abroad. He is the social networking specialist for the Association of Integrative Coach–Therapist Professionals (AICTP).

Gordon Jinks is a principal lecturer in the School of Psychology at the University of East London, where he is the programme leader for the MA/Postgraduate Diploma in Counselling and Psychotherapy. He is an integrative counsellor and trainer with particular interest in the client's experience of therapy.

Carolyn Mumby is a qualified and experienced coach–therapist, trainer and supervisor, with over 20 years' experience of facilitating personal and organisational development. She has a particular interest in developing the Personal Consultancy model for use with young people and works directly as a Personal Consultant with adults, particularly those in the creative industries.

Lesley Symons is an executive coach practising in Australia and the UK. Her background includes a 20-year career in management in the retail and fast-moving consumer goods sector, then subsequent training as a psychotherapist. For the past seven years Lesley has coached leaders across a wide range of industries in the business sector focusing on general management and chief executive officer level. Lesley heads up the international division at the Association of Integrative Coach–Therapist Professionals (AICTP).

Preface

Nash: How do new ideas and concepts come about? Two conditions seem to be necessary: growing dissatisfaction with existing concepts and ideas is one; and a sometimes chance trigger that unleashes this dissatisfaction in an act of constructive creation is another. In my case, dissatisfaction had been brewing for a long time, probably from the beginning of my career as a one-to-one practitioner. The inadequacy of the very names used (counselling, therapy, coaching) contributed to this dissatisfaction; however, in retrospect, probably the most important factor was the failure in many cases to see a tangible behavioural change after internal conflicts were explored and successfully addressed. The chance 'trigger', on the other hand, was a question. After I published a polemical article in *Therapy Today* in 2001, I was contacted by a colleague and friend with whom I had studied existential counselling and psychotherapy years before. He said that he was getting trained in CBT to complement his way of working, and he asked me what I was currently practising.

This question made me stop and think. It occurred to me that, whilst I still held the existential way of working in high regard, I certainly did not practise 'pure' existentialism. And yet, alarmingly, this way of practising was never clearly formulated. I was always aware that this profession had a strong tacit element, but, for the sake of clients and practitioners alike, an open and clear formulation of one's way of working is required. To achieve this I had to 'clear the table' and start from the absolutely necessary conditions for any one-to-one practice. This quickly led to visual representations (diagrams) of the Personal Consultancy model. One of them was sent to my friend as my reply to his questions. However, it took years to check the validity of the model and refine the arguments in support of this way of working.

The first attempt to publish the results of this endeavour was not successful. The article was rejected. 'Integration? No, thank you.' The time was not right. This did not last long, though. More and more practitioners recognised that integration was on the cards, especially since coaching had become a reputable player. With some minor modifications, the original article was published for the first time in 2007. Since then, Personal Consultancy has attracted increasing interest, as evidenced by voluminous correspondence as well as a steady influx of practitioners who wanted to be trained in this approach even though no formal accreditation was offered. More publications followed, but all of this was more like a ripple than a real wave – that is, until Debra appeared on the scene. She was instrumental in pushing the whole issue of integration to a different level, so I would like to hand the rest of this preface to her.

Debra: I can't claim any credit for creating the Personal Consultancy model as this really is Nash's brainchild. However, since being interested and involved I've helped to develop and refine it. Perhaps my biggest contribution has been my passion for the model that has been the driving force behind launching it onto a bigger stage. More recently, as my conviction and confidence has grown, this has been a deliberate process. But initially my journey began as a curious and somewhat naive outsider. My interest in Personal Consultancy developed quite by accident. I'd had reservations about keeping the disciplines separate due to an experience with a coaching client whose pattern was to be highly motivated for a few weeks and then lose all confidence and almost break down in every sense of the word. He would disengage from the process and then emerge and want to try again. The repertoire available to me under the coaching umbrella just didn't offer the opportunity to explore in any depth what might be derailing him in this way and I thought that if I could wear my counselling hat for a couple of sessions he might very well develop important insights into these patterns. However, my supervisor at the time was adamant that doing this would be outside the boundaries of the coaching contract and that if he needed therapeutic input he should get it elsewhere. I followed the guidance offered by my supervisor but it didn't sit right with me. So, when required to write an essay about ethical dilemmas for the Masters Programme I was studying at Hull University, I chose the experience with my client to explore as an ethical dilemma. While doing the research for this, my frustration grew when I realised that, even if I made the choice to work across the boundary of coaching and therapy, at the time appropriate support from the professional bodies was not available.

However, a chink of light came into vision when I unearthed the article about Personal Consultancy. I remember thinking it seemed somewhat radical at the time but I also remember feeling very excited. This was the beginning of my journey. My interest was ignited, I wanted to explore the topic further and the focus for my Master's dissertation became what other practitioners thought about the concept and practice of Personal Consultancy. Around that time I had just joined LinkedIn and, as a somewhat social networking novice, I posed a question on one of the groups to see what response I would receive. My thoughts were that this could be the way to test the water about this subject. I was overwhelmed by the response both in terms of numbers but also in the passion it aroused in practitioners on either side of the coin. The thread later enabled me to find people to interview and helped me to shape my questions for my research. However, the unintended result was that it gave people who believed in coach–therapy integration a voice and something of a platform.

Looking back I think it was the start of a new community of practitioners who had previously been operating beneath the radar, in isolation and sometimes even in fear. Since then Nash and I have combined our resources to take the Personal Consultancy model further. We have shaped and refined it and considered different applications. We've talked at conferences, universities and written an article – and now this book – in the hope of reaching a wider audience. The most important thing is, though, that we do not feel alone any more. The community of integrative practitioners is growing on a daily basis, but that is another story.

Acknowledgements

Our special thanks go to the contributors to this volume, who have made Personal Consultancy come alive by providing varied contexts for its application. We are grateful to the team at Routledge for helping us make this project a reality and a pleasant journey; we would particularly like to thank Katharine Atherton and Joanne Forshaw for their guidance and Chris Shaw for his patience and warmth. It is also important to express our gratitude to Professor Stephen Palmer, who very generously read through our first draft and gave valuable feedback. Last – but certainly not least – we thank our clients, who have been an ongoing inspiration and without whom Personal Consultancy would not have been created.

On a more personal level:

NASH: I would like to thank my partner Wendi Adamek for her feedback and continuous personal, emotional and professional support.

DEBRA: First, I'd like to thank my grown up kids, Francis and Abigail for their enduring support and belief in me; my sister Jayne who has been part of this journey and most of the other important journeys in my life; and finally, my husband Gordon for his patience, encouragement and love and because he is and always will be an inspiration to me.

Introduction

Personal Consultancy and integration

This book is about the concept of Personal Consultancy – an integrative approach to *one-to-one talking practices.* 'Integrative' in this context refers to the range of approaches currently encompassed by counselling, psychotherapy and coaching. Thus, Personal Consultancy is a framework that not only integrates counselling and coaching, but also various counselling and psychotherapeutic approaches. Such integration is a focus of considerable interest at this time in the UK and across the globe.

The book is intended for practitioners who are interested in working in an integrative way and for undergraduate and postgraduate courses and programmes. In the past, counselling and coaching training have been clearly demarcated. However, there are a growing number of undergraduate and postgraduate programmes that have started offering both (e.g. coaching modules on counselling programmes). There is little doubt that integration is a hot topic in need of materials that addresses the subject in a systematic and coherent way.

The Personal Consultancy model is offered as a framework for integration. The purpose of this volume is to describe Personal Consultancy as a framework for integration from a theoretical perspective and also in terms of how to use it with clients. Case study examples are provided to illustrate its application in a variety of contexts and with a variety of issues. This model is already much discussed on courses, at conferences, in seminars, networking meetings and professional forum sites. A number of articles and a book chapter on the topic of Personal Consultancy have already been published. Moreover, both authors are founder members of the Association of Integrative Coach–Therapist Professionals (AICTP) that attracts interest around the world. This professional body has been established to support and guide those practitioners who already choose to work in an integrated way or wish to pursue this direction in the future. So the aim of the book is to contribute to this growing trend and to satisfy a demand for material that will inform practitioners about how they can advance their practice, how they can define themselves professionally and how they can position themselves in the marketplace.

The context

In order to understand the need for such integration we will situate Personal Consultancy in the context of current and past developments. In Chapter 1 we summarise some existing approaches that this framework draws upon. However, we also think that some philosophical, scientific, social, cultural and political factors need to be acknowledged. It seems to us that Socrates, for example, has at least as much right to a place at the table as Freud when considering an approach that values personal development and operates on the principle of helping the client to help themselves. Facilitating individual growth and development through the 'practice of talking and listening' is not a recent invention and has its roots in Ancient Greece. We will turn to this first.

Philosophical

Socrates revolutionised our world in many ways, but what is particularly relevant to our practice is his method of enquiry. Before Socrates, most people exercised persuasion (often forcefully) by the strength of their arguments, and they still do. It is in our nature to believe that if we think we are right, everybody else should think the same. Socrates took a different route. He was posing questions rather than proving pre-contemplated answers – 'I know I don't know, so let's arrive to a conclusion together' was his way. Such a radical departure from the usual attempts to influence people resonates with one-to-one practices today, where the aim is to facilitate deeper insights and help the client get to the bottom of a situation. So-called 'Socratic dialogue' is a common practice among many professionals in this trade.

There is another fundamental discovery that occurred in the distant past. The Roman Emperor Marcus Aurelius, influenced by the ideas of the Greeks and the Stoics, articulated it in the following way: 'If you are distressed by anything external, the pain is not due to the thing itself, but to your estimate of it, and this you have the power to revoke at any moment.' In other words, it is not the *problem* that is the problem but the way that we look at it. This insight is pivotal to what we, as professionals, do and its value can never be underestimated. In many respects this is the foundation of one-to-one talking practices today, influencing just about every approach. Rational Emotive Behaviour Therapy (REBT), based on the premise that if people are able to change their beliefs, they can change their feelings and behaviour, is an obvious example.

Scientific and technological

There is no doubt that the scientific and technological revolution has changed the world. It has also changed one-to-one practice, sometimes in obvious and sometimes in subtle ways. For example, Pavlov, Watson and Skinner's attempts to put psychology on a scientific footing gave rise to Behavioural Therapy. Freud, too, was influenced by the focus on causality and reductionism in science. The nature–nurture debate and the issue of free will is at the heart of any one-to-one practice. We all have to think hard about where we stand in this respect. After all, if it were all about our genes, would not our profession be redundant? Technological breakthroughs are also changing the world at an ever-increasing rate and present new challenges and opportunities to professionals. How to use Skype™, e-mails and other technological devices in our practice is something that our predecessors did not need to think about.

Social and educational

Beside the philosophical and scientific roots we would also like to acknowledge contributions of other social practices and professions that focus on helping, caring, educating, guiding and developing. This is not the space to go into detail on a subject that deserves a volume of its own, so we will mention just one example of a Brazilian educator, Paolo Freire. In the tradition of Rousseau and Dewey, he instigated an approach to teaching and learning through self-discovery, experimentation and creativity – principles that are nowadays also at the heart of coaching practice. Such cross-fertilisation of various social disciplines and practices is likely to continue. We find the influence of systemic theory based on the premise that an individual can only be fully understood in the context of their family and culture particularly promising.

Cultural

In fact, probably the whole of Western culture would benefit from being seen in a more systemic way. There is no doubt that it has influenced other cultures, but in turn it has been influenced and shaped by other cultures too. The same applies to talking practices. For example, Erikson (1968) developed his conceptual model 'Psychosocial stages of development' after fieldwork with Native Americans (see Chapter 9). The Navaho Native Americans and Australian Aboriginal communities may be examples of societies in which different generations are far better integrated (Walker, 1993; Leonard, 2011), with the elders usually playing a greater role especially in educating the youth. Learning from mechanisms that other cultures use to help those who are going through difficulties could contribute to our profession opening up to innovative solutions and being more creative. For instance, professional healers such as *shamans* stay with their 'clients' with psychological issues as long as necessary – there is no time limit to their session! Some of our colleagues in this country are now using the same principle. We hope to see more cross-cultural exchanges that could enrich our practice.

Political

Political shifts and social movement in the second half of the twentieth century also had an enormous influence on one-to-one talking practices. After the Second World War a good part of humanity was traumatised by the horrors of the Holocaust, atomic bomb and other atrocities, as well as the potentially even worse consequences of the ensuing Cold War. For the first time psychotherapy was used on a massive scale. Carl Rogers, the founder of person-centred therapy, admitted that his way of working was greatly influenced by the experience he had with war veterans. This period was also characterised by massive technological advancements, better standards of living and the steep rise in individualism that took psychology and psychotherapy into the uncharted territories of the human psyche. Every decade since has brought further social and political changes and our profession has had to adapt to them quickly.

The 1950s saw changes such as the struggle for colonial liberation, racial and gender liberation and cultural liberation (especially prominent in music). These trends continued with even greater force throughout the 1960s. Challenging the establishment become a norm rather than an exception on popular media such as radio and television at that time. By the late 1960s there was social unrest around the world, the anti-war and anti-racial segregation demonstrations in the United States, riots in Paris and Prague, and the first strikes by female workers demanding equal pay in the UK. The mood of the time also brought a different perspective to one-to-one practices as individuals were experiencing greater independence than ever before. This was echoed in a gradual move away from focusing on the pathology and seeing the practitioner as an expert. Michel Foucault, Thomas Szasz and R. D. Laing challenged the fundamental assumptions and principles of psychiatry, asserting that definitions of diagnoses and disorders are an inadequate way of understanding and intervening in mental health. One result of this 'anti-spychiatry' movement was a more holistic and empowering way of approaching problems in one-to-one practices. Individualism, but also greater awareness of difference and diversity, and a need to consider the kinds of support that diverse groups and individuals might require led to an unprecedented proliferation of approaches: psychoanalysis that had dominated the field for decades became just one approach among many. Practice became more complex, but this complexity also indicated greater maturity – 'coming of age'.

In the 1970s, the two world wars were included in history textbooks in UK schools – they became history in the real sense of the word, especially for new generations. Buzz words of the time were freedom, independence, opportunity and possibility. Social class was no longer seen to be something that was fixed as it had been in the past and there was a sense (for some people at least) that if a person worked hard enough they could shape their own destiny. Education was no longer seen as a privilege of the few and grants were available in the UK to support young people who wished to go to university. In parallel, consumerism became a norm and young people of the time were no longer prepared to save and wait in order to fulfil their desires as their parents used to. At that time, counselling, largely based on the principles of humanistic psychology, and moving further away from pathologising clients, became a force to be reckoned with.

The 1980s witnessed the collapse of communism in Eastern Europe as well as a fresh wave of optimism and belief that wealth and affluence can keep increasing indefinitely. The name 'yuppie' was coined for a burgeoning new breed of young urban professionals who had in common a hunger for social status and material wealth, excessive consumption and, some might say, a lack of taste. For those who were left behind, cheap loans and credit cards were readily available. Perhaps unsurprisingly, coaching appeared and rapidly grew in this period. It was sometimes even considered a status symbol for aspiring leaders and executives. Because of the focus on performance and goals and the association with the business world, coaching held none of the stigma attached to therapeutic approaches. Despite a number of crises and an ever-increasing gap between the rich and the poor, the march of confidence and optimism continued unabated for a while. This also fuelled, at the turn of the century, the meteoric rise of Positive Psychology that focuses on well-being, happiness and an individual's strengths rather than on problems, weaknesses or deficiencies. Now we can consider not only how to get from minus to zero, but also how to get from zero to plus – a great contribution that coaching embraced wholeheartedly. However, no party lasts forever.

Party is over, hopefully the hangover, too – now it is time for sobriety

The IT bubble burst first in 2001, and then the collapse of the housing market in the USA in 2008 triggered global crises throughout the so-called developed world. At this moment, the jury is still out on whether the worst is over, but one thing is clear: we all, including one-to-one practitioners, need to look at the mixed bag we find ourselves in with sober and realistic lenses. As things stand, though, society is more confused now than ever before. We still live in a consumer society but most people have been impacted in one way or another by the current economic climate. On a daily basis, individuals juggle conflicting feelings of hope and fear for the future. Indeed, nobody can provide assurances or predict the future, which threatens to be more volatile than ever. However, it seems that what our clients want and expect is becoming clearer. The common-sense wisdom of those who receive our services is unambiguous. We need to work with weaknesses and strengths, with nightmares and dreams, with inner tabulations and behavioural changes; and all our lives, without exception, have both sides of the coin. If we want to do our job well, we need to be willing and capable of addressing both. It is only right that clients expect to get 'value for money' (or value for their time, in the case of free consultancy) and this means the whole package. Few clients these days are interested in lengthy therapy that is supposed to reveal some hidden parts of themselves with little effect in real life. The assumption that, when the depths are sorted out, 'the surface' will take care of itself has never been proven in practice. On the other hand, clients soon become disillusioned by the short-term effects of practices that are built on weak or non-existent foundations. Most clients want to explore their depths but also make constructive, practical changes. Personal Consultancy is an attempt to provide a model broad enough to satisfy such requirements. Its integrative character is what distinguishes this one-to-one practice from most approaches to counselling or coaching.

Structure of the book

We have divided this book into three parts. The first part is theoretical: it deals with the case for the Personal Consultancy framework and examines the model itself in detail. The second part is more about practice: it includes edited chapters from different contributors on the application of the model in various situations and with other approaches, as well as a chapter on research. The third part in a way puts the theory and practice together: it begins with a critique from the standpoint of a 'critical friend'. We chose to do this because we believe that this new concept is still evolving and we would like to encourage dialogue in this respect. We include in our last chapter some responses to the critique and our thoughts about developments for the future.

Overview of chapters

Part I: The Personal Consultancy framework

Chapter 1: A brief overview of one-to-one talking practices

This chapter reviews the current field of one-to-one talking practices: counselling, psychotherapy and coaching. It is necessarily an incomplete guide, but attempts to set the scene for Personal Consultancy by providing an overview of the field. It is suggested that some therapy approaches may be closer to coaching than to other therapy or counselling approaches. A number of established models (such as the Skilled Helper model or SFBT) that already allow practitioners some degree of integration are examined.

Chapter 2: Coaching and therapy: integration and differentiation

This chapter defines and critically evaluates eclecticism, integration, differentiation and fusion in the context of counselling, psychotherapy and coaching. The pros and cons and the implications of these approaches to managing the relationship between therapy and coaching are considered. The issues of ethics, training, boundaries and public perception related to each of these concepts are also explored. The argument is made that since Personal Consultancy maintains a clear sense of what is being done and when, integration and differentiation need not be mutually exclusive.

Chapter 3: Why Personal Consultancy?

This chapter provides evidence and develops arguments supporting the need for an integrative model such as Personal Consultancy. It starts from a simple premise that, although it may be possible to divide the activities of counselling and coaching, it is not possible to divide the client! Whatever the issue is, it is rare for a client to want or be able to restrict their focus on work that is either only restorative or only proactive. It is argued that Personal Consultancy is specifically designed to meet the full spectrum of a client's needs and is therefore more likely to provide a balanced, rounded and complete service. In addition, the chapter discusses research showing that many practitioners are already working in an integrated way but without a coherent model and are potentially 'beneath the radar' of professional bodies or clinical supervisors. The benefits of a model that would bring some clarity to both practitioners and clients are highlighted.

Chapter 4: What is Personal Consultancy?

Here, Personal Consultancy is defined and demarcated from other approaches and models. This chapter also illustrates how Personal Consultancy can provide a coherent framework for one-to-one talking practices that combines elements from both disciplines; how it can allow practitioners to integrate the depth perspective offered within therapy with an opportunity to make more practical and constructive changes usually associated with coaching; and how it can provide guidance for managing the boundary. Why the term 'Personal Consultancy' might be more adequate than other terms currently used is also clarified.

Chapter 5: The model

In order to minimise a possible ideological bias, Personal Consultancy starts from three necessary dimensions of any one-to-one practice: client, practitioner and relationship. These dimensions are used to map out the 'space' within which Personal Consultancy operates. The three dimensions are defined as bi-polar constructs, the modalities associated with each dimension are explained and their inter-relatedness is discussed. On this basis the underlying structure of the Personal Consultancy model is delineated.

Chapter 6: The stages of the process

Four stages of the Personal Consultancy process and skills associated with each are discussed:

*   authentic listening
*   rebalancing
*   generating
*   supporting.

This chapter explains how bearing these stages in mind enables practitioners to be aware of where they are and what they are doing in the process. The exploration of each stage includes relevant examples and appropriate techniques for that stage. The process of moving between stages and the essential non-linear nature of the model are discussed.

Chapter 7: Where are the boundaries?

In practice counselling and coaching can have different boundaries and an integrative approach needs to balance the shift in boundaries that can occur when moving from one modality into another. The practicalities and implications of working in this way are discussed, with examples. Given that the boundaries may be different depending on the type of work one is engaged in, it is important to manage the boundaries in a way that is clear, easy for the client to understand and safe. Appropriate ethical principles for Personal Consultancy are discussed.

Chapter 8: The process

Case studies are used to illustrate the kinds of issue that can arise for the practitioner and client when moving from one stage to another in this process. A detailed description of a first session with one client is offered, alongside a study of the work over a number of sessions with another. Examples are given to illustrate the choices to be made in managing the Personal Consultancy process and moving through the stages. This chapter provides clear guidance for using the stages of the model in a collaborative and flexible way which is in line with the evidence base for the effectiveness of both disciplines.

Chapter 9: Integrating other concepts, techniques and processes

This chapter explores how various techniques and concepts from other approaches can be incorporated into the framework of Personal Consultancy. Examples and brief case studies are used to illustrate the arguments. Examples of specific techniques and approaches which can be integrated into particular stages of the Personal Consultancy model are discussed in some detail. The ways in which the model can be used as an over-arching framework for the integration of other approaches and conceptual frameworks are also discussed.

Part II: Context and application (with edited chapters from contributors)

Chapter 10: Should we offer Personal Consultancy? An exploratory dialogue between practitioner and organisation

JAYNE HILDRETH AND SIOBHAN DUNLEAVY

This chapter offers the reader access to a number of conversations held over a period of time in response to the above question, through a series of 'snapshots'. The dialogue begins with a simple organisational need for understanding what Personal Consultancy is. This leads to more in-depth questions exploring how it works and with whom. There is also discussion of some of the more practical aspects of managing and marketing such an offering. Through the process of this conversation understanding grows and with this understanding the level of organisational engagement develops. This leads to the decision to add Personal Consultancy to the services currently on offer.

Chapter 11: Below the surface: an integrative approach to leadership coaching

LINDA ASPEY

Incorporating an integrative approach in coaching executives and leaders offers the opportunity to work on a number of levels if the client wishes. The journey towards achieving their potential as a leader – or maintaining their success – can be challenging in many ways. A 'managed eclecticism' approach to integration, underpinned by the Thinking Environment and in conjunction with Personal Consultancy is outlined as a way to achieve the optimal balance for the client to generate and articulate their own thinking, free from interruption, judgement or overemphasis on coaching goals.

Chapter 12: Personal Consultancy with young people: 'Are we bothered?'

CAROLYN MUMBY

As front line services for young people disappear or face great threat, discussing the need for a new integrative framework for counselling and coaching adolescents might seem to be the modern day equivalent of 'fiddling while Rome burns'. To adapt Catherine Tate's ubiquitous teenage Lauren phrase, 'Are we bothered?' But, as resources for supporting young people dwindle and are targeted on those with the highest need, it is more important than ever that we identify new, innovative, efficient, cost-effective and swift responses that can support all young people as they develop and change. Carolyn explores the arguments for using the Personal Consultancy model to provide an integrated service for young people which meets their needs, responds to their preference and is sufficiently flexible to cope with the rapid fluctuations of teenage life.

Chapter 13: Personal Consultancy with addictions
ANN COLLINS

Ann examines the application of the Personal Consultancy framework to working with women in the probationary service for whom addiction is part of their issue. Using two case studies, she explores how the framework is applied integrating various approaches and techniques. The chapter demonstrates the flexibility of the Personal Consultancy framework with these particular clients. It allows the reader to see that, despite the complexity of the client's issues, incremental change occurs which commences with clients gaining a different perspective that they had not previously considered. This chapter endeavours to demonstrate how the Personal Consultancy framework allows a more integrative approach in supporting the client's needs, at both a 'depth' and a 'surface' level, whilst still respecting a safe and ethical practice of working with these vulnerable women.

Chapter 14: Comparing existential perspective on integration with Personal Consultancy
YANNICK JACOB

Existential philosophy has informed many approaches to therapy and counselling. Its recent advance into the realm of coaching inspired Yannick to explore the relationship between these different approaches to helping-by-talking with a focus on integration. Starting with an outline of existential thought and going through the fundamentals of working existentially with clients, the chapter then explores differences, commonalities and potential overlap between existential coaching and counselling, followed by a discussion of the framework's capacity for integrating aspects of each into a coherent whole-person approach. Existential practice is then compared with the Personal Consultancy model and the chapter concludes in a short case study of existential integrative practice.

Chapter 15: A postcard from Down Under: an international perspective on practising as an integrative executive coach–therapist
LESLEY SYMONS

Lesley has been practising for some years in Australia, explicitly defining what she offers as coaching, informed by psychotherapy principles and her own business experience. She therefore occupies a particular place on the therapist–coach continuum of integrative practice. Coaching and psychotherapy are both unregulated professions in Australia. In order to understand where Australia stands in the world of integrative coach–therapy, Lesley explores the regulations and qualifications required for practising as a coach or psychotherapist in a few major world markets. The chapter also focuses on the key principles that underpin Lesley's practice as an integrative executive coach–therapist. These principles include: listening, clean language questioning, transference, business experience and reflective practice. Finally, due to the multi-cultural nature of Australia, the chapter touches on using this modality when coaching across cultures.

Chapter 16: Listening to the practitioners about integration
SARAH BAKER

This chapter introduces recent research into coaches', counsellors', and therapist–coaches' perceptions of the boundaries between counselling and coaching. The research entailed interviewing counsellors, coaches, therapist–coaches and Personal Consultants to gain a deeper understanding of practitioners' experience of identifying and working with boundaries in practice. From listening to the practitioners, it was apparent that some coaches and counsellors strongly believe that differentiation between the approaches was fundamental to maintaining discrete coaching and counselling professions. However, conflicts, dilemmas and discomfort were evident for many practitioners when they described managing boundaries in practice. Blurring the edges and holistic integration were discussed by several counsellors and therapist–coaches. Some expressed a need for guidance on how to integrate effectively and others explained that they had developed their own practice model. Personal Consultants discussed the benefits of using the Personal Consultancy model to facilitate the integrative process and working with the framework to accommodate their skills and abilities.

Part III: Critique and future developments

Chapter 17: Some reflections on Personal Consultancy
GORDON JINKS

This chapter offers a response to the concept of Personal Consultancy and the Personal Consultancy model as described in Part I of this book, from the perspective of a 'critical friend'. The case for integration of this type is considered along with the extent to which we need a specific model or framework to guide its practice. The underpinning principles and philosophy of the Personal Consultancy model are discussed and its structure is reviewed. An attempt is made to identify the strengths of the model as it is currently formulated, and some suggestions are offered as to areas for future development. The reader is encouraged to engage in their own critical evaluation and some questions are offered to guide the process.

Chapter 18: Areas for development

The authors make a brief response to points made in the critique. They also consider future development(s) of the Personal Consultancy model, in particular in relation to the areas of supervision, training and professional standards.

We hope you will find this book interesting, stimulating and, at least in parts, challenging. We encourage you to read it with an open and enquiring mind while reflecting on your own practice or aspirations. We see that the purpose of Personal Consultancy is to provide a framework for integration that is safe, ethical and creative, and that preserves the integrity and authenticity of the practitioner. However, this is a work in progress and we hope it will always be; it will keep evolving based on practitioners and clients' feedback. So, let us know what your experience is and what you think – we will listen.

Part I

The Personal Consultancy framework

Chapter 1

A brief overview of one-to-one talking practices

Introduction

In the 1880s a young Viennese physician was trying to establish himself as a specialist in so-called nervous diseases. Enduring extreme mood swings himself, he tried everything – from cocaine to electrotherapy and hypnosis – to help himself and his patients suffering from hysteria. Gradually, he abandoned all these props and realised that listening and talking to a patient is what really mattered. The interaction between patient and therapist seemed to have a curative power. His name, of course, was Sigmund Freud and the 'talking cure' was born. However, his approach was very unusual for that time and it took a while to be accepted by the medical and scientific establishment. Just over a hundred years later, it is estimated that there are over 400 different approaches to one-to-one practice. In this book we will refer to some of these approaches as well as the methods and techniques that they use, so it may be helpful to start with a brief overview of the field.

Traditionally, and mostly for historical reasons, one-to-one practices are organised in three categories: psychodynamic approaches, cognitive-behavioural approaches and humanistic approaches (some sources also add integrative approaches, constructivist approaches, systemic approaches, etc.). We follow this fashion to a degree, but we also recognise the need to be fluid in this respect. Any categorisation of a human endeavour that has been evolving organically by individuals and groups of different temperaments, ideological backgrounds and working in different historical periods and social circumstances is in danger of oversimplifying the real situation. We will suggest later on, though, when the Personal Consultancy framework is introduced that, from a practical point of view, there might be a more fruitful way to group different approaches. Putting this aside, there is one important difference from other similar overviews: we include coaching as a valuable contribution to one-to-one practice and on a par with other approaches. All approaches are situated in historical context for two reasons: one is to show that every approach is to some extent the product of its time (which is not to say that it cannot have a lasting value), and the other is to highlight the fact that the field as a whole is constantly evolving. So, the journey continues!

Before moving on, we wish to make clear though that we do not see sufficiently compelling reasons to make a distinction between counselling and psychotherapy (referred to from now on as therapy). With due respect to those who wish to maintain boundaries between these practices, we concur with the prevailing view in the UK (although not necessarily in the USA) that these professions overlap to a large extent, so we use these terms interchangeably. Without getting into details, we take the view that the similarities between them, in regard to their aims, functions and methods, seem to be much greater than their differences.

Psychodynamic approaches

Freud's ideas and ways of helping his patients were innovative, even revolutionary for that time. However, Freud wanted recognition, and this was hard to achieve for a Jewish doctor in conservative Viennese professional circles. So, even if the Greek myths meant more to him than empirical research, Freud tried hard to align himself with the scientific, medical model. And, in the spirit of the time, 'scientific' meant causal: gravitation causes an apple to fall, some chemical reactions cause explosions, natural selection causes biological evolution. Following his logic, if we want to help patients with mental health problems, we (and they) first need to find the cause of their troubles. It is assumed that understanding the cause will lead to recovery. This is linked to another assumption in psychoanalysis, namely, that we all go through certain developmental stages in early childhood and that sexuality plays a major role in this respect. This process is not straightforward and easy though. When moving from one stage to another, we can have all sorts of conflicting and even disturbing feelings towards those close and dear to us. Sometimes we develop defence mechanisms, or lock away or suppress our feelings and thoughts in order to cope with them. Not managing to negotiate our way through this process successfully can cause a neurosis later in life.

So where do we look, according to Freud, if we want to find the cause of our troubles? We look inward and we look into the past, usually early childhood. Freud's truly ingenious (although not completely original) answer to a question of where we hide our unwanted materials and the roots of troubles from ourselves was the unconscious mind. He famously compared the mind to an iceberg. Most of it is under the surface! Freud had never satisfactorily defined the unconscious, but still this idea revolutionised our understanding of the mind and therapeutic practice. As an archaeologist's task is to painstakingly dig out our collective past buried under the layers of sand and soil, the therapist's task is to help the patient bring to the surface (into their full awareness) those hidden experiences and aspects of their personality. The role of the therapist is to provide an environment in which clients feel safe to lower their defence mechanisms – the guards that have become jailers – so that those underlying processes and drives can resurface. The most common methods to do so are free association and dream analysis. Both techniques clearly aim to establish some sort of communication with the unconscious. So the therapist interference is minimised (which is why, in the past, the therapist would sit outside the visual field of the client, a practice now largely abandoned). The therapist listens attentively and perhaps helps the client later to interpret or analyse the content. Nevertheless, the relationship between the therapist and client is deemed to be an essential part of the therapeutic process. This is partly because trust is a key ingredient, but also because there is an apparent tendency for clients to project their early relationships with significant others onto the relationship with the therapist (known as transference).

As soon as this practice was established, it diverged into a number of approaches (e.g. Jung's Analytical psychology, Adler's Individual psychology and Ericson's Ego psychology being best known examples). So, psychoanalysis, still most faithful to its origins, is considered nowadays as a member of the family of psychodynamic approaches.

These approaches once dominated the field but not any more – according to the latest survey in the UK only 12 per cent of therapists subscribe to them. There are a number of reasons for this: psychoanalysis is notorious for its lengthy treatment – therapy can last for years and in some cases a client has up to five sessions a week, although this is less and less common. A consequence of such a way of working is that it is expensive – only the well-off can afford psychoanalysis and it is largely beyond reach of the public sector too. Moreover, there is no conclusive evidence that psychoanalysis actually works. No doubt it has helped many clients, but the assumption that changes in one's inner world (insights and realisations) would spontaneously lift 'neurosis' and lead to tangible changes in the affective, cognitive or behavioural patterns of the client has never been proven beyond reasonable doubt. Freud himself did not do much empirical work, so his theory is often considered philosophy rather than hard science. This is reflected in the fact that Freud is still widely taught at universities, except in psychology departments! Nevertheless, the influence and importance of psychodynamic approaches can never be overestimated. Any attempt at integration would be incomplete without taking them into account.

Behaviourism

At the time when Freud was developing his approach, a physiologist on the other side of Europe was doing something very different but with equally important consequences for psychology and one-to-one practice. His name was Ivan Pavlov and he used the experimental method (mostly on dogs and occasionally orphaned children). The way he conducted his experiments would cause an outcry nowadays (because of quite invasive surgical procedures that were involved) but nevertheless the impact of his findings was far reaching. In a nutshell, Pavlov discovered that dogs would salivate in response to a food-associated stimulus whether they were fed or not. The concept of a stimulus–automatic response pattern became known as Classical Conditioning. To understand how powerful classical conditioning is we only have to think of certain smells or sounds that immediately evoke an emotional and sometimes behavioural response. The relevance for one-to-one practitioners is that it can not only help us understand a client's seemingly 'irrational' behaviour but it can also lead us to help clients to recondition themselves so that they can associate a positive response to a stimulus of their choosing. Pavlov's work took the central stage in psychology in the early twentieth century thanks to John B. Watson who started a psychological school of Behaviourism in the United States. Behaviourism was further developed by B.F. Skinner who introduced the concept of Operant Conditioning: here, in brief, behaviour is maintained or modified by its consequences. For instance, if rewarded, it will be strengthened and more likely to be repeated; if ignored, it may fade away. This may be useful to practitioners who, for example, want to help clients to improve performance.

The major tenet of Behaviourism, which reigned for fifty years, was that human beings are born as blank slates and are fully shaped by the environment. So nurture, rather than nature, rules. The mind, in fact, became seen as something unscientific, not to be bothered with – all that mattered was scientifically observable behaviour. Behavioural practice (best known for the use of the 'exposure' technique) still exists today but is usually integrated with cognitive approaches, which are known as Cognitive Behavioural Therapy (CBT) or Cognitive Behavioural Coaching (CBC).

Cognitive Behavioural approaches

In the 1950s Ellis developed Rational Emotive Therapy (RET) and Beck founded Cognitive Therapy (CT). While rooted in rather different theories, Behavioural and Cognitive Therapy have shared their enthusiasm for experimental research. It was recognised that these two approaches can complement each other so nowadays their hybrid Cognitive Behaviour Therapy (CBT) is amongst the best-known and recognised approaches to therapy and coaching.

CBT is very different in its philosophy and practice from psychodynamic approaches. It is goal-oriented and practitioners are not shy in taking a more directive or guiding role. Compared with their psychoanalytic colleagues, CBT practitioners may be less interested in the past of their clients or the causes of their troubles. The focus of this approach is on the present and the future. Moreover, the assumption is that our feelings and emotional reactions are mediated by our thought patterns and interpretations. For example, if we think negative thoughts we may feel depressed; if we focus on perceived danger we are likely to feel anxious. So, changing maladaptive thinking leads to changes in affect and in behaviour (although recently the emphasis is on changes in one's relationship with maladaptive thinking rather than changes in thinking itself; Hayes et al., 2011).

A number of techniques are used to help individuals challenge and replace their maladaptive reactions, beliefs and thinking patterns (e.g. over-generalising, magnifying negatives, minimising positives and catastrophising) with more realistic and effective thoughts, thus decreasing emotional distress and self-defeating behaviour. Modern forms of CBT include some traditional techniques such as exposure and Ellis's ABC model, but new ones are often added to its repertoire (e.g. using imagery, cognitive restructuring, relaxation training, acceptance and commitment method, etc.; Hoffmann, 2011).

CBT is currently widely used in health-care (the NHS in the UK) because it is considered cost-effective and evidence-based. However, the full picture is more complicated. CBT is often criticised for being somewhat superficial – it focuses on changing manifestations or symptoms without necessarily dealing with deeper issues and causes. So, even if CBT can be very effective in, for example, changing certain thought and behavioural patterns, it is sometimes claimed that these changes are short-lived. One study, for example, found that, two years after treatment, two-thirds of those who had CBT had relapsed or sought further help (Westen et al., 2004). Moreover, CBT doesn't suit everybody – some clients find this approach and some of its methods (e.g. being asked to do 'homework') too directive and feel that their emotional issues are not always addressed adequately. That said, the effectiveness of CBT interventions probably depend on the skill and sensitivity of the practitioner and to what extent this style of working matches the expectations and preferences of the client. We are in no doubt that many CBT techniques and methods can enrich the repertoire of one-to-one practitioners especially those who choose to work in an integrative way.

Humanistic movement

In the mid twentieth century a sort of revolution happened in the field of psychology and therapy. A number of new approaches appeared as a reaction to the by now established approaches of psychoanalysis and behaviourism. Although these two schools differ dramatically, they have certain common characteristics which came from the prevailing scientific paradigms of the time. Both schools try to observe the person objectively, assuming that there are discernable laws of human nature that direct individuals' behaviour, and are essentially reductionist, relying on one or more determinants of human behaviour (such as sexual drive or conditioning). However, it appeared to some psychologists and therapists that human beings do not seem to be completely determined, that we are self-actualising organisms and active players in shaping our destinies. As the French existentialist Sartre famously put it 'We are condemned to be free.' This opened the way towards recognition of the importance of individuality, choice and personal responsibility. It was quickly realised that taking account of this self-actualising tendency and adopting a more holistic approach would have profound effects on the therapeutic process, so many new approaches appeared. They are often considered under the banner of humanistic psychology, although some, such as Gestalt therapy (which we will consider shortly), or Psychosynthesis that included a spiritual or transpersonal element, developed independently. What they all had in common was moving away from seeing the therapist as an expert and pathologising the client. In their view clients were the experts in their world and given the right conditions they would spontaneously strive towards actualising their potential. This reflected other social changes towards greater racial, sexual and gender liberation that took momentum at that time. The person-centred approach, founded by Carl Rogers, is the lasting legacy of the humanistic movement.

Person-centred approach

Person-centred perspective on the therapist–client relationship is nowadays a foundation for most counselling training programmes. Person-centred (originally called client-centred) therapy emphasises 'being with' and listening to a client rather than trying to do something, which is probably the greatest temptation for many counselling trainees and novice practitioners. The assumption of the person-centred approach is that clients know themselves best and that they, rather than the practitioner, are in the best position to help themselves and find solutions to their problems. All people have a natural tendency and capacity to develop, so the role of the therapist is to provide the right conditions for this process to unfold spontaneously at the client's pace, rather than try to force it to happen. Metaphorically speaking, the therapeutic process can be compared with helping a plant or a tree to grow – pulling it up will not do! The therapist's genuineness, unconditional acceptance of the client's 'real self' and empathic understanding is what enables the client to take responsibility for their own life and develop in the direction of greater fulfilment and realisation of their potential.

The above assumptions are sometimes charged with being somewhat naïve and not evidence-based, and it is argued that they don't always take into account the darker side of human nature or its limitations. Some clients, too, feel frustrated because of the perception that the therapist is 'doing nothing' – they never offer advice or make suggestions. Nevertheless, the principles of the person-centred approach remain a cornerstone of most one-to-one talking practices and rightly so. Convincing evidence has accumulated that an accepting, understanding and caring relationship as experienced by the client is a key factor in successful outcome (Duncan et al., 2010).

Gestalt approach

Gestalt psychology was one of the most productive and influential schools of psychology between the two world wars. However, it took a maverick, chain-smoking (yes, during sessions too) psychiatrist Fritz Perls to make and popularise a therapy with the same name. The important contributions of Gestalt psychology was the recognition of two human tendencies: to form a 'gestalt' (a 'whole') out of an experience and to seek 'closure' (a tendency to mentally finish any incomplete form). This was first related to our perceptions (e.g. seeking a triangle when presented with three dots), but later on the importance of 'emotional closure' was also recognised. Gestalt therapy shares with humanistic approaches the stress on self-actualisation and the importance of an authentic relationship with the client.

The individual is seen in context and cannot be properly understood outside it. Self-awareness – but experiential rather than cognitive, in the 'here and now' (what we would nowadays call mindfulness), is emphasised in this approach too. So, a Gestalt therapist doesn't only pay attention to the content of what the client is saying, but also to the form: facial expressions, posture and how language is used (the choice of words, intonation, gesticulation, etc.).

It is fair to say, though, that this approach is not for everybody. If the therapist is not very skilful, some clients might find it irritating. Even the client from the now legendary recording of sessions with Rogers, Perls and Ellis – 'Gloria' – was annoyed with Perls, although she chose him over others to continue working with (a decision she later regretted). Gestalt therapy may not be so popular today as it used to be, but its huge influence on more recent approaches (such as NLP) and contribution to the fields of therapy and coaching should not be underestimated.

Existential counselling and therapy

Existential therapy has many similarities with humanistic approaches in its theory and the way it is practised. It is hardly necessary to say that existential therapy is based on existential philosophy. Unlike many other approaches, it treats ups and downs in human life as a normal part of human life and experience, rather than as a sign of neurosis in need of a cure. Uncertainty and anxiety, nothingness, death, ultimate separateness from others and responsibility that comes with freedom and choice are seen as unavoidable challenges of the human condition. The therapist helps the client to embrace life in all its complexity and to live life more authentically, rather than in 'bad faith'. Clients are assisted in becoming aware of their assumptions, clarifying their world-view, and creating their own sense of meaning in their lives. The therapist does not rely on any specific techniques – it is more about the attitude – although phenomenological reduction or 'bracketing' is a method worth mentioning and will be discussed later in the book. This approach remains very strong in the UK with a number of training courses established, now including Existential Coaching.

The main limitation of this approach is that it is heavily based on a particular philosophical framework, whose conclusions and assertions may or may not be true (they can be and have been challenged many times). There is a danger that an existential therapist may unwittingly impose certain beliefs upon clients who may not want to see the world in that light. Moreover, existentialists do not believe in the unconscious and mainly focus on the 'here and now', which makes it difficult to work with suppressed materials or issues that stem from early childhood. Van Deurzen writes that 'people who directly want to relieve specific symptoms will generally find the existential approach unsuitable' (in Dryden, 2007, p.215). Still, any serious attempt at integration would be incomplete if the contributions of this approach are ignored.

The Skilled Helper model

This model is included here as a well-known example of an integrative approach (see Chapter 2 for further discussion of the concept of integration). Gerard Egan's work (Egan, 2010) is based on humanistic principles, particularly with regard to the qualities of the helping relationship, but he also asserts that the practitioner's role ought also to include encouraging client direction, helping to establish goals and action plans. Since the Skilled Helper model was first developed in the mid 1970s it has had a huge influence on one-to-one practices and many therapy and coach training providers use it as a core model. Every few years there is a new edition of the Skilled Helper book and after nearly forty years it is still going strong (the tenth edition has now been published). Almost every edition has been changed to reflect and incorporate the latest research and trends (e.g. the seventh edition introduced some elements of Positive Psychology). However, Egan remains faithful to his basic model for managing problems and developing opportunities, consisting of three stages:

- identifying and exploring the current situation;
- helping clients determine what they need and want;
- helping clients develop strategies to accomplish their goals.

The Skilled Helper is essentially an a-theoretical approach but it is strongly influenced by person-centred principles on the one hand and the cognitive-behavioural approach on the other. So, it is one of the first attempts at integration – responding to the needs and demands of clients. The Skilled Helper is an attempt to integrate a receptive, empathic aspect of helping with a more proactive, solution-focused or problem-management aspect. This may be the secret of its popularity and lasting appeal. Many clients want both: a chance to explore their inner world and resolve inner conflicts but also a chance to make a tangible change in their lives and develop their strengths and opportunities.

Not everybody, though, is completely comfortable with what they see as Egan's focus on skills and solutions. An existential practitioner, for example, may say, 'there is more to life than that!' The Skilled Helper model is also charged with lacking depth, which may not be fully justified if the subtleties of the steps or tasks identified within each stage are taken into account. Moreover, the model is offered as a framework and there is room within the framework to go into as much depth as it is necessary, and to use the framework in a flexible way, moving back and forth between the steps and stages as needed by the client. Egan also suggests that the model can be used to enable integrative practitioners to use concepts and techniques from other approaches within a coherent overall structure which provides containment for the client and the process. The Skilled Helper model is a good example of how a clear integrative framework can be a great help for practitioners and clients alike.

Solution Focused approach

Solution Focused therapy started in the 1980s in the USA but is now widely used throughout the world. The essence of this – sometimes seen as a radical approach – is to move away from focusing on the problem and focus on solutions, exceptions to the problem, client strengths and resources instead. The practitioners discourage 'problem talk' – they phrase questions in such a way so as to maximise the chance of gaining a positive response from the client. This is an extreme departure from many traditional therapies that spend most of the time exploring and analysing clients' problems and the roots of those problems. There are a number of interventions that solution-focused practitioners use:

- exploring what the client is already doing that is helpful (seeking exceptions);
- encouraging a client to do something different from what they usually do;
- encouraging clients to imagine their future without the problem (miracle question);
- scaling, measuring progress (usually using a scale from 1 to 10);
- giving positive feedback about the client's strengths, qualities and accomplishments;
- negotiating between sessions tasks.

This type of approach is appealing not only because it can be effective but also because it aims to be time-efficient (at most 5–6 sessions – and sometimes only one!) – an aim which fits well with the spell of the 'efficiency curse' under which many of us now live. However, its strengths are its limitations too. Sometimes it is important to focus on the problem and some issues need more time and depth to deal with them properly. To use a metaphor, consider the example of a professional tennis player who is losing matches. He is aware that his forehand is really good – that is what he does well, his strength. However, his backhand is his weakness, his problem. Obviously, he needs to capitalise on his strength, but he also really needs to pay attention and improve his backhand in order to start winning. We see the Solution Focused approach as being very well suited for some clients, but usually most useful when integrated with other approaches.

Neuro-Linguistic Programming (NLP)

In the mid 1970s another revolution started in the West that we all are now part of – the IT revolution. Not surprisingly, many tried enthusiastically to model the human mind in this new way. Factionalism appeared in the philosophy of the mind, and Cognitive psychology (which took the mantle from Behaviourism around that time) was heavily influenced by computer models. One-to-one practices were not an exception. NLP (created by a linguist and an IT expert) is indebted to Gestalt Therapy and the Hypnotherapy of Milton Erickson, but the formative role of the new technology was undisputed and acknowledged in its very name. The basic assumption of NLP is that we all model our experience; the role of the practitioner is to help a client with the process of remodelling when things go wrong. Language and its use play a crucial role in this process, hence 'linguistic'.

In the decades since, NLP has become very popular. One reason for this is that NLP was not perceived as therapy (and thus avoided stigmatisation in some circles) even if it was doing a similar job. The other reason is that NLP, unlike many other approaches, is an open system – almost any technique that could be useful can be and has been added to its repertoire. So NLP has become a toolbox for many practitioners. On the other hand, NLP has been heavily criticised and characterised by some as a questionable pseudoscience. These charges are not unfounded – for example, 'neuro-' in its name has no clear meaning. NLP is not more 'neuro' than any other approach though it may create the impression of scientific aura. Nevertheless, NLP is worth including in this overview not only because of the wide range of techniques that it offers to practitioners, but also because of its influence on coaching, to which we turn next.

Coaching

There is general consensus that the name coaching was derived from sports coaching. In the boom of the financial sector in the 1980s, the industry expected a high performance from its staff akin to top sportsmen. So sports coaches seemed a natural ground to look for inspiration as they were dedicated to 'fine tune the mind to ensure maximum mental and physical performance' (Dexter et al., 2011). Benjamin Karter, a college football coach turned motivational speaker, and Timothy Gallwey, captain of the Harvard University tennis team, paved the way for the current movement in business coaching, executive coaching and life coaching.

Coaching very quickly became a big industry itself. It appealed to many people, especially in the business world because it does not have a connotation of deficiency (as therapy has had). To put it simply, there has often been a stigma around therapy in the workplace whereas having a coach is sometimes seen as a status symbol. There have been legendary accounts of the exuberant fees that top coaches are able to charge and coaching became also an appealing career option. Many coaching training schools and programmes are now available worldwide, with online or distance learning being an increasingly popular option. Although still popular in the business world it is now being used in a variety of contexts (e.g. state-run organisations such as the NHS, the third sector and the general public). Present-day coaches come from a variety of backgrounds, such as counselling and therapy, human resources, business, clinical and occupational psychology, and more recently specialist coaches may come from the field of their expertise, such as health, education, etc.

So what is coaching about? Coaches offer their clients a supportive and motivating environment to explore what they want in life, how they might achieve their aspirations and fulfil their goals, often related to improving performance. The role of the coach is to assist the client in committing to action and to support them in maintaining motivation. Two types of coaching are usually distinguished: life (or personal) coaching, and executive (or business) coaching. However, in practice, they often differ only by the context and the focus. Business coaching is always conducted within the constraints placed on the individual or group by the organisational context. Life coaching is a practice that helps people identify and achieve personal goals.

Critics contend that life coaching is akin to therapy without the training, oversight or regulation. It is true that, for example, the quality of coaching training programmes varies greatly (Peltier, 2010). In order to address some of the above concerns coaching psychology was developed. Its current working definition is: 'Coaching psychology is for enhancing well-being and performance in personal life and work domains underpinned by models of coaching founded in established adult learning or psychological approaches' (Palmer and Whybrow, 2006).

Clearly, coaching psychology intends to situate itself within the wider field of psychology. This is an important step in the evolution of coaching practice. However, perhaps an unforeseen consequence is that we now witness the building of parallel structures for various coaching approaches on the basis of existing therapeutic approaches (e.g. cognitive-behavioural coaching, existential coaching, etc.).

Routes to coaching

Although coaching sprung and borrowed its name from sports coaching, the profession, as it evolved, can be now situated within a historically far longer tradition. Since ancient times many cultures have had mechanisms for transmitting their understanding of how to lead a good life. Socrates, Aristotle, the Stoics and many other philosophers were primarily interested in this issue. Young men used to have their mentors who would educate them in this respect. The moral element was central at the time, which is, arguably, not the current purpose of coaching; nevertheless, the emphasis on learning, personal development and growth align coaching within this tradition. For example, one of the oldest 'interventions', so-called Socratic dialogue – a skilful use of questions to help a person draw their own conclusions rather than being told what is right or true – is used more and more by coaches and other practitioners.

In more recent times, coaching has found its natural ally in Positive Psychology, which also attempts to move away from the medical model and focus on growth. Positive Psychology is commonly defined as a study of optimal human functioning (Seligman and Csikszentmihalyi, 2000). Rather than being preoccupied with pathology, disorders and how to treat these, Positive Psychologists are interested in building strength and virtue, increasing sustainable positive emotion and promoting well-being in individuals and institutions. Positive Psychology has had a huge influence on coaching, and in turn coaching has influenced organisational development and human resources. It seems that due to such influences an increasing number of organisations are gradually embracing cultural change. Rather than being appraised on a yearly basis, employees often take part in professional development where they consider their strengths, achievements, aspirations and goals and develop plans to meet them. Instead of having top-down feedback from their line manager they now engage in a two-way process, often using '360 degree feedback' that includes the opinions and suggestions of everybody – those above as well as those below. More and more organisations and teams try to match individuals' strengths and roles so that more people can take responsibilities that make the best use of their talents. This is a far cry from business efficiency techniques such as 'time and motion' activities of yesteryear which largely focused on establishing standard times for activities and improving work methods but were criticised for neglecting individual differences and passing initiative and control from employees to the management. This process of change, however, is not straightforward and many challenges lie ahead. Hopefully, though, coaching will continue to play a part in finding the right balance between the needs of individuals and the needs of organisations for the benefit of both.

The use of tools and techniques

Being solution oriented, coaching has adopted, adapted and created many new techniques and tools (e.g. wheel of life, value elicitation, matching and mirroring). The use of these interventions has many benefits:

* they are relatively easy to learn;
* it is easier to structure a session and know what to do with the toolbox at hand;
* many clients are more comfortable with interventions than with an introspective type of work; and
* it is relatively easy to evaluate their effectiveness.

On the other hand, there are concerns that some, especially inexperienced practitioners, rely too heavily on such techniques, that they may produce quick but often superficial or short-lived results, that some of them are even based on largely discredited or outdated ideas, such as that changing the behaviour will automatically change thoughts and emotions, and that some 'tricks of the trade' (e.g. mirroring) are used inappropriately.

Limits of coaching

Coaching is still a relatively young and evolving discipline. No doubt in time many present shortcomings and challenges will be overcome. However, this would still leave one issue unresolved. Peltier (2010) writes 'High performance athletes are coached – sick, weak, or crazy people get therapy.' If only life was so simple! In fact, probably very few would endorse such a crude way of making the distinction between these two disciplines. Still many coaches would like to believe that there is a clear distinction between their clients and counselling/therapy clients. This belief seems unfounded though. Based on their research, Coutu and Kauffman (2009) claim that 'companies may not hire coaches to attend to issues in executives' personal lives, but more often than not personal matters creep in'. In the same research report Grant (2009) writes, 'Studies conducted by the University of Sydney, for example, have found that between 25 per cent and 50 per cent of those seeking coaching have clinically significant levels of anxiety, stress, or depression.' According to the Townsend-Handscomb (2013) research conducted in the UK:

> 72.29 per cent of surveyed coaches had perceived that at least one prospective or existing coachee had mental health symptoms, with 40.36 per cent having experience of both. Of those who attempted to say how many prospective and existing coachees had mental health issues, by far the majority had experience of more than one in each category.

It is also worth mentioning that, of course, counselling clients do not always have mental health issues, but experience difficulties in their relationships, careers or personal (and sometimes even spiritual) development. In conclusion, the evidence from different parts of the world points in the same direction: there is not such a clear cut distinction between counselling and coaching clients as some would like to believe (and, even if there was, it would be very hard indeed to demarcate them). For this and other reasons we will discuss later in the book, we believe that the greater crossover between the disciplines is the better.

We would like to acknowledge at this point that there has already been some interest in integrating more of a therapeutic dimension within the coaching field. De Haan's (2008) *Relational Coaching* and the work of Elaine Cox and Tatiana Bachirova from Oxford Brooks University spring to mind. They are all aiming to enhance the attention given to underlying issues that clients may have and develop a more holistic approach. However, they are definitely locating themselves within the coaching profession, rather than the broader integration that Personal Consultancy is about.

Conclusion

As already stated in the introduction to this chapter, this brief outline covers only a selection of the most widespread approaches. No book (let alone a chapter) can be comprehensive in this respect. This is no reason for pessimism though. Many approaches are variations on the same theme or are specialised approaches for a particular type of clients, so we believe that this is a fairly representative selection. All the above mentioned perspectives have something to offer to integrative practitioners, but they all also have their own limitations. No approach seems to do the trick on its own and therefore some sort of integration has to be worth considering. This is already recognised by practitioners. The latest survey shows that, of four major approaches, 21 per cent are Integrative, 19 per cent Person-centred, 12 per cent Psychodynamic and 12 per cent Cognitive Behavioural. It seems that the majority of practitioners already work integratively. So it is worthwhile examining what integration is, what forms it can take, its advantages and possible disadvantages. We will turn to these questions next.

Chapter 2

Coaching and therapy

Integration and differentiation

Most people would agree that there are clear areas of overlap between coaching and therapy in terms of basic skills, processes, psychological roots and the significance of the client–practitioner relationship. However, coaching and therapy have different histories and to some extent a different purpose, so it was perhaps inevitable that in the last few years arguments about to what degree they are the same and to what degree they are different have intensified. For some people the extent to which they are similar adds to a case in favour of integrating these two activities. For others it flags up a need for further clarity around definitions and a demarcation line between them.

The issues relating to differentiation and integration have to some extent become conflated over the last few years in that a position favouring coach–therapy integration might equate to both disciplines being essentially the same. Although some may make a coherent argument to support integration on this basis there are other practitioners who practise integratively but still see both disciplines as significantly different. This chapter will attempt to unpick and make sense of the complexities and subtleties of both of these arguments.

Examining how far the field has got with establishing definitions of the two disciplines seems a good starting point. There is no doubt that a great deal of energy has gone into attempts to define and differentiate the two disciplines. The amount of available literature indicates that those in the field are interested and concerned with this subject (Price, 2009; Maxwell, 2009b). So the first step in distinguishing between these two disciplines would be to compare their definitions. However, it is apparent that there is ambiguity, lack of clarity and sometimes dissension in attempts to pin down either of these practices. Feltham (1997) recognises this as a problem in relation to therapy when he states, 'I wish to demonstrate that it is extremely difficult to define counselling in a way that fairly, unambiguously and accurately places it beyond misunderstanding and reasonably distinguishes it from other activities.'

The British Association of Counselling and Psychotherapy (BACP)'s lengthy description identifies therapy as a response to client problems, dissatisfactions or difficulties and as a method of enabling choice, change or reducing confusion in clients. Emphasis is placed on the private and confidential nature of the interaction as well as the importance of client autonomy (BACP, 2008). Feltham (2011), having acknowledged that there is no agreed definition for counselling as yet, offers the following:

> Counselling and psychotherapy are mainly, though not exclusively, listening and talking-based methods of addressing psychological and psychosomatic problems and change, including deep and prolonged human suffering, situational dilemmas, crises and developmental needs, and aspirations towards the realisation of human potential.

Bayne et al. (2008) suggest the phrase 'helping people to help themselves' as a starting point for a definition.

Turning now to coaching, despite a great variety of definitions with different areas of focus, there seems to be some consensus around its goals. The International Coach Federation (ICF, 2008) and several authors cited in Jarvis et al. (2006) all agree that coaching is a process which facilitates the improvement of individual performance and growth. Another area of agreement is that coaching is goal oriented (Russell and Dexter, 2008; ICF, 2008; Jarvis et al., 2006). In addition, Russell and Dexter (2008) and Parsloe (as cited in Jarvis et al., 2006) highlight the importance of facilitating learning and development. An understanding of behavioural change by the coach is also indicated as being important (Russell and Dexter, 2008; Kampa and White, as cited in Jarvis et al., 2006).

A general point that can be drawn from the above definitions is that therapy is often seen as an activity that helps the client to address problems or issues, whereas coaching can be seen as goal oriented and future focused. The fact that clients usually seek counselling when in some distress is not disputed and is sometimes seen as its defining feature. Hubble et al. (1999) write that '[clients] come to therapy when they are unable to engage in (these) procedures to a sufficient extent to generate a restorative function in everyday life'.

In comparison, some authors suggest that coaching is sought more typically to aid with development or growth. Biswas-Diener and Dean (2007), for example, state that 'Coaching has long been a powerful force for transformation in people's lives … coaching is about harnessing the best in people and inspiring them to live out their potential.'

However, the argument that a key difference between coaching and therapy is the focus of coaching on 'positive' does not convey the whole picture when the range of counselling approaches is examined in more detail (as we will do later in the chapter). Whilst the reasons and routes that take a client to counselling are more likely to lead to problem-focused work (at least at the beginning), many counselling approaches are positive in both theoretical underpinning and/or process. Carl Rogers (1999), for example, believed that therapy is about growth and fulfilling potential: 'Gradually my experience has forced me to conclude that the individual has within himself the capacity and the tendency, latent if not evident, to move towards maturity.'

Solution Focused therapy focuses on strengths, achievements and goals and actively discourages engaging in problem-focused talk. In describing the work of its originators, O'Connell (1998) states that they 'chose to concentrate more on non-problem behaviour, client competence and personal strengths, in the belief that people tend to behave well when treated well, to act competently when treated competent'.

Egan's (2006) view is that effective *helping* is concerned with both problem management and opportunity development: 'Helpers are effective to the degree that their clients, through client-helper interactions, are in better positions to manage their problem situations and/or develop the unused resources and opportunities of their lives more effectively.'

The attempts to differentiate coaching and therapy can be compared with that of the counselling/psychotherapy debate which has rumbled on for years. This suggests that it may be very difficult to reach a consensus. Both debates can get very highly charged as practitioners from different camps are perhaps to some degree motivated to favour one argument over another on the basis of what best suits their existing way of practising. Garvey (2004) explores the discussion about what is meant by the terms coaching, counselling and mentoring, and asserts that the language and terminology of helping is 'being subject to extreme "spin" by those with vested interests'. He warns that this can only lead to confusion for practitioners and clients and adds to difficulty in assessing effectiveness, standards and value for money. He asserts that it is more important that the *meanings* behind the terminologies are communicated in ways that are clear to understand: '[T]he name does matter but perhaps what matters more is the meaning we place on the name. If we are buying a rose we should at least know what type of rose or we could end up with a bramble!'

Several other authors (Bachkirova, 2007; Summerfield, 2002, 2006; Price, 2009) acknowledge difficulties in differentiating between the two disciplines. Bachkirova and Cox (2005) seem to agree with Garvey's point about competing camps. Their article 'addresses the forced estrangement between coaching and counselling' and suggests that *coaches* are invested in distinguishing themselves from counsellors to make their services appear more attractive. They see this as giving coaches the benefit of a niche market that capitalises on an 'anti-counselling orientation' in order to promote quick and easy performance enhancement and avoid association with pathology. On the other hand they see *counsellors* as being invested in seeing the similarities in order to lay claim to the territory that they see coaches trying to annex. They outline an argument suggesting that coaching is just counselling under another name, but that it lacks the ethical, training and regulatory infrastructure. Such debates raise the question of how practitioners who are both coaches and therapists and offer an integrated approach position themselves in this respect.

We contend that if it is challenging to define each discipline individually, as can be seen from our exploration of definitions, it becomes even more difficult to compare and contrast both at the same time.

Three different points of view

In favour of seeing the two disciplines as being different

Those who believe in keeping coaching and therapy separate seek a clear boundary to delineate and differentiate the two disciplines. For example, Buckley (2007) notes that the relative function or dysfunction of the client can be a key differentiator and that the mental health boundary has often been classified as a major difference between coaching and counselling. Fairley and Stout (2003, p.32) refer to a minus 10 to plus 10 scale (minus 10 = high psychopathology, 0 = normal and plus 10 = fully functioning). They suggest that clients between minus 10 and 0 are suitable for the realm of therapy whereas those in the 0 to plus 10 range are better suited to coaching. This argument is reinforced by several authors including Grant (2001) and Williams (2003). However, differentiating clients in this way seems to hinge on adherence to the medical model. As Buckley (2007) notes, this is the dominant paradigm in the West regarding mental health and psychology, so it is small wonder that it is also powerful in the area of coaching and counselling. Joseph (2006) suggests that because the fields of counselling psychology and clinical psychology have adopted the medical model as an 'underlying meta-theory', coaching psychology, linked to their clinical and counselling cousins, has unintentionally adopted it too. However, he provides a convincing argument as to why he thinks the medical model is flawed and unsuitable for coaching: such a model necessitates taking an expert stance and this disempowers people. In contrast, he presents a strong argument that the 'meta-theoretical' ethos of the person-centred approach (aiming towards optimal functioning) is much better suited to the field of coaching psychology. This is consistent with the ethos of coaching psychology as seen by Palmer and Whybrow (2006) who describe it as being 'grounded in values that aim to empower those who use their services'. This and some other candidates that are suggested as the boundary between therapy and coaching will be addressed in Chapter 3.

An argument often proposed in favour of differentiation is the danger of the practitioner slipping into areas that they are not trained or competent to deal with (Jinks, 2010). There have also been suggestions that keeping the disciplines separate provides more of a specialised offering equating to a higher quality of intervention for the client as opposed to being 'all things for all men' where the danger may be that neither is carried out as effectively as if they were kept separate. Martin (2001) claims that an integrated coach–therapy approach provides 'a poor dose of each, in other words, a confusing and unhelpful mish-mash that does not have useful or long term effects'.

This suggests that the coach–therapist is a 'Jack of all trades' sort of practitioner, implying insufficiency in their skills, knowledge, training and experience. This is curious given that many of those who promote such an argument are coaches who are also therapists and indeed offer both disciplines themselves, albeit separately (Jinks, 2010). Surely, separating clients does not make them more skilful with either group! We do not equate therapy and coaching, but, considering a degree of overlap between them, we would argue that it is possible to be sufficiently skilled to effectively navigate in both domains sometimes even within the same session. However, to achieve this, being a 'good therapist' and being a 'good coach' is not sufficient. It also requires learning how to bring the two together in the best interests of the client.

In favour of seeing coaching and therapy as being the same

The other extreme emphasises the similarities between coaching and therapy and holds the view that both disciplines and activities are essentially the same. These practitioners work in exactly the same way with coaching clients as they do with therapy clients because they consider that what they *do* is the same regardless of what it is called. For example, Solution Focused practitioners frequently state that for them there is no difference. In a recent review of Solution Focused training Jacobs (2012) noted that all three trainers stated unequivocally that coaching and therapy from their perspective are the same. Similarly, Joseph (2006) asserts that the process of person-centred coaching psychology is the same as that of person-centred counselling. He claims that the names are interchangeable simply because the focus of the practitioner (irrespective of where they may sit on the continuum of psychological well-being) is to facilitate the client towards optimal functioning. He acknowledges that there may be some differences in practice simply because clients are likely to bring different material to coaching than counselling. However, he claims that from the person-centred perspective both disciplines are actually inherently integrated and in fact the only way they can be defined or differentiated is by the client in terms of the context in which they seek help or the content they bring. This more holistic way of working avoids the possibility of the 'straying' from coaching into therapy by default.

In favour of focusing on the 'grey' area

An increasingly popular view particularly amongst those coaches who are also therapists is that coaching and therapy are not completely the same but nor are they completely different. This camp is interested in the 'grey' area of the overlap. Despite efforts made to demarcate the two disciplines there is little doubt that there is a 'grey area' between coaching and counselling. Hart (2001), for example, recognises the large degree of overlap between the disciplines especially (and not surprisingly) among coaches who were formerly therapists or practice coaching and therapy concurrently. Summerfield (2002, 2006) compares the boundary between the two with 'walking the high wire' and in particular focuses on the challenge for coaches in 'managing the coaching/counselling mix'. Exploring the difficulties of working in the field and separating between the two disciplines, Summerfield (2002) concludes that a coach may continuously move between coaching and counselling within the course of a single session.

Price (2009) conducted research with the purpose of gaining greater understanding of the boundary *as perceived* by coaches in practice. There was almost a fifty-fifty split in his sample of coaches who had therapeutic or psychological training and those who did not. He found that despite coaches stating they were able to differentiate between the two disciplines many of them involved in his study were actually engaged in practice which could be characterised as therapeutic. This strongly suggests that while it might be possible to construct a theoretical distinction between the two disciplines it is much harder to hold to it in practice.

Perhaps some approaches or models seem better suited to working with the area of overlap than others. Egan's Skilled Helper model is a generic model that offers a framework which can be used by coaches, counsellors and indeed anyone working within the helping professions. It is probably intentional that throughout ten editions of his book, *The Skilled Helper* (Egan, 2013), he has not engaged in discussions on differentiation and that he usually refers to practitioners (of whatever persuasion) as 'helpers'. Egan's interest seems to be in the commonalities of the *helping process* rather than in exploring the specifics of different possible 'brands' of helping (Egan, 2010). However, he does recognise that 'helping' takes place in a wide variety of contexts, some more formal than others.

In addition, De Haan's emphasis on the interpersonal aspects of coaching is certainly reminiscent of counselling (De Haan, 2008). His argument that the relationship is a critical factor in terms of success is consistent with counselling and psychotherapy research findings. In fact, De Haan draws his conclusions about what factors are successful in coaching from research and meta-analysis in counselling and psychotherapy, as he states that coaching in part has its historical roots in therapy (ibid.). Of course, the conclusion that research which pinpoints what works in therapy can be transferred to coaching is open to challenge. It will be useful to have similar research/analyses into what works in coaching to unequivocally confirm this.

However, he presents a plausible argument to support his claim so it makes sense, at least for the time being, to consider how these findings might impact on those practitioners who choose to work in the area of overlap between coaching and therapy. One particular conclusion is of interest to us: the strong indication that working on issues that the client sees as important in ways that make sense to them at any point has a strong positive effect. It could be argued that a strict imposition of the coaching/therapy boundary would interfere with the client and practitioner's freedom to follow that principle. This could call into question the pro differentiation camp argument that coaching and therapy being separate offerings is in the best interests of the client. Such arguments that seem to be about safeguarding the client's welfare could actually easily override the client's best interests by denying them access to a fuller service that might meet all their needs.

What do these three stances have to contribute to the reality of sitting down with a client and trying to do some useful work?

Which of these three positions a coach–therapy practitioner takes is not the most important issue, in our view. Understanding reflectively the subtleties of the arguments and taking a stance based on what resonates most for them is what matters. Since the quality of the relationship has been proven to be central in terms of positive outcomes (Hubble et al., 1999) we assert that the authenticity of the practitioner is also key, as it plays such an important part in determining the strength of the relationship. It is therefore vital that the practitioner is comfortable with whatever position they take and that it fits with their value system.

Perhaps the message that we most want to communicate in this respect is that differentiation and integration do not have to be mutually exclusive. Whether the practitioner sees the two disciplines as being broadly the same or essentially different it is possible to integrate coaching and therapy effectively and safely when it is done in a thoughtful and considered way using a guiding or overarching framework. This is what Personal Consultancy attempts to achieve: an integration that recognises a 'grey area' but also some differences between various disciplines.

What is it useful to think about if you are going to integrate coaching and therapy?

It is clear that many practitioners have reservations about coach–therapy integration based on the assumption that it will result in a 'confused … mishmash' (Martin, 2001) and/or reduce the quality of both the coaching and therapy intervention. We will explore the different ways of approaching integration in order to present a robust counter argument to this. However, it may be important to consider first what *not* to do and how *not* to integrate.

We do not propose an ad hoc 'pick and mix' approach to any form of integration. Nor do we subscribe to integration that is solely based on practitioner intuition. We strongly contend that the practice of coach–therapy integration should be considered and intentional as well as based on feedback received from the client, so that the choice of direction or a particular intervention is in the client's best interest. This means involving the client in discussion and working collaboratively so that they understand the process, and are given choices about what they might like to focus on, what might be useful and what might not be. Although we recognise that intuition based on practitioners' experience may play a part, we caution against use of this word because it is unclear. Any intuition is almost certainly based on a conglomeration of verbal and non-verbal cues received from the client (at present or in the past) that is difficult to verbalise and may not always be right. So we contend that it is useful when heading in a particular direction to be as clear as possible about *what* the evidence is that has prompted us to do so. This can guard against work that is lacking in intentionality, which can be confusing and demotivating for the client.

The concepts of integration and eclecticism

It is perhaps important to recognise that terms such as integration and eclecticism do not have an absolute meaning and different authors and practitioners use them in somewhat different ways. In very broad terms, eclectic counsellors choose from a range of concepts, ideas, approaches and techniques to meet the client's needs in the moment. Integrative practitioners 'form a coherent whole' by integrating two or more theories or concepts or by working with an established framework to which a range of approaches and techniques can be applied (Bayne et al., 2008).

The issue of purism versus integration and eclecticism in therapy has been debated for many years. One of the most prominent arguments from the purist camp has been that different theoretical and epistemological underpinnings are likely to lead to confusion or inauthenticity (McLeod, 1998). However, the common factors evidence about what works in therapy (such as the relationship) actually provides strong support for the way of practising that is consistent with integrative or eclectic approaches (Bayne et al., 2008).

Integration and eclecticism both share the act of combining concepts, approaches and/or techniques to create something better or unique, and practitioners who adhere to them do so because they believe that a single theory or purist approach does not meet all of their clients' needs (McLeod 1998).

Eclecticism

Despite eclecticism being popular in the 1970s it dropped out of fashion in favour of integrative approaches perhaps because integration suggested a greater rigour and more robust approach. However, reducing eclecticism to a 'pick and mix' approach may be an oversimplification. 'Technically eclectic' approaches such as Lazarus's Multimodal model draw from a number of psychological theories and systems as well as empirical research findings (Palmer, 2012). This is an example of how eclecticism can be systematic, rigorous, versatile and flexible.

Eclecticism has seen a growth in popularity in recent years, particularly in the field of coaching, (Palmer, 2011). In fact, Grant (2011a) goes so far as to describe coaching as being 'an essentially eclectic practice', in that coaches use a wide range of tools and techniques depending on a client's specific needs. He makes the point that it is not whether coaching should be eclectic or not but rather *how* it is carried out. We share his concern that 'unsystematic eclecticism' or an arbitrary blend of methods could lead to confusion. However, there may well be an argument for using technical eclecticism as an approach for integrating coaching and therapy given its flexibility and rigour; and that models such as the Multimodal model can be applied effectively in both coaching and therapy, as well as in practice that combines the two.

Integration

The concept of integration as applied to one-to-one practices requires careful examination as it can be potentially confusing. Horton (2012) has a useful way of cutting through such perplexity in that he distinguishes two different types of integration: 'fixed system' and 'open system'.

He describes a fixed system of integration as combining identifiable and specific aspects of models or approaches in a pre-determined and explicit way. On the other hand, open systems integration uses an overarching framework or trans-theoretical concept that provides internal consistency, yet at the same time provides a map or framework to allow assimilation of a range of theories, approaches, techniques and tools. So fixed system integration puts together two or more approaches to make something new. Horton (2012) gives the example of Cognitive Analytic Therapy (CAT) that has systematically combined identifiable aspects of both cognitive and analytic models. On the other hand, Egan's (2006) Skilled Helper model is an example of an open system integration in that the practitioner has the freedom to be able to incorporate other concepts and approaches within the overarching framework or map that Egan provides.

When considering the specific issue of integrating coaching and therapy another 'option' emerges. This option is the application of a 'single theoretical framework' which can be applied across both disciplines as a foundation for both activities. Within this perspective there may be a range of views on the question of differentiation. For example, as mentioned above, Solution Focused practitioners might see no difference at all between the activities; Joseph (2006) claims that from a person-centred perspective any differences arise solely from context or client material. On the other hand some Existentialists may see coaching and therapy as being different, but apply a single theoretical model across both activities.

Open system integration

We promote the argument for an open system approach to coach–therapy integration because integration and differentiation within such an approach do not need to be mutually exclusive. In other words, we suggest that it is possible to integrate coaching and therapy effectively regardless of whether they are seen as the same, similar or completely different. Open system integration is a pragmatic and inclusive approach to integration that takes into account that no one has all the right answers and that opinion is often subjective depending on a range of often unfathomable variables. A framework or map can help the practitioner with direction and focus and to navigate through the process. In particular, it facilitates understanding of what is going on at any particular time and how the process is unfolding. Because the practitioner can be confident about the overall purpose, aim and focus of the work they have the flexibility and freedom to be more responsive to the client and their needs. We suggest that this approach is especially useful when dealing with complex and chaotic situations. This is because an overarching framework can give the practitioner confidence to make necessary steps in such situations when the time is right. Furthermore, the open system approach to integration is responsive and flexible to change, enabling the practitioner to incorporate new findings and new ideas. This allows and perhaps even encourages the practitioner to not only draw on new research and literature to inform and enhance their practice, but to contribute to the body of evidence themselves. According to Cox (2011), allowing us all to be researchers can help in overcoming the domination of theoretical paradigms. Such a pragmatic, reflexive approach serves not only the practitioner and their clients but also the field itself.

Where does Personal Consultancy stand on this?

Personal Consultancy is an example of an open system model of integration in that it provides a framework into which the practitioner can insert activities that are similar to coaching and also those that are more usually associated with counselling and therapy. Thus, it does not pin colours to the mast around stance on differentiation and definitions and it recognises that people will have varying opinions and perspectives. This framework is more concerned with the issues of surface *vs.* depth, being with *vs.* doing with and restorative *vs.* proactive, and delineates stages and dimensions which are pragmatically useful in helping the practitioner keep track of where they are. Rather than getting caught up on names, the Personal Consultant is more focused on what is happening in a session at any given time and the general flow of the process.

Chapter 3

Why Personal Consultancy?

John

John was a manager at the central office of one of the largest estate agents in the country. He was also a regular cocaine user. John was recently married and had a daughter. Before the marriage he and his wife used to take cocaine together, which in John's words 'spiced up their sex life'. However, once she became pregnant she stopped. John had not, so she urged him to seek help. John also worried that somebody at work might have noticed that he was using the drug. He had had an executive coaching experience at work, which had given him the idea of finding a life coach to deal with his addiction (he did not dare to bring the drug issue to a coach at work). The life coaching worked really well. John had really liked the down-to-earth, 'concrete' approach of his coach. He had seen the coach for about ten sessions and was off cocaine after the fourth session – for about three months. He resumed his old habit within a month or so of his coaching sessions coming to an end. He said he could not cope with the pressure of work and family life, but was too ashamed to go back to his coach. When the Personal Consultant asked about his background, John talked about growing up on a council estate. His father was in and out of prison for petty crimes. John said: 'I remember a lot of shouting when I was a kid, but all things considered (giggle), I think I had a tough but ok childhood. I don't remember much though.' He had been introduced to 'soft' drugs when he was 12, but got his act together and managed to get through college and was proud to be 'the first middle-class member of his family'. When asked if he had talked about his parents and his past with his coach, he responded: 'No, why should I?'

Melissa

Melissa came to Personal Consultancy because of her regular drinking. She said she used to drink much more. Her first drink would be in the morning before going to work, 'just to get [her] through the day'. Then she would have some wine at lunch, and couldn't wait to get home and 'relax properly' – which involved a number of G&Ts or at least one bottle of wine. At weekends Melissa would go out with her friends and would hardly remember getting home (if she got home). Melissa had had no relationship beyond one-night stands for years and she was not happy with the direction her life was taking. Melissa had been in counselling for over a year and had managed to cut down on drinking ('I don't make an idiot of myself anymore') but still drank every day, which started to affect her work and health.

PC: *How was your counselling experience?*

MELISSA: *Wonderful, but hard work. There was so much pain in me, so many issues to sort out. I didn't have a clue what a mess I was inside. I feel now much more together.*

PC: *So, if you don't mind me asking, why do you still drink?*

MELISSA: *I don't know ... Just a bloody habit I guess.*

In Chapter 1 we outlined some approaches to one-to-one practices. This was only a relatively small (but arguably a representative) selection. As already mentioned, it is estimated that there are more than 400 approaches, so it is reasonable to ask why we need something else. The purpose of this chapter is to answer that question by making a case for the following two points:

- The field of one-to-one practices is still evolving, so there is scope and need for further development and improvement.
- It is perhaps true that we don't need a new approach (although it is unlikely that they will stop popping up). However, practitioners may benefit from a framework or model that can help them make sense out of the huge number of varying perspectives, methods and techniques, and incorporate what is best into their own practice.

Some limitations of existing approaches

It is a thankless task to make generalisations in this respect, but on closer inspection it seems possible to make some inferences, with due respect to possible exceptions. Starting with their very names, existing approaches seem to be confusing and not fully adequate, especially to clients who have not had previous experience with them. For instance, one thing that counsellors are not supposed to do is counsel, or *advise* (see, for example, the UK official graduate careers website: Taylor, 2007). This can be difficult for new clients to comprehend. The term psychotherapy, on the other hand, has a connotation of deficiency, implying that there is something wrong with a 'patient' and a need for a remedial intervention, akin to the work of physicians. This often puts off potential clients and undermines the developmental work that psychotherapists do. The name coaching may also leave a wrong impression because of its association with sports coaching that is highly directive and instructional – something that life or business coaches tend to avoid.

Names, of course, are not the only issue. Although there is ever-increasing evidence that one-to-one practices can be beneficial, there is often a sense of the incompleteness of the process among practitioners and clients alike. For instance, counsellors and some therapists (notably from client-centred and existential perspectives) customarily take a reactive role (Whitmore, 1997). No doubt this has many benefits: for example, if clients are considered to be their own best 'experts', they are more likely to take responsibility for themselves, which in turn will lead to long-term change (rather than just a short-term fix, lasting only as long as a practitioner is around). However, this attitude is not a panacea for everything. In fact, it is sometimes perceived as apparent 'passivity', which can be a cause of frustration for clients. Anecdotal evidence indicates that a reason frequently given as to why clients decide to leave or change their counsellors is that 'they do nothing'. This is not to underestimate the skills required to provide so-called 'active listening' – that may seem effortless from the outside. Only, for many clients, this may not be enough. Let us be clear, though, that this is not only about client perceptions. One-to-one practitioners sometimes can – and need to – do more as already argued in the past (Egan, 1994, e.g., accepts that Rogers's conditions for change are necessary but not always sufficient) and is evidenced by the popularity of practices that take a quite different attitude.

Some practices, such as Cognitive Behavioural Therapy, Neuro-Linguistic Programming (NLP) and coaching, are usually far more proactive, but, according to some critics, at the expense of paying insufficient attention to deeper underlying issues. A humorous take on superficial coaching can be seen in the novel *Who Moved My Blackberry?* (Kellaway, 2005), in which a coach uses many popular techniques that are supposed to help the client achieve his goals, only to reinforce his false self-image and misguided perception of his situation. This is, of course, a work of fiction, not based on empirical findings, and should be taken with a pinch of salt. Nevertheless, it is plausible that something similar may happen in reality if practitioners do not help their clients to examine and question their underlying perceptions, values and conflicts.

Coaching, a relative newcomer to the field, is especially vulnerable in this respect. Criticism of coaching often goes along these lines: the briefness of currently unregulated coaching courses can produce newly minted professionals who cling to techniques and tools to see them through a session. This may not be conducive to genuine interaction, and some of these techniques even contradict what we know from psychology research. For example, a number of training courses in life-coaching emphasise an explicit commitment from clients to undertake an action, often by asking them to sign a commitment form, or by attaching an external reward to a desired behaviour. Whilst this may be effective in the short term or when carefully used in conjunction with other support mechanisms, research warns us about the long-term costs of relying on extrinsic motivation that can undermine personal agency and intrinsic motivation (Ryan and Deci, 2000).

This sort of criticism may highlight some important issues but it is only contingent. After all, coaching, as a profession, is still evolving. Increasingly thorough and quality-driven training programmes are being put in place, along with new regulatory bodies, so we can reasonably expect that some of the criticisms will soon become obsolete. Still, very few would disagree that the essence of coaching remains and will remain different from counselling. In a nutshell, coaching is more interested in performance and behavioural change than internal conflicts, and more focused on defining and achieving new emotional, cognitive or behavioural patterns than examining the old ones (see Chapter 2 for further elaborations of this point). Yet, more often than not, we cannot secure a lasting change without dealing with deeper issues that may be the roots of particular behavioural manifestations, as already recognised by some coaches themselves (e.g. Jenny Rogers, 2008). In other words, a change is unsustainable if addressed in isolation, without paying attention to the whole person. Rebuilding a house without at least examining its foundations is simply unwise.

These limitations should not, by any means, cast doubt on the good work put in by various individuals and organisations towards establishing ethical and professional standards in coaching and particularly coaching psychology (Palmer and Whybrow, 2006). Nor should the comments above undermine the value of proactive practices that can provide a more focused approach and the 'scaffolding' for personal development and improvement of already well-functioning individuals. Again, as in the previous case of more 'reactive' approaches, our intention is only to highlight the areas of possible incompleteness. Concentrating on action and producing measurable outcomes quickly is unlikely to be fully beneficial to most clients if the underlying issues and conflicts, as well as the validity of clients' goals, are not examined, and if a natural dynamic of change is ignored.

Why integration?

As the above extracts from two initial Personal Consultancy sessions show, more often than not clients need to deal with internal conflicts and external/behavioural issues. This is rarely contested, but a frequently heard response (especially from coaches) can be summarised in the following way: 'Well, if a coach recognises that a client has an issue that he or she is not qualified to deal with, he or she should refer the client to a counsellor or therapist.'

This response, however, is not satisfactory for several reasons. To highlight them let us start with an illustration: a client comes to a coach to improve his organisational skills (he often misses deadlines, his desk is a perpetual mess and he frequently feels that time is slipping through his fingers). This is surely something that a coach can handle. One or two sessions go well, but then the client stumbles across an underlying issue – his deep dissatisfaction with the sort of job he is doing, realisation that he started on that career path only to prove something to his father, and the feeling that it is too late to do anything about it. The client starts crying. At this point, the coach may feel out of his depth to deal with the situation. Yes, he can suggest that the client arrange an appointment with a counsellor, but in such an acute situation that would appear somewhat cold-hearted. It may take weeks before the client gets to the point of actually seeing somebody – and he is crying now! It would be hardly surprising if failing to attend to the situation straight away were to be perceived as unprofessional. Not to mention that dealing with the client's organisational skills without addressing these underlying issues would be futile and possibly even harmful: greater efficiency and better time-management may, in a case like this, intensify an internal conflict.

The other potential issue is pragmatic. The fact is that it is not so easy to find clients, especially for new practitioners. It is reasonable to surmise that some coaches may not want to refer their clients (and source of income) to somebody else, even if they feel out of their depth. They may try to deal with the situation without being properly trained to do so, or they may just ignore it with a hope that things will return to more familiar terrain soon – and so retain the client. Furthermore, if clients notice that the practitioner is unresponsive, they may collude with the practitioner and return to the 'surface'. They may even apologise for crying, and bury even deeper those underlying conflicts and issues. The need to be able to do both is already recognised. Summerfield (2002), for example, asserts that 'a good coach may be constantly switching between coaching and counselling during a single session'.

The question is, how many practising coaches have enough training, expertise and experience to be able to accomplish this switching so that it is beneficial to clients. Admittedly, *coaching psychology* is evolving in a direction that, to some extent, addresses the above concerns. However, the possibly unintentional result of this perspective is that parallel structures for various coaching approaches (e.g. cognitive coaching, existential coaching, client-centred coaching, etc.) are being built on the basis of existing psychological approaches. This can be seen as a form of theoretical integration (after all, client-centred coaching, for example, is supposed to be based on the same theoretical premises as client-centred counselling). In fact, as some practitioners readily admit, this is little more than a licence for counsellors and therapists to enter the field of coaching. In other words, they do the same as they have been doing all along, but under a somewhat different name. Even if this is not the case, this integration does not go far enough. A practitioner who extends his or her own approach to include some elements of coaching will still miss out on possible benefits to practice that other approaches can bring.

This is not to say that all these different approaches can be or should be blended. Although we recognise that all one-to-one practices have something in common, to some extent rely on similar skills and have partly overlapping domains, it needs to be recognised and acknowledged that there are substantial differences between them that cannot be ignored. But where do we draw the line? There are already various attempts to find a way of demarcating the boundaries, especially between counselling and therapy, on the one hand, and coaching, on the other (Kampa-Kokesch and Anderson, 2001). Let us consider some of the criteria used and their validity:

- *A temporal perspective:* it is claimed that counselling and psychotherapy deal with the past, while coaching deals with the present and future. There are many counsellors and therapists who would disagree with this. Solution Focused therapy and CBT, for example, very much deal with the future, and Gestalt therapy and Existential therapy are focused on the present. It is also highly unlikely that a coach, hearing a client talking about his or her past experience, would say, 'Sorry, I don't work with the past.'
- *Specifying a client group:* working with people without vs. people with mental health issues. This is highly controversial and perhaps more applicable to a difference between psychiatrists on one hand and counsellors, therapists and coaches on the other. Even if we take on board that this distinction refers to neurosis rather than psychosis, we have to acknowledge that these are fuzzy categories with many shades of grey. There are simply no satisfactory and reliable criteria to decide who is normal and who has mental health issues. For example, a young man has a problem in school; he is lagging behind and finding it difficult to motivate himself. Is this a job for a counsellor or a coach? Is this a common case of poor teenage organisational skills or an early sign of schizophrenia? How quickly can we make this assessment? And, if we discover later on that our initial assessment was wrong, would it be ethical to drop the client, because this is not what we are supposed to be doing?
- *Therapy as a remedial activity:* this is sometimes contrasted with the performance-improvement objective of coaching (Carroll, 2003). Again, it is difficult to say where one activity stops and the other begins. What is remedial for one person may be improvement for another, depending where the goal-posts are. To return to the above example, if we are helping somebody who has an issue with organisation, is this remedial or improvement work? Moreover, even if we somehow manage to separate them, does it mean that counsellors who are doing developmental work on a regular basis should be criticised for not sticking to the 'remedial'?
- *Problem-focused vs. solution focused:* This is also a somewhat puzzling distinction. After all, every client and practitioner work towards some sort of solution or believe that they can achieve a solution or resolution. Nobody is interested in problems as ends in themselves. Still, one can say that some therapists, for example, believe that a solution is reached only through dealing with the problem, while coaches believe that there is no need to dwell on the problem at all and that we should focus on the solution straight away. This may be the case, but it needs to be recognised that these two perspectives existed long before coaching appeared on the scene. For example, traditionally the difference between psychoanalysis and CBT is seen in this light. So, if

this distinction is to be taken on board, the demarcation line should not be between therapy and coaching.

Indeed, this is perhaps why it is so difficult to separate counselling and coaching – the demarcation line may be elsewhere! After all, there are a number of counselling approaches that share more with coaching than with other counselling approaches. The reason why this is not widely recognised and why many are still struggling to find a way to keep these professions apart is not empirical or rational. Rather, since the names (or labels) are already attached to these practices, there is vested interest among those who use these names to protect their respective territories. Thus the form (the name) is prioritised over the content (the practice itself).

We suggest, therefore, that focusing on differences within the one-to-one practice as a whole rather than between the professions may be more meaningful. For example, one such difference could be an emphasis on being with the client versus doing with the client; the other could be an emphasis on internal conflicts and examining existing patterns vs. external issues and forming new patterns. We will clarify these differences further in Chapter 5. For the time being, it suffices to assert that putting aside ideological baggage associated with some approaches (and their subdivisions) and combining their strengths in a meaningful way is beneficial for practitioners and clients alike. Personal Consultancy is an attempt to do so, by creating a new integrative approach to working with clients. What Personal Consultancy is and its aim are the topics of the next chapter.

One question needs to be addressed before we continue, however: 'Are there not already some frameworks or models that can help with this sort of integration?' To the best of our knowledge, there are not many that have sufficient conceptual and practical coherence. Egan's 'Skilled Helper' model, discussed in Chapter 1, might be seen as an exception. Indeed, these two models share some common ground, but Personal Consultancy has a different starting point (which we will discuss shortly) that seems to be conducive to building a more balanced model.

As we could see from John and Melissa's cases at the beginning of the chapter, many clients want and need both: to explore their inner depths and look for the causes of their issues, as well as make a tangible behavioural change. In the case of addiction, for example, there are two related but separate issues: the reasons why somebody, for instance, drinks excessively (which may be buried deep in the past) but also it is a habit that has been formed in time. Different approaches may be needed to deal with these issues: humanistic or psychodynamic therapy may be a good choice to deal with the first issue, and CBT or coaching may be more effective with the second. In any case, our assertion is that we need to help our clients address both, if we want to maximise their chances to get where they want to be. This, of course, does not apply only to addictions but to almost any other issue that a client may bring, such as relationships, motivation and organisation, emotional and mood difficulties (e.g. depression and anxiety), phobias and so on.

Chapter 4

What is Personal Consultancy?

The following excerpt is not taken from our practice (as in other cases) but from the novel *Who Moved My Blackberry* by Lucy Kellaway (2005). The novel satirises, among other things, the coaching industry, but at the same time raises some serious issues about our profession and its aims (i.e. should we *always* help clients feel better and achieve their goals, no matter what they are?). We will explore some of these issues in this chapter.

From: Martin Lukes

To: Pandora@CoachworX

Hi Pandora

You ask what would money give me that I don't have already? Easy! I'd like an Aston Martin DB9. I'd also like to upscale my real estate. A substantial residence in Atlanta, with smaller pads in London, Antigua and Aspen, Colorado. I am not into being flash with money – I certainly would never want my own plane. But I think I would like my own art collection, or something classy like that, which is as much about taste as money.

22.5 per cent better than my best

Martin

[...]

From Pandora@CoachworX

To: Martin Lukes

Martin –

I'm a teensy bit disappointed that you haven't grasped what this exercise is all about. I was asking what emotions – happiness, security, freedom, you thought money would get you?

Think again: Why do you want more money?

The reason Martin, has got to be: BECAUSE YOU'RE WORTH IT!

If you don't believe that, you can throw away all your hopes of getting the package of your dreams. What is money? Money is a symbol of someone's confidence in you! If you want more money you are going to have to have Extraordinary Confidence in yourself, so that others will have Extraordinary Confidence in you!

Strive and thrive!

Pandora

Definition

In a nutshell, Personal Consultancy is a general framework for different types of 'one-to-one' (or 'helping by talking') practices that enables their integration. The term *consultancy* is defined as a meeting which is held to discuss something and to decide what should be done about it – this, in our view, describes one-to-one talking practices better than other terms (e.g. counselling, coaching or therapy). *Personal* signifies that it is about focusing on the person and personal matters that, of course, may include social and professional issues as well.

What sort of integration Personal Consultancy is

The theory of practice

Traditionally, Personal Consultancy would probably be categorised as a 'technical (open or practical) integration' rather than a theoretical integration. Theoretical integration is an attempt to integrate theoretical assumptions from two or more approaches and then develop a coherent practice out of it. The assumption is that without such a theoretical basis the practice would have shaky foundations. A theory usually involves several elements such as a view of human nature (or image of the person), conceptualisation of psychological disturbance and health, selection criteria, etc. Thus, we can see that such theories are client-based theories (see Chapter 2).

Personal Consultancy does not follow this route. The human being is arguably the most complex phenomenon in the known universe, so any approach that starts from a conceptualisation of the person is likely to be reductionist in one way or another. This is not to say that attempts to understand human nature are useless – far from it. They are very valuable and we are grateful that there is now a whole array of disciplines, from biology and neuro-science to philosophy that contribute to this field. However, we believe that any theory is too narrow to encompass the complexity of the human being as experienced in one-to-one practice. Moreover, as we hinted in Chapter 1, many theories, as they are largely shaped by the particular views of their founder(s) and the social circumstances within which they were created, are prone to ideological bias, which can make integration very difficult indeed.

This is not to say that we consider the Personal Consultancy model a-theoretical. It is only that this model is based on the theory of the practice rather than the theory of the person. In other words, the theory is about the interactive process of practice rather than an attempt to *explain* the client. This is a radical departure from some other theories, so we need to consider possible objections to this. One objection might be that we cannot practise without a clear idea of what it might mean to be the person. This assumption is questionable though. In fact, we believe that such 'knowledge' can often be more of a hindrance than a help. When we try to fit a client into our theories and categories we inevitably leave much out resulting in a somewhat 'blinkered' view. Instead, we take a phenomenological perspective in this respect, avoid diagnosing or interpreting clients, and attempt to approach the person as a whole. We find that the experience of being human and interacting with other human beings (which by default we all have and do) is a richer source of understanding than a theory. We do not deny that various theories may be helpful from time to time in working with clients, but they have to remain firmly in the background. While most approaches derive the logic of practice from the concept of the person they have generated, Personal Consultancy theory is formulated from the practice itself. Thus, Personal Consultancy is not a-theoretical, but its theory is 'practice-based' rather than 'client-based'. This theory will be discussed further in Chapter 5.

Demarcated integration

There is another difference between this approach and many other approaches that follow the path of theoretical integration. Most of these approaches tend to blend, at least to some degree, their constitutive elements in a manner similar to a cocktail. Personal Consultancy takes a somewhat different path to integration. Individual ingredients can be kept separate and used at different times during a consultancy process with the client. In fact, sometimes integration is not necessary and just one approach/method is sufficient. To use a comparable metaphor, this is more like drinking tequila. Salt comes first, the drink next and then the lime. Thus, Personal Consultancy is not about a fusion between counselling and coaching: the demarcation line still exists (although, as argued in the previous chapter, perhaps not where it is usually drawn).

Open model

As we illustrated in Chapter 2, many theoretical integrative models are closed models – that is to say there are self-imposed limits to what can be incorporated. In this respect they are similar to a purist position. The assumption is that preserving some fidelity is important, even if more than one ingredient is involved. On the other hand, Personal Consultancy is an open model. This means that new approaches or interventions can be situated within its framework. This is not to say that Personal Consultancy is eclectic: although the view that something has to have a practical value in order to be incorporated is shared with eclecticism, Personal Consultancy moderates this pragmatic stand with other criteria that need to be clarified.

Non-linearity and diversity

The client–consultant relationship is considered a non-linear system. This means that any new element introduced affects the whole and leads to realignment of existing elements. For example, if the consultant uses a new technique, this will affect not only the client as a whole but also the relation-dynamic with the consultant. Everything needs to be somewhat adjusted so that the new can be incorporated. One reason for this is the time–space limit of such an interaction. For instance, considering that a session is normally time limited, in order to introduce a new intervention some other choices of what to do in the session may have to be excluded. So not only the past and present but also the future dynamic can be affected in many subtle and complex ways. The Personal Consultancy model tries to reflect this non-linearity as much as possible and is not, therefore, just a tool-box of various interventions. Every practitioner is expected to take responsibility and think carefully where and when the new element that they want to include will fit, and how it will affect everything else. This means that, even if the core is the same, Personal Consultancy practice may differ somewhat from one practitioner to another. In other words, there are as many variations in practice as practitioners! We welcome diversity within Personal Consultancy framework and we do not wish (nor would we be able) to impose uniformity or top-down control. This is, of course, not to say that Personal Consultants should not strive to forge 'shared philosophy' but, as Cox (2012) puts it, this should be 'shared philosophy built by a community of practice; a community of practice founded on evidence based practice and practice based evidence'.

Multiple integration

So, what does Personal Consultancy integrate? The subtitle of the book indicates that this is integration between counselling and coaching, but such shorthand may be slightly misleading. Personal Consultancy is an integration of one-to-one practices – not only integration between counselling and coaching, but also integration between different counselling approaches.

However, any attempt at integration inevitably has to sacrifice something. Integrating various approaches intact would be unmanageable from a practical point of view and probably incoherent from a theoretical one. In the case of Personal Consultancy, the sacrifice is the ideologies that usually stem from theoretical assumptions. The integration seems much easier without ideological baggage. We believe that this move is justified because it is unlikely that we will ever be able to come up with a grand unifying theory that is foolproof. Let us consider just one example. Transpersonal psychology and Psychosynthesis, for instance, are based on an assumption that we all have a 'higher self', spirit or soul, and practitioners believe that no practice can be complete if this aspect of the human being is not taken into account. But is there conclusive evidence (rational or empirical) that such a level really exists? It does not seem so. In fact, some psychologists and therapists (e.g. from psychoanalytic or existential orientations) would consider that we only perpetuate the 'bad faith' of our clients and do not deal with real issues if we take such dubious notions seriously. But is there conclusive evidence that a transpersonal aspect of the human being does not exist? Again, this does not seem to be the case. The so called 'mind–body' problem still ruffles many feathers.

If we take this into account, there are two ways forward: one is accepting the multiplicity of 'truths', wherein each practitioner can choose whatever suits their beliefs and sensibilities – such a relativism has its own ideological baggage though ('there are no universal truths' is itself an assertion of a universal truth). The other option is to take our clients as they come and concentrate on the truth of our practice or the dynamic truth that arises from the interaction rather than pre-supposed truths based on our own beliefs. Let us take an example of a client who believes in fairies and a practitioner who does not. The practitioner may make an assumption (based on his own beliefs) that the client is delusional. And they may be right – but would it be helpful? We suggest that practitioners' primary concerns should be whether the relationship with the client is true rather than congruence between their respective beliefs. So, if the client is telling us about seeing fairies, the truth is that he is *telling* us that he is seeing fairies – it is the truth of his phenomenological experience, which may correlate to the 'objective reality' to a lesser or greater degree. The consultant does not need to accept that fairies exist in order to accept the truth of the client's experience. This does not mean colluding with the client's beliefs. The consultant may challenge the client's view, but only if an incongruence transpires either in the client's world-view or in their interaction – not just because they have different beliefs. The same principle applies to even less-benign situations, such as a client reporting that he hears voices that are telling him to kill himself. In this case, the consultant does not try to prove to the client that these voices are not real, but tries to help him arrive at the point of recognising that he still has a choice and that he does not need to follow these voices blindly (see also Chapter 7).

The aim of Personal Consultancy

In order to clarify the aim of Personal Consultancy we will start from the aims of counselling and coaching. It is difficult to find a single definition of counselling that everybody is happy with (see Chapter 2), but the following one encapsulates a fairly common view: according to the British Association for Counselling and Psychotherapy (BACP) official website the aim of counselling and therapy is to 'help [clients] bring about effective change or enhance their well-being'. Turning to coaching, despite a great variety of definitions, there seems to be some consensus in this respect: the aim of coaching is usually seen as to assist clients to improve performance of specific tasks and enhance the quality of their lives.

We can see that the aims of counselling and therapy on the one hand and coaching on the other have two interrelated components that overlap to some extent: both aims involve helping clients enhance their well-being (the quality of their lives). However, the emphasis in the other component (effective change/ improving performance) is somewhat different. 'Bringing about effective change' is (perhaps deliberately) vague. We can assume that this is not about a change of job, country or a partner, but an inner, psychological change. Improving performance is also a change, but a behavioural change that may or may not be associated with some internal change, such as changes in our thoughts, beliefs, emotions or perceptions. Personal Consultancy also recognises these two components, but in order to integrate the above aims somewhat different terminology needs to be used. So, the aim of Personal Consultancy is to facilitate the process of internal as well as external harmonisation and personal development. We will clarify these terms next, starting with 'the internal' and 'the external'.

Demarcating the internal and the external is not straightforward because these two domains permeate each other, but from a practical point of view the following heuristic characterisation may be helpful: everything that is not directly observable can be considered internal. What we have in mind here are clients' thoughts, beliefs, feelings, dreams, desires, values, memories or intentions. These mental processes are not directly accessible to practitioners – we can only extrapolate about them from what clients tell us and from their body language. On the other hand, clients' behaviour, performance and other actions (including some emotional reactions) are, in principle, observable (although, of course, *we* don't need to always observe them). Let us take an example of somebody who has a phobia. The internal work may involve helping the client examine and deal with the inner processes that the phobia is rooted in (e.g. maladaptive beliefs or associated past experiences). The external work may involve helping the client make behavioural changes and overcome the phobia, as it were, in practice. These two are of course related, but change in one domain does not necessarily lead to change in the other, so both need to be addressed.

Harmonisation corresponds to enhancing the well-being or quality of clients' lives in the above definitions. We find that 'well-being' and 'quality of clients' lives' are overly broad terms, however. After all, painters and decorators, waiters, doctors and teachers also enhance the well-being of their service users in one way or another, so we need to be more specific about the way that one-to-one practitioners enhance clients' well-being. We propose that we do so by helping clients resolve or deal with their internal and external conflicts. There is a whole tradition in philosophy and psychology that defines well-being or happiness as harmony, peace of mind or minimising personal conflicts (see, e.g., White, 2008). This is exactly where our profession makes its contribution. Let us, this time, take a client with an addiction as an example. Obviously, such a client is not happy with his addiction (otherwise he would not come to see the consultant). The consultant's aim in this case is to help the client resolve emotional, cognitive and behavioural conflicts associated with this issue. Whether this will lead to abstinence or moderation is not up to the consultant to decide. Peace of mind or harmonisation is compatible with both, while addiction is always in a conflict with the client's agency.

Turning to the other component of the above definitions, we need to clarify why we believe that the term personal development (that, of course, may include professional development) is better than 'effective change' or 'improved performance'. Very often counsellors and coaches explicitly acknowledge or implicitly assume that the aim of their practice is to help a client make a change *of their own choosing*. This seems to be common sense. Surely, the practitioner has no right to impose a type or direction of change on the client. However, a client choice might sometimes create an ethical dilemma. Let's take a typical coaching situation: a client wants to improve their performance. But what if the client is a Mafia boss or a drug dealer? Should we help them improve their performance? Admittedly, the chances of working with a Mafia boss are very small, so it is tempting to dismiss this question by simply saying that we would refuse to work with such people. However, less extreme cases are not uncommon and they can lead to similar dilemmas. An example might be a CEO whose more efficient performance could mean more misery for his employees or family, or even society in general or the environment, and might even make him unhappy in the long run. This is satirised in the novel *Who Moved My Blackberry*, the source of the excerpt included at the beginning of this chapter.

To put it simply, the question is: how might we work ethically with goals that may not be ethical? The issue becomes even more complicated if it is accompanied by another question: who decides what is ethical? From the Personal Consultancy point of view, we cannot impose our own values on clients. Let us consider one example to make this point: a consultant is against abortion as a matter of principle, and his client is contemplating whether she should have an abortion or not. Clearly, in this and many other cases attempting to impose one's values would not be conducive to the aims of Personal Consultancy. However, it would also be irresponsible to follow clients blindly in any direction they want to go. This is why we think it is crucial to help clients examine their goals and intentions and their underlying assumptions and values, as well as possible associated internal conflicts, before we help them embark on any tangible change. So the purpose of this practice is not only to lay good foundations for change but also to secure the validity of one's goals. Examination may not necessarily bring either a change of a client's beliefs or a change of behaviour, but will almost certainly contribute to their personal development.

The basic tenets of Personal Consultancy

Complexity

Personal Consultancy embraces the complexity of human nature. From this perspective we believe that starting from our own assumptions and judgements about the client is not conducive to the consultancy process. We do not advocate some sort of radical relativism here, only that shared features or 'universals' are expressed in unique and specific ways in any individual. To put it in more concrete terms, we all, irrespective of our culture, age, gender, race or sexual orientation, have abilities and capacities to think, feel, relate, make decisions, etc., but these universal human capacities are developed to various degrees and combined in unique ways in each individual. So, rather than the relationship being based on certain pre-set truths, truth emerges from the relationship with the client.

We should point out again that this does not mean that we disregard the work of scholars who have had valuable insights into human nature. It is not that the various conceptualisations in this respect that have developed throughout the history of one-to-one practices are necessarily wrong, but we take the view that they are incomplete and almost always reductionist. So, rather than saying 'this or that is wrong', our response to various theoretical perspectives is 'yes, but this is not all – the human being is more than that.' After all, every psychology textbook contains an array of various theories for a good reason. Let us take an example: psychologists have spent much time and energy on the nature–nurture debate. And yet, after all that effort, what appears to be accepted wisdom nowadays (and has made sense all along) is that both nature and nurture need to be taken into account. Moreover, the Personal Consultancy perspective holds that not only nature and nurture but also the self-actualising tendency emphasised by humanistic psychology, and even those aspects of human nature that are the focus of transpersonal psychology, all play a part. To what extent and how differs from individual to individual. This, of course, is only one example – there are many other aspects of human nature that contribute to this complexity. Various attempts to conceptualise them may be worthwhile, but we need to be aware that such conceptualisations are always simplifications. What matters in practice is to be open to engaging with this complexity as it is revealed in the relationship with the client.

Time

Various approaches to one-to-one practice usually emphasise either the past, or the present, or the future. For example, in psychoanalysis the past plays the crucial role, Gestalt therapy is present-oriented, and coaching is mostly concerned with future goals and achievements. Personal Consultancy takes the position that all of them are equally important. One clarification may be needed at this point. While we can think and talk about the past, the future and the present, we can only ever live in the present. So in the one-to-one practice setting we need to distinguish two presents: the client's present (whatever present issues they bring); and the present of the immediate interaction (whatever is happening in the consultancy room). At this point, we will focus on the former; the latter will be discussed in the following chapter. The client's present is a part of their overall narrative; it makes a continuum with the past and the future and they all influence each other. So focusing on only one of them is deemed incomplete. The consultant should be able to work with the past, the present and the future, but not in a haphazard way. Some stages of the consultancy process require emphasis on the past, some on the present and some on the future. The question may be asked: who determines when to focus on the past, present or future, the client or the consultant? Our view is neither or both – again, this is determined by the interaction and the process itself. The consultant needs to be aware, however, that different skills and mind-sets may be needed when focusing on the past, on the present or on the future and should be comfortable with switching from one to the other, when required. The Personal Consultancy framework can help the practitioner navigate through this process.

Selection criteria: with whom do Personal Consultants work?

We mentioned in the previous chapter that specifying a client group is sometimes used to demarcate some approaches to one-to-one practice (e.g. counselling and coaching). Conversely, certain selection criteria are often used to assess a client's suitability for a particular approach. They often boil down to expecting from the client an explicit or implicit acceptance of a particular model and its rationale. This is not unreasonable – after all, how can somebody work with a client who does not accept the assumptions and principles on which one's practice is based? Moreover, congruence (or compliance) in this respect may greatly increase the success rate of an approach (Duncan et al., 2010). However, the 'my way or the highway' attitude does not necessarily serve clients best – especially when they do not always have much choice (which is usually the case in the public sector and not uncommon in the private sector as well, except in urban areas). To be fair, though, many approaches use broader criteria, but this still raises the issue of their reliability. Let us consider some randomly chosen criteria that are suggested by other approaches (Dryden, 2007):

- Is the client really desirous of change?
- The patient's ability to get actively involved with the therapeutic process.
- The client's difficulties must be current and predictable.

However, we must ask: can we really find out within the limited time of an initial session whether clients fulfil the above criteria? Most likely not; the best we can hope for is to learn is whether a client is there voluntarily or not – and even this is not always certain and straightforward. For these reasons, we find using selection criteria unnecessary and problematic. Personal Consultancy works with a very broad group of clients. In fact, there are no selection criteria beyond the willingness of a client to voluntarily engage in the process and the caveat that they don't present a physical danger to themselves or others, including the consultant. One of us recalls an initial session with a teenage client who did not say a word throughout. She could have been dismissed as uncooperative, but continued working with her turned out to be worthwhile. This, of course, does not preclude or affect self-selection in any way. Consultants are expected to be explicit in the initial session about their way of working, so that the clients can make an informed choice about whether they want to engage with such a process.

What sorts of practitioner are suited to working in this way?

Obviously, Personal Consultants are generally expected to have some training and experience in counselling, as well as coaching or other more proactive approaches. However, there is a more subtle but equally important issue. As explained above, the Personal Consultancy model is not a specific approach, but a framework for various approaches and methods that embrace the complexity of human nature. For many practitioners, however, being well versed in a particular approach gives them a sense of security and confidence. Adopting an open model can be anxiety-provoking. The Personal Consultant needs to be prepared to work *with* that anxiety rather than trying to get rid of it. In fact, we believe that a reasonable level of uncertainty and ensuing anxiety keeps practitioners alert and is conducive to the process. Personal Consultancy practitioners need to accept that there is no way we can map out in advance what will happen in the session and that we will not always know what we will do – we need to embrace some uncertainty and the possibility that we may be frequently surprised, no matter how experienced we are. Personal Consultancy is for those who see this as an advantage rather than a difficulty, and as something that makes the profession more interesting.

Chapter 5

The model

An initial session with a new client

Teresa

CONSULTANT: What do you expect from Personal Consultancy?

TERESA: I want you to unscrew my head, put it on the table, fix it and then put it back (she laughs).

CONSULTANT: (laughs too) Well, I can't do that ...

TERESA: I know, that was a joke, but seriously I need help. Can you help me?

CONSULTANT: No, I can't.

TERESA: Excuse me?!

CONSULTANT: I can't help you, I can't fix you. I can only help you to help yourself. We need to work together. Please consider carefully if you want to work in this way, because this is the only way I can work; I wouldn't like you to be disappointed if you have different expectations.

We could see in Chapter 1 that the whole field of one-to-one practices has been oscillating between *being* with the client (e.g. client-centred approach) and *doing* with the client (e.g. CBT); between the problem-focus (e.g. psychodynamic approaches) and the solution-focus (e.g. coaching). This is exactly what Personal Consultancy attempts to integrate, but we have come to this point from a different direction. As already argued in the previous chapters, we believe that the major obstacle to a fruitful integration is the seemingly incompatible ideological positions and assumptions that various approaches hold. In an attempt to minimise any ideological biases, the Personal Consultancy model starts from the basic components of one-to-one practice that are absolutely necessary, irrespective of which approach one is using. We suggest that there are three such components:

- the client;
- the practitioner;
- the interaction between them (relationship).

No one-to-one practice, whether counselling, therapy, coaching or consultancy, can happen without these three components. This is what they all have in common without exception, and thus is taken as the foundation of the model. These three components provide three dimensions of the process, which is graphically presented in Figure 5.1 (note that the model is three-dimensional, so the relationship axis is not in between the client and consultant axes, but is the third, 'in-depth', dimension).

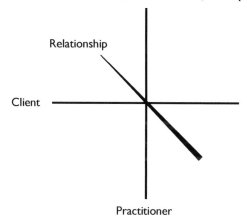

Figure 5.1 The dimensions of one-to-one practice

Each dimension has its polar properties that are shown in Figure 5.2.

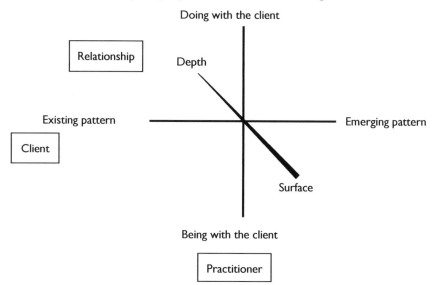

Figure 5.2 The properties of the dimensions

The *vertical axis* relates to the consultant and encompasses two basic modes:

a) being with the client – a non-directive, reactive, defused mode;
b) doing with the client – a more directive, proactive, focused mode.

The *horizontal axis* relates to the client and encompasses the following modes:

a) existing emotional, cognitive and behavioural patterns (which can include the present and the past);
b) desired, strived-for patterns (which can include the present and the future).

The *in-depth axis* relates to the relationship that operates on two levels:

a) the depth focuses on the intra-psychic, inner world of the client;
b) the surface focuses on the client's reality (the external manifestations and events) and behaviour.

We will now examine each of these dimensions.

The vertical access (the consultant)

As stated above, this axis relates to the consultant, and encompasses two basic modes: *being with the client* and *doing with the client*.

Being with the client

One of us recently encountered a person who was very enthusiastic about making a computer programme that could act as a counsellor. He talked much about how, in principle, it would be possible to programme a computer to ask the right questions or make the right comments on cues from the client. Leaving aside the question of whether this is really possible, our assertion is that it would not do the trick. Even if such a programme were created, it would not put any one-to-one practitioner out of work for a simple reason: a machine can never 'be with' the client. The presence of another human being is an irreplaceable quality of one-to-one practice. This is not to say that the use of modern technologies is out of the question. Physical presence may be most conducive to this process, but in our experience it is not absolutely necessary – using media such as Skype, for example, may not always be ideal for everyone but is still a viable option. Phone consultancy may be less effective although still possible, and e-mail consultancy is really very close to missing this mode all together, because of the time lapses between e-mails.

So, why does being with the client matter? This mode, if conducted well, can be rich in meaning and content: by being with the client, practitioners give space for reflection, attention, empathy and support that are intrinsically beneficial. However, this mode is probably the most intricate aspect of one-to-one practice – particularly in relation to attention and empathy, because they have to be genuine and cannot be simply learned as any other skills. There are some attitudes, however, that are helpful in this respect, such as a resolve to be fully present and open.

As mentioned above, this mode is a non-directive, reactive, defused mode. This means that we need to resist, when in this mode, any temptation to do something, fix a problem, jump to conclusions and offer solutions. We should not underestimate how challenging this can be. To bring home this point let us imagine that a client is struggling with finding an answer to how much two plus two are. Of course, no client ever actually struggles with such problems, but it sometimes may feel as if they cannot put two and two together. The temptation to enlighten them with what seems obvious to the consultant can be very strong. Yet we know that this would not work, because it would be the practitioner's answer and not the client's answer. The process of arriving at an answer counts as much as the solution.

Doing with the client

Doing with the client is a more directive, proactive, focused mode that brings different challenges. When we try to do something with the client we inevitably take responsibility, which can be anxiety-provoking. Let us say that we want to use an intervention. Nagging questions may appear in the back of our minds such as: is this the right time for this intervention? Would the client accept it? Will it work? And we do not have the luxury of time to consider these questions carefully – we need to make a decision there and then. So this mode requires courage. Not the reckless courage of somebody who has learned a few tricks of the trade and is eager to implement them; or the arrogance of somebody who is hiding behind the established procedures of their particular approach. Rather, we need to cultivate a mindful courage similar to that of a surfer who braves waves but is continuously sensitive to any feedback from the environment.

The horizontal access (the client)

The *horizontal axis* relates to the client, and encompasses the following modes: the mode of existing emotional, cognitive and behavioural patterns (which can include the present and the past) and the mode of desired, strived-for patterns (which can include the present and the future).

Existing pattern

Clients inevitably come to a session with their story, their narrative. That narrative usually includes their past and present. The point that we should bear in mind is that the client does not only have an issue; they have a life, too. From the Personal Consultancy perspective, looking at an issue without considering the context is unlikely to be very helpful, even if the context does not seem to have direct bearing on the issue itself. A green colour looks different depending on whether the background is blue or yellow. Similarly, the same issue may appear differently depending on the client's context. So, becoming familiar with the client's story (that inevitably reveals some existing emotional, cognitive and behavioural patterns) is an important part of the process. Needless to say, this is not only about what clients say but also *how* they say it. How a story is told can be more significant than the content (e.g. emotional fluctuations when speaking about personal failures and personal achievements may indicate an unstable self-esteem).

Emerging pattern

By and large, clients also have their aspirations. Human beings have a capacity to project their lives into the future; they have wants beyond their immediate needs. We tend to take it for granted, but it is amazing that we are able to want to be different than we are, or want to achieve long-term goals. Without this capacity one-to-one practices would not exist. If clients did not want to make changes, they simply would not seek our services. This aspiration is situated in the present and in the future; the future cannot be taken in isolation as it always stems from the present. Though seemingly obvious, this point is important because we have to keep in mind than any future goals are provisional. Just like everybody else, clients only live in the present (whether or not they acknowledge this) and we, as practitioners, need to be aware that any change in the present may modify their future aspirations as well. In other words, even when clients are able to explicitly state a goal (which is certainly not always the case), it should not be taken that the goal is set in stone. The Personal Consultant needs to be sensitive to possible change and be flexible enough to embrace it. Some approaches start from setting goals and then treat them as solid ground on which the rest of the work is to be built. However, reality is different. There is no firm ground. Goals, actions and environmental feedback are in constant interplay and modify each other. Treating goals set with a coach or counsellor as exempt from this interplay may not be the best way forward. Sometimes it may be better to reconsider one's goals than to stick with them, and we should not close off that option to our clients.

The in-depth axis (the relationship)

An abbreviated excerpt from one Personal Consultancy session:

Diana

CONSULTANT: *So, how was your holiday?*

DIANA: *Great! The weather was marvellous, no rain at all! The accommodation was lovely as always, and everybody was so nice and kind. The kids were really behaving; they found their own friends and were no trouble at all.*

CONSULTANT: *How was the holiday for you?*

DIANA: *Crap! This was my first time being there without John and it was really depressing. I was wearing my dark glasses all the time so that the kids wouldn't see my eyes were swollen from crying. That, or being bored lying on the beach on my own and trying to read books that I was not interested in at all. Couldn't wait to get back – at least I have something to do here or someone to talk to.*

Some practices pay only perfunctory attention to the relationship between the practitioner and the client, while others consider it to be the most important (even the only important) aspect. As is often the case, the truth is likely to be somewhere in the middle. We do not think that the practitioner–client relationship is a panacea for everything or sufficient on its own. A good relationship does not guarantee constructive change, but it is very important. In fact, so important that we believe it is conducive to think that in any one-to-one interaction there are three players: the client, the practitioner and the relationship itself (hence, the three dimensions of the Personal Consultancy model).

Two basic levels of interaction are proposed in the relationship (which, of course, does not mean they are the only important aspects of the interaction). The depth level of interaction focuses on the intra-psychic, inner world of the client (their experience). The surface level focuses on the client's reality (the external manifestations and events) and behaviour. To put it simply, the depth is about a subjective truth (the truth of one's experience) and the surface is more about factual truths. The segment of the session with 'Diana' at the beginning of this section illustrates how these two can be very different. However, these terms do not have value connotations. We do not consider that depth is intrinsically superior to the surface, or vice versa. It is not always appropriate or necessary to go into depth, but it is also sometimes futile to stay on the surface. Consultants need to be comfortable with both and to be able (sometimes almost imperceptibly) to switch from one to another.

There are many characteristics of the practitioner that can contribute to a good relationship with the client: being genuine, reliable, trustworthy, conscientious, acting with acceptance and integrity. However, the bottom line is that the relationship is a tacit component of the process that mostly depends on the practitioner's experience, talents and sensitivity. Techniques that are supposed to help in this respect can often be more of a hindrance than a help, because they may lead to losing spontaneity and authenticity, essential ingredients of a good relationship.

Mirroring, for example, is still used by some practitioners. In simple terms, it consists of mimicking the body language of the client. It has been known for some time that people who are on the same 'wave length' during their interaction tend to spontaneously mirror each other's body language. The logic behind deliberate mirroring is that this may work the other way around as well: if body movements are synchronised, then greater psychological congruence between those who interact may occur. However, even if this is true, the problem is that mirroring not only often affects spontaneity, but it also borders on manipulation and *if* recognised can have the opposite effect – clients may become more suspicious and shut down. One of us recently had an encounter with a window-glazing salesman who tried to use mirroring. Needless to say, it did not help at all with the sale! We believe that the most conducive attitude for a good relationship is to let the relationship develop spontaneously. However, this is not so easy as it may seem. There are a number of challenges to authenticity and spontaneity. Let us consider some of them in the following sections.

Distractions

Being engaged with the client is absolutely crucial. Engagement is the mortar of the relationship – it is difficult to see how the relationship could be built without it. It is not easy to remain fully engaged all the time, however. Our unwanted thoughts often intrude upon us – and this is an aspect of the practice that can always be worked on. Of course, the first step in this respect is catching ourselves as soon as possible when we are not fully engaged. However, this creates a paradox. We need to focus fully on the interaction with the client, but in order to do so we also need to be aware of ourselves – our thoughts and feelings. So, from the Personal Consultancy perspective, the engagement is precisely the balance between absorption or flow and a 'larger perspective' or mindfulness of everything that is going on at any given moment (including one's own internal processes). This 'larger perspective' can help us recognise what is conducive to engagement and what is not. For example, we may be distracted by our own problems (e.g. a family member being ill) or pre-occupied by something else (e.g. hosting a dinner party after the session). These distractions need to be put aside during the session – a skill that is gradually developed through practice. Many professionals have their own strategies to help them in this respect. For example, a word or a sentence (e.g. 'I am here for the client') can be used, or imagination (e.g. imagining putting one's thoughts in a box or on a shelf), or a body movement (e.g. leaning forward). This may vary from person to person and consultants need to experiment until they find what suits them best. Of course, this only applies to distractions that are clearly ours. Sometimes the distractions are a result of the interaction (e.g. picking up on the client's distraction), in which case it may be worthwhile bringing this experience up (e.g. 'I notice I'm feeling distracted ... do you think we should talk about it?').

Boredom

One of the perks of one-to-one practice is that it is an interesting and engaging job – most of the time. Occasionally, though, practitioners may experience moments of boredom with some clients. Their perception may be that a client keeps repeating him- or herself, or goes in circles, or fails to recognise the obvious, or just keeps talking incessantly. It is important to recognise that these are not client or even practitioner issues – they are relationship issues. Boredom is a response to the immediate interaction. The challenge here is that the practitioner can hardly be completely authentic and spontaneous in this respect (i.e. just admitting 'I am bored'), because this could have a negative effect, especially on vulnerable clients. On the other hand, trying to endure or suppress boredom is not conducive to building a good relationship. So what can be done if we feel this way? We suggest the following steps: they are not prescriptions, but more like indicative suggestions designed to inspire consultants to reflect on and develop their own strategies:

- Boredom is often the result of being disengaged, closed or not understanding sufficiently what the client is saying. So, the first step is to make an earnest attempt to engage more, open up and understand the client better (e.g. by asking relevant questions). This may not necessarily alleviate the sense of boredom, however. We might even feel that boredom is justified. In this case it may be worthwhile to consider how to address the issue without being judgemental of the client. These are some examples, although we encourage every consultant to find his or her own approaches:
  o My impression is that we are going in circles. How do you feel?
  o You seem to be bringing many issues at the same time. Do you think it helps?
  o You seem to be coming back to this story again and again. Is there something there that we have failed to address?
  o I feel a bit lost. Can I ask you to clarify what you mean by … ?

It should be noticed that all the above examples take the form of questions. This is not an accident. As this issue is ultimately about the relationship, these are open-ended invitations to the client to address whatever is going on *together*. Sometimes this can even be used as a springboard to work, in the safe environment, on related issues 'out there' in the real world.

Eagerness to help

Another challenge to the relationship is overzealousness. Everybody comes to this profession with a desire to help others. Most prospective students, when asked at their admission interview why they want to study counselling (or therapy, consultancy, coaching), reply that it is because they want to help others. This is a noble aim, and without such enthusiasm the profession would be next to useless. However, as with many other good intentions in life, this one also has its shadow that needs to be kept in check.

Eagerness to help can negatively affect the relationship for several reasons: it can tilt the balance of power, it can lead to either client or consultant closing down (albeit for different reasons), it can be patronising, and most importantly it can undermine the client's agency. This is why it is important to always bear in mind that we are not there to fix clients. Our work is always a cooperative effort. Even when the end result is positive, if the practitioner has been taking the lead then the client has missed the process of getting there and is therefore unlikely to be able to transfer this achievement to other situations. This, in turn, would tend to encourage the client to develop dependency on the practitioner, which in the long term could outweigh any positive results. So, even if the consultant is completely confident about what the client should do, they need to bear in mind that it is not a good idea to transport the client there – they have to get there together at the client's own pace.

Being attracted to a client

In the popular TV series *In Treatment,* a therapist and a client become attracted to each other with quite undesirable consequences for both, even though they do not act on their feelings. In popular imagination one-to-one practice is full of such situations, but this is most likely an exaggeration. We all may like some clients more than others, but falling in love or being obsessed with a client is arguably a rare occurrence. Nevertheless, if it does happen it may have serious consequences for both sides, so it is worth addressing.

The common response to this issue (if discussed at all) is that we have to behave professionally – which is true, but it needs to be acknowledged that this may be a challenge when we also need to maintain spontaneity, openness and authenticity with the client. Thus, it may be a good idea to consider what can be done in such a situation:

- The intensity and duration of these feelings needs to be taken into account first. If they are slight and fleeting, the practitioner can notice, recognise and let them go, reminding themselves of their role and purpose in this interaction. Of course, it is important to avoid feeding these feelings further with any fantasies (however innocent they may seem). As Russell and Dexter (2008) put it, 'Don't fan the flames!' Focusing on the whole person rather than just the sexual element may also help (ibid.)
- If these feelings are enduring or intense, consultants are advised to address the issue with their supervisors. There may be some underlying (counter-transference) issues at play.
- If this does not work, consultants may consider referring the client to somebody else – this is likely to be less harmful than any other alternative.

Tiredness

We would be very surprised to meet a practitioner who has never felt tired during a session. Some practitioners readily admit that they sometimes struggle to keep their eyes open. This is of course not good for the relationship; clients will probably feel offended if they notice that the practitioner cannot engage properly. So, what to do in these situations? First of all, there is no point in trying to stifle obvious signs of tiredness (e.g. a yawn) – it is likely to be noticed anyway, and trying to hide it just makes the situation worse. It is acceptable for clients to notice that the practitioner is tired as long as it is not interpreted to mean that the practitioner is tired of them. Glancing at a watch more frequently than usual is also to be avoided because it may be misunderstood (and it does not make one less tired).

On the other hand, engaging in a dialogue (if appropriate) may be helpful. Research shows that we all get slightly aroused when we talk, which in turn make us more alert. After all, it is easy to fall asleep while listening (or intending to), but very difficult to do so while talking. Sometimes it may be necessary to be open about feeling tired or under the weather, to make sure the client knows it is not about them, but this needs to be only mentioned as a matter of fact and played down to avoid an undue influence on the session.

The best remedy for tiredness, however, is to be well rested when working with clients. Nowadays it is popular to cram our working days with as many tasks as possible – we all live under the spell of the 'efficiency curse'. But this mode is not conducive to our type of work. Consultants are advised to compare themselves with athletes in this respect: an athlete may train hard, but is unlikely to do a good job if tired. The same applies to Personal Consultants. This means that a break between sessions should not just be filled up with paperwork, but should also involve a change that enables rest, such as a brisk walk, meditation or even a short nap!

Disliking a client

It is unrealistic to expect that every practitioner will always like every client. Occasionally, clients' thoughts or behaviours may go against our own values or preferences. Practitioners are and should be professionals, but they are people too. Again, this is not to say that there is something wrong with the client or with the practitioner. This is a relationship issue. Some personalities just rub each other up the wrong way. These feelings should be recognised, acknowledged and ideally let go or put aside. Reminding ourselves that we are there for the client may help. However, the problem is that it is not always easy to make ourselves discard certain thoughts and feelings. This is where positive emotions (such as compassion) may play a role in countering negative ones. But it is difficult to have positive feelings on demand, especially if we dislike somebody. How can we generate genuine compassion? First, we need to bear in mind that, even if we do not like somebody's behaviour, this does not preclude our feeling compassion for that person. Parents are in this situation with their children frequently, but where does compassion come from with relative strangers?

It comes from shared humanity between the client and the practitioner. We are all human beings who struggle to make sense of our lives and the world around us.

We often make mistakes, are misguided in our responses to life-challenges or fail to resist temptations. However, we are all more or less in the same boat. Deep down, beneath the individual differences, we all share a journey – awareness of this can be the source of our compassion. This certainly does not mean putting up with anything. If a client has really bad breath, it may be beneficial (for the client and practitioner) to address the issue, but it is easier to do so if one feels compassion for that person. For more serious cases (e.g. ethical issues that the consultant feels strongly about), again, discussing the issues in supervision and even referring the client to somebody else may be necessary.

Feeling under 'attack'

Sometimes practitioners may feel under 'attack'. A client may keep asking for advice or personal questions, trying to cross the explicit or implicit boundaries that are established. This is not uncommon and an almost knee-jerk reaction is to deflect such questions by another, counter question. From the Personal Consultancy perspective this is not a good practice. Clients easily recognise this as a defensive response, which is not good for the relationship. Attempting an honest answer that one is comfortable with may be more constructive in the long term. These are some examples:

- *I am not sure what I would do. I am not in your situation.* OR
    - o   I can't give you advice, because I can't take responsibility for your choices and actions.
    - o   I don't think it would help if I answered your question.
- *No, I am not married. I am divorced, but have two children.* OR
    - o   I don't feel that it is appropriate to talk about myself in our session.
    - o   I understand that you may be curious about me, but it would be unprofessional of me to engage in such discussions.

Afterwards the consultant may explore further the reasons behind the questions, but they should not forget that it is only human to want to know the answers or to be curious.

These are, in our view, some major challenges to developing a good relationship, but the list is by no means fully comprehensive and could never be. We are in no doubt that Personal Consultants will face other challenges in their practice or will deal with these ones in a somewhat different way. As already mentioned building the relationship is largely a tacit process and can never be fully captured in words. We are grateful for that though – this is what makes the work interesting and never a mechanical activity. Overall, this chapter has explored the dimensions of the Personal Consultancy model and its characteristics. In the following chapter we will focus on the stages of the process, which are derived from these dimensions.

Chapter 6

The stages of the process

This is an excerpt from one of the sessions that influenced the development of the Personal Consultancy model. In this case it was deemed more appropriate to use the first person singular:

Sarah

SARAH: What we did last time was really helpful. Do you remember?

I panicked. I did not. I remembered her story in minute detail, I remembered her issue, but what I said or what I asked, I could not recall. My immediate reaction was to reach out for my notes, but that was, of course, not an option.

Sarah was a very intelligent woman, very interested in self-awareness and self-development, a pleasure to work with. But she was going through a really difficult period. Life seemed to be hitting her from all directions. The relationship with her partner was on the rocks, she had issues with her ageing mother (who disapproved of her relationship, among other things), she was losing confidence in her work (as a teacher), her daughter from a previous relationship was playing up, her health was giving up, and she had financial problems, bouts of anxiety and low motivation as well as succumbing to 'solutions' such as smoking cannabis and drinking alcohol. Whenever we started working on one issue, something else would crop up and the sessions felt like working in an emergency ward – patching up whatever was the most urgent at that point. This session was not an exception. I had to be honest.

'I am very sorry, actually I can't remember. Can you please remind me?

Sarah took it well, but I couldn't help noticing she was a bit disappointed that what was important for her did not seem important enough for me to remember. It dawned on me there and then that we, as practitioners, need to keep in mind not only where the client is going but also what we are doing.

These stages are introduced in the Personal Consultancy framework because we believe that consultants need to have some orientation, a map of the territory. It is helpful to know where we are in our journey with the client. Without it, both the client and the consultant may lose a sense of where they are going or even if they are going anywhere at all. Some practitioners might say that this is fine, that we need to embrace 'not knowing' and uncertainty. We agree with such a view only up to a point. Even if we accept that our sessions cannot be and should not be fully predictable and pre-determined, we also believe that the consultancy process as a whole should progress (rather than, e.g., going in a circle). After all, how many clients would take on our services if we told them that we don't really care whether we get somewhere or not? Thus, we believe that delineating the stages of the consultancy process may be helpful in providing some orientation. It needs to be clarified, though, that we are not talking here about the stages of achieving the client's goals (as is the case in, e.g., the Egan model). We do not believe that there are universal stages in this respect. Some clients may have fluid goals, or not have explicit goals at all! Thus, the stages of the Personal Consultancy process *may or may not* coincide with the client's steps towards their goal. While goals are usually linear (sequential), these stages are non-linear. For example, going from stage three (Generating) to stage two (Rebalancing) does not mean going backwards! It is also sometimes necessary to go through all the Personal Consultancy stages a number of times before a client reaches their goals. Understanding that the process of a client's personal change is not the same as the consultancy process has practical implications as well. For example, it is reasonable to discuss where the client wants to be in five weeks, but we do not think that it is helpful to speculate where the consultancy process will be in five weeks.

The stages of the Personal Consultancy process are based on the dimensions discussed in the previous chapter. However, as already mentioned, the relationship is largely tacit and all-pervasive (it matters at all stages in equal measure) so, for the sake of simplicity, we have not included this axis in Figure 6.1. However, we will consider how these stages relate to the levels of the relationship.

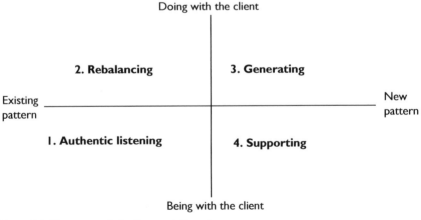

Figure 6.1 The stages of the Personal Consultancy process

While the relationship is mostly about the 'how' of the interaction, the other two axes (the client and the consultant) are more about 'what' – the content (although, of course, this is not and does not need to be a sharp distinction). These two dimensions provide four quadrants that can be identified with the stages of the Personal Consultancy process, as represented in Figure 6.1. Each of these stages can involve four domains of interaction: perception, emotions, thinking and behaviour.

Authentic listening

Natalie

NATALIE: I had a lunch with my friend Sam and I got really angry with him afterwards. I am not sure why ...

Almost six months previously Natalie had broken up with her boyfriend. Around that time, a friend, Sam, arrived in London from their native country and they met up and acknowledged that they had feelings for each other – but she was going through a difficult break-up and he had a girlfriend. A few months later he sent her a text message saying that he missed her and would like to see her. Some time after that they met for lunch. In the meantime the relationship with his girlfriend ended. The Personal Consultant's immediate assumption was that Natalie was irritated because he hadn't proposed a date given that they were both free. The PC was aware, however, that this was his conclusion not his client's, so he bracketed it and went on exploring the events further – in particular the client's feelings around the text message from Sam prior to their meeting. It transpired that she believed that sending such a message while in a relationship with somebody else is inappropriate even if completely innocent. The PC now realised that she perhaps got angry with Sam because she didn't completely trust him anymore, and trust was very important to her. So the PC now had two competing 'explanations', but they were not the client's, so they both needed to be bracketed.

PC: OK, let's return now to your angry feeling and consider together what it is all about ...

Listening, needless to say, is ubiquitous in one-to-one practices. However, we believe that the listening that we would name 'authentic' deserves its own quadrant because of its unique emphasis: it is listening that is an end in itself, not a means to an end. This means that listening at this stage is not a mere means to help us figure out what to do with the client. It is not some sort of precursor to other stages. The Authentic Listening stage is part of the process, as valuable in itself as any other part (enhancing self-reflection being one benefit among others). The term *authentic* indicates the need for a genuine focus on what the other person is communicating (rather than, e.g., applying techniques or procedures that are supposed to add to an impression of listening). As Figure 6.1 shows, authentic listening is defined by *being with the client mode* and *existing pattern*.

As already mentioned, the 'existing pattern' is largely about the (client's) past and present. This does not mean that clients cannot talk about their future goals or changes that they want to make in their lives at this stage. However, our assertion is that the new pattern cannot be fully understood and addressed adequately without first getting some idea where the client is right now, and how they got there. In other words, the context affects the outcome. The issue (and how it is defined) affects the solution. Even if a client has a very clear and specific goal, there are many reasons why the past and the present may be relevant, such as: to determine if the goal is realistic, to determine mitigating and restricting factors, to determine possible causes, influences and triggers, and so on.

The *being with mode* indicates that this stage is primarily about giving space to clients, letting them talk and express themselves, cognitively and emotionally. This, of course, does not mean being completely passive, which is why some practitioners call it active listening. Such participation can be achieved in the following four domains:

- The domain of perception may involve observing body language and facial expressions and noting their (in)congruence with what is being said.
- The cognitive domain involves understanding which can be facilitated by clarifying some issues, summarising what has been said or categorising information into themes. Methods such as free association, drawing or visualisation (e.g. to describe an emotion) may sometimes aid the process. Phenomenological reduction (used in, e.g., existential therapy) is also suggested as a valuable tool. It consists of bracketing one's own assumptions, judgements or expectations, in order to gain insights from experience rather than existing mental constructs (for a further description, see e.g. Young, 2000, p.75). It is important, though, to refrain from offering any insights that the consultant may have at this stage. This is not only because the consultant may be wrong, but also because the client may not be ready for that insight and therefore not be willing or able to internalise it. As the above excerpt hints at, the client and the consultant need to arrive at an insight together, and the consultant should not leap in front of the client.
- The emotional domain requires empathy or emotional understanding that helps the client feel safe to express their feelings (see Chapter 7 for further discussion on empathy).
- Several attitudes can assist in the behavioural domain: genuine interest and engagement, respect (including self-respect) and (non-attached) involvement. 'Non-attached' means that the consultant is not detached, but they also do not let themselves get attached to clients and their stories.

Regarding the relationship dimension, at the Authentic Listening stage the consultant can focus on the *surface* (the story, facts, issues of the client) or on the *depth* (the client's experience of the story, facts or issue).

Rebalancing

Rebecca

Rebecca was a professional in her early thirties. Her relationship had recently broken down and she was devastated. The relationship had been rocky for a while, she had harboured doubts about it herself, but when her boyfriend pulled the plug she was extremely distressed. She mostly blamed herself for what had happened and frequently engaged in 'if only I did/didn't ... ' scenarios. Over time these scenarios were repeated with more and more details and idealised outcomes, causing greater and greater anguish for her.

PC: *We've been there already ... Does it help going over and over what could have been?*

REBECCA: *No, it doesn't, I know, but I can't help it!*

PC: *What about your present and future?*

REBECCA: *My present and future? There is nothing really to tell ... I go to work and try to put on a brave face, come back home, watch TV or come to see you (wry laugh) and dread the approaching weekend with nothing to do. And the future ... (she sighs) just more of the same.*

PC: *(smiles) You seem to reverse time.*

REBECCA: *What do you mean?*

PC: *Normally, we have one past and think about a number of possible futures. You think about many possible pasts and see only one future.*

REBECCA: *Hmmm, interesting ... but I am not sure how this can be changed?*

PC: *Who can change it?*

REBECCA: *I knew you would ask that! Me, I know, but how?*

PC: *You tell me.*

REBECCA: *OK, I suppose whenever I start thinking about what could've happened, I should say to myself 'The past is fixed; think what you can do in the future!'*

Rebalancing is defined by *doing with the client* and *existing pattern* (see Figure 6.1) and consists of the consultant helping clients to locate and resolve internal conflicts. These conflicts can be cognitive, emotional, behavioural or complex (e.g. a conflict between one's thoughts and feelings). For instance, in the above case the client was stuck in her way of thinking in a state she did not want but felt powerless to change. While we consider that the use of interventions and techniques might be of limited value in the 'being with' mode, many techniques can be used to assist the process at this stage. As in the previous case, Rebalancing can operate in all four domains:

- Perceptual distortions can be addressed, for example by challenging negative biases (e.g. an 'is the glass half full or half empty?' type of intervention), or helping the client take a larger perspective (e.g. seeing a particular problem with their partner in the context of the whole relationship).
- In the domain of thinking, the client may be assisted to reveal some hidden assumptions or beliefs that may be inadequate. Dream interpretation, or laddering (see, e.g., Personal Construct Therapy in Dryden, 2007) may be used for that purpose. Also, possible inconsistencies, incongruence or incompleteness of the client's views may be addressed.
- Bringing to the surface and acknowledging suppressed emotions and developing acceptance may contribute to resolving emotional conflicts. This process can be aided by interventions such as focusing (Gendlin, 1981), reliving past experiences or systematic elimination (Popovic, 2005).
- Behavioural conflicts can be tackled, for example, by exploring possible causes of undesirable behavioural patterns or by helping the client to set priorities (e.g. long-term goals vs. short-term gratifications).

Regarding the relationship dimension, the consultant may focus on *surface* (horizontal) conflicts triggered by an immediate situation (e.g. a client wanting to confront their bullying boss on the one hand, and fearing for their job on the other), and/or they may focus on *depth* (vertical) conflicts with deep-seated beliefs, values or attitudes that may originate in a distant past (e.g. the client may have been brought up never to challenge authority, making it difficult to challenge their boss).

Generating

Rebecca (cont.)

PC: How was your week?

REBECCA: Good, I tried to do that thing 'The past is fixed ... ', remember?

PC NODS

REBECCA: So I rang my sister ... I haven't been in touch with her for a while; she lives in Devon with her husband and two kids ... To cut a long story short, she invited me to visit them and I spent last weekend there! On Saturday evening I volunteered to baby-sit for them ... My sis and brother-in-law haven't been out without kids for years, so they were really excited, and finally pleased to have me there (she laughs) ... So, I spent Saturday evening watching all three Shrek movies with two kids ... I cried my eyes out ... I'm sure the kids think I am nuts.

PC: *So how do you feel about it?*

REBECCA: *No, it was good, better than staring at my bedroom ceiling all weekend, but I can't drive there all the time, I think I've run out of ideas.*

PC: *Shall we try brainstorming to see what else can be done?*

REBECCA: *OK.*

PC (BRINGS AN EMPTY TIN AND A SMALL BAG OF DRY BEANS): *Take a handful of these beans and whenever you have an idea throw a bean into the can and I will do the same. Remember, no judging whether the ideas are good or feasible, it could be anything that you fancy.*

REBECCA (TENTATIVELY THROWS IN A BEAN): *I can go and see my parents.*

PC (THROWS IN A BEAN): *You can become an astronaut.*

REBECCA: *That's silly!*

PC: *No judgements at this stage! Would you like to be an astronaut?*

REBECCA: *No, not really ...*

PC TAKES A BEAN OUT.

REBECCA: *I could go to Egypt and have a photo taken of me on a camel in front of the Pyramids! When I was with John I wanted to travel but he was always busy ...*

REBECCA (ANOTHER BEAN): *And I can learn scuba-diving, in Egypt too! Apparently, it is magical! ... I can also become a new J. K. Rowling, write something even better than Harry Potter! I can take a course in creative writing ... I can go clubbing this weekend if–*

PC: *No 'if' at this stage, please.*

REBECCA: *Ok, I can visit China ... I would like to do some charity work too ... I can write a letter to John and tell him to fuck himself ... I can go on a date!*

This continued for a while. The PC asked Rebecca to write down all the ideas she remembered and then take each of them and think how they could be put in practice. Almost none of them were, but Rebecca soon had two dates.

REBECCA: *I can't decide yet who I really fancy, but when I do we are definitely going to Egypt!*

The Generating stage is defined by the *doing with the client* and *new pattern.* 'Generating' focuses on personal change and achievement – in other words, on developing more constructive patterns. As in the previous case, ideally all four domains (perception, thinking, affect and behaviour) should be addressed:

- The domain of perception can involve gathering accurate information, encouraging self-monitoring behaviour, prompting the client to take their situation as a challenge (a chance for change or growth), and recognising his or her strengths and competencies.
- Setting or clarifying goals, identifying and exploring options, choosing solutions, developing an action plan can all be relevant to the domain of thinking. Coaching provides a range of techniques in this respect.
- On the affective side, the consultant can help the client learn how to alter and control their affective states by utilising, for example, guided visualisation, relaxation techniques, breathing exercises or meditation.
- Well-known methods such as desensitisation, exposure or dis-identification (Popovic, 2005) can be used to modify one's behaviour. Organisational and motivational techniques belong to this category (e.g. identifying social, personal and health benefits of the new pattern).

Regarding the relationship dimension, the consultant can focus on a client's aims and goals (*surface*), or a client's real needs or values that underpin these goals (*depth*). This will be discussed further in Chapter 8.

Supporting

Melissa

Melissa (a client already mentioned in Chapter 3) turned up at a session very distressed.

MELISSA (ON THE VERGE OF TEARS): *I failed. I am deeply, deeply, ashamed of myself. And I was doing so well.*

PC: *I can see you are very distressed ...*

MELISSA: *Last Friday I went out with the girls. We had a really good time, I was drinking Coke to start off with, was really a good girl. And then we decided to go to a club. As soon as we got there Joanne got shots of vodka for all of us. I said no, but she started egging me on, 'Come on! Don't be a spoil-sport! One won't kill you!' You know, that sort of stuff ... and I took it. From then on, it was just a slippery slope. I ended up drinking more than anybody else, 'just like old times'. The whole evening became a blur. Next morning was awful, one of the worst ever. I had a nice cocktail of hangover, guilt and disgust with myself. I wanted to scream, I bit my hand, I cried, I was slapping my head, and swearing at myself. And you know what? I really want to go out and get a packet of fags and a bottle of vodka and drink myself into oblivion again – just to have a break from these feelings. I even got dressed, but I stopped myself. I don't know how.*

PC: *So what happened then?*

MELISSA: *What do you mean? Wasn't that enough? I fucked up!*

PC: *You got drunk on Friday. Today is Tuesday. Have you had another drink in the meantime?*

MELISSA: *No! Every time I thought of it, I was so angry that I kept shouting 'Fuck you, fuck you!'*

PC: *So, you gave in to a temptation, but managed to get through the next few days without a drop even though you felt really bad? Is this a fair account?*

MELISSA: *I guess so ... Are you trying that 'a glass is half-full, not half-empty' with me?*

PC: *Not trying anything, just summarising the facts. You don't fail if you lapse, but if you give up. Are you giving up?*

MELISSA: *No.*

PC: *Then you haven't failed.*

MELISSA WAS SITTING IN SILENCE AND THEN LOOKED AT THE CONSULTANT: *Are you not disappointed with me?*

PC: *You know I don't judge clients ... I am with you through this ...*

MELISSA REMAINED SILENT.

PC: *Would you like us to consider what you can do next time when you find yourself in a similar situation, or would you prefer to sit here quietly for a while?*

MELISSA: *I would like first to sit quietly for a while ...*

As with the previous stage, this one is about new patterns; unlike the previous one, it is about *being with the client* (as in the case of Authentic Listening). Therefore, the range of techniques or interventions that the practitioner might use at this stage is limited. Nevertheless, it is possible to associate some support mechanisms for different psychological domains such as:

- Assisting the client to maintain positive outlook (hope and optimism) in the domain of perception.

- In the thinking domain, the consultant can help the client identify what can provide support (e.g. family members), and on the other side of the coin help them do a prediction check (what can go wrong, what can sabotage their attempt to make the change).
- In the affective domain, the consultant can be there for the client, to provide stability and acknowledge difficulties that the client may be experiencing when putting their intentions into practice.
- In the behavioural domain, constructive feedback and encouragement (e.g. focusing on benefits) can help the client sustain a desirable change.

Regarding the relationship dimension, the consultant can support the client in making a change (*surface*) and/or assist them with their experience of change (*depth*). For example, a client may be doing well in trying to free themselves from an addiction, but may feel low or even depressed during that transition period. In such cases the consultant may stay more on the depth side of the relationship axis.

Moving from one stage to another

Rob

Rob was a heroin addict and HIV+. His health was deteriorating rapidly and yet he was not able to disengage from using drugs, smoking and drinking. He engaged in the consultancy process but was not motivated to do much and was very pessimistic. He had already tried counselling on a number of occasions and was 'tired of repeating the story of his life over and over'. Although the PC did not engage in an attempt to make a diagnosis, depression did come to mind. This was all a part of stage one. However, in order to motivate the client the PC made the decision to skip stage two (Rebalancing) for the time being and move to stage three straight away.

PC: *Is there anything else you would like to do in life besides drugs?*

ROB: *Hmmm ... I would like to have dinner in a nice restaurant; I haven't done it in years.*

PC: *Can you tell me how that would look? Is there anybody you would like to be there with you?*

ROB: *Yes, my sister ...*

Rob was encouraged to describe this fictional experience in detail. Later on he was asked to vividly describe his ideal day and where he would like to be in a year. Rob brightened up after talking about these positive 'experiences' that he slowly turned into his goals. After a while, we had to visit stage two, but he commented that he found that early session particularly refreshing as, for once, he was not focusing on his issues, on what was wrong with him. This encouraged him to work towards a change – as he put it, 'It helps to see some light at the end of the tunnel, even if I never get there.'

The consultancy process should ideally follow the pattern 1, 2, 1, 3, 1, 4, 1 ... Returning to Authentic Listening is essential. For example, it would be a mistake to point out certain inconsistencies in a client's views (stage two) and then immediately jump to Generating different options (stage three). The client may need time to absorb what has been discussed and the consultant needs to check if the new insights have been internalised before moving on, which requires listening first. This is not to say that all these stages are always necessary. Sometimes a process may end with Rebalancing (stage two), or certain specific practical issues may need only a brief visit to the same stage. It also seems that there are cases when it is useful to go straight from stage one to stage three and only later visit stage two, as in the above example. So, this map of the territory does not have only one trajectory – there are a number of options available. Nevertheless, it is important not to lose sight of any of them all.

The timing

Timing, or deciding when to move from one stage to another, is an essential element of the process. To be sure, many practitioners, even those who do not practise Personal Consultancy, may spontaneously move from one stage to another. We believe that timing is indeed to some extent an intuitive decision based on experience and that we should not be overly prescriptive in this respect. Nevertheless, there may be some useful pointers to keep in mind. For example, we always need to be aware of what stage of the process we are in and clear about when we are moving between stages as it happens. The other issue is that although the process can shift between stages even within one session, it is not helpful to blur the boundaries between them. For example, the consultant should not challenge the client on certain perceived inconsistencies (which may happen in Rebalancing at stage two) before both the client and the practitioner feel that the client has been understood (in other words, while still in Authentic Listening stage one). This is because what is perceived as inconsistency may only be a misunderstanding on the consultant's part. Of course, emotional understanding is also important – the client needs to be given enough time to express their emotions about an issue before moving on.

The move from the Rebalancing stage to the Generating stage is especially sensitive. Some may even see this as a move from counselling to coaching. This move should happen only when both the client and the consultant feel that the client has reached an optimal level of balance or inner harmony in relation to the issue at hand. In other words, when they feel that good foundations have been laid for future work. This is because it is very difficult to deal with internal conflicts and external (behavioural) issues or goals at the same time. As the example in 'Why integration' (Chapter 3) illustrates, it is hard for someone to build their organisational skills and motivation if they have conflicting feelings about their job. Determining when to move from the Generating stage to the Supporting stage is probably easier, but is not by any means straightforward. The earliest that moving to this stage can be beneficial is normally when the client starts putting goals and strategies into practice. For example, if the issue is phobia of pigeons, the Supporting stage should commence when the client takes the first steps toward overcoming his or her phobia in the real world, outside the Personal Consultancy sessions. Of course, it may be necessary to revisit the Generating and/or Rebalancing stages, perhaps several times, and it is always necessary to return to the Authentic Listening (stage one), before the Supporting stage is completed. Finally, it should be mentioned that going through the whole cycle a number of times with the same client (perhaps in relation to different issues) is quite common.

The topic of the stages and particularly the timing raises another issue: use of boundaries when working with this model. This subject will be addressed in the following chapter.

Chapter 7

Where are the boundaries?

What do we mean by boundaries?

From a professional perspective boundaries are about the practitioner being clear with themselves and their clients about what might be expected from each other and therefore communicating that they are reliable and trustworthy, which helps to establish rapport. Boundaries create a framework within which the relationship can develop and thrive and which the client and practitioner can both refer back to. They allow clients to *know* (rather than guess, surmise or have anxieties about) what is expected of them and what they can reasonably expect of the practitioner. Relevant boundaries include time, frequency of sessions, location, confidentiality agreements and contracting. They help to create stability and safety for the client by communicating the notion that all relationships have limits including a coaching, counselling or coach–therapy relationship. They protect the client and practitioner from exploitation and from potentially 'messy' situations that could have a negative impact on the interaction and outcomes. Frequently clients are very unclear about what to expect from therapy or coaching so it might be reasonable to assume that offering an integration of the two potentially increases the possibility of confusion. If this is not managed well at the outset (and throughout the relationship) then the quality of the work and the potential for a positive outcome could be compromised.

Although we often hear practitioners extolling the importance of boundaries we wonder if they are always applied with sophistication. We think there is merit in exploring the true nature of boundaries with all their facets and complexities in more depth so that we can offer a refined understanding of their *purpose* as well as how and when they might be best implemented, in ways that are of the most benefit to client and practitioner. For this reason we want to step outside of coach–therapy for the moment and examine boundaries in other contexts.

Managing and negotiating boundaries is something that we all do on a daily basis whether we are conscious of it or not. Put simply, a boundary can be seen as being a 'line in the sand' or something that demarcates one thing from something else. Its purpose is to bring some clarity about what is expected of us, what is acceptable and what isn't. In society we deal with explicit and implicit boundaries all the time. Explicit societal boundaries include the laws of the land that we all mostly abide by, with clear sanctions if we don't. Implicit societal boundaries are the *invisible* lines drawn between what is generally acceptable and what is not. Despite being implicit these boundaries are often very clear because we have grown up knowing what they are and how to manage them. However, because different cultures and different people have varying ideas about where the lines should be drawn, in some contexts there are times when we are uncertain about where a boundary might be or if we might have crossed it unwittingly. Despite being implicit, most of us recognise them and navigate through them on the basis of our experience. Similarly, we have probably all experienced boundaries being crossed by others who may have had different notions about where the lines are. We may experience a feeling of anxiety when this happens and uncertainty about what to do. These are precisely the situations in which questions arise about where we draw the line, who draws it and how flexible it is.

We negotiate boundaries explicitly and implicitly within the family, school, work and personal and professional relationships. They consist of spoken and unspoken agreements that exist to communicate what each party expects and hopes for from the other and they serve to make us feel safe in a variety of different contexts. They help us feel secure, because we can predict what might happen in a given context and can be better prepared if a situation does not go the way we expect or hope for. We are able to plan our day-to-day lives because to a certain extent we know what to expect. People usually inform us if they are unable to attend a meeting, training is expected to start at a prearranged time, and we may want to make sure that a lunch with a friend is arranged at a time and place that is convenient for both; if we meet in a restaurant, we know what to expect from the staff there, and how we are expected to behave as customers. Boundaries also help us to deal with unexpected situations or crises. For example, when involved in a road traffic accident we know that we should be insured, that we must swap insurance details, inform the police in certain circumstances and not admit liability. These explicit and implicit boundaries allow situations to be contained and avoid further confusion, chaos and conflict. These are only a few examples of how boundaries help to grease the mechanisms of our lives and the world around us. If there were no boundaries and no rules of any kind, then life for everyone would be chaotic or even dangerous and society would probably grind to a halt!

Returning then to the practitioner perspective, we might ask what we should be thinking about so that our boundaries with clients will be safe, ethical and meaningful, and managed with purpose and intentionality. We can reasonably apply what we understand about personal and societal boundaries to our professional work. For example, boundaries like those that help to prevent arguments when there is a traffic accident can also help the therapist, coach or Personal Consultant and their clients to negotiate the unexpected as and when it occurs.

The working alliance

To help give meaning and some shape to the setting and maintaining of boundaries on an ongoing basis we refer to Bordin's (1979) concept of the 'working alliance'. Bordin identifies the key elements of the working alliance as the *empathic bond* and agreement about the *goals* and *tasks* of the work. If the empathic bond is strong and there is a high level of agreement about the goals and tasks, then the practitioner and the client are 'on the same page' about important aspects of their work together, the relationship is collaborative, and positive outcomes are more likely to occur. Dryden (2006) builds on Bordin's ideas by identifying a fourth element: agreement on the *views* taken of the client's issues. Holding these in mind when contracting at the outset and throughout the relationship helps us to clarify and therefore more effectively keep track of and understand the subtleties of boundaries. We see this as being vital when working as a Personal Consultant or as an integrated coach–therapist because it necessitates moving between different types of work, where aspects of the working alliance may be different. This perhaps most obviously relates to the tasks, but as we illustrate below the elements may need to be considered.

Empathic bond

We propose that empathy is something we should communicate in subtle ways and that the boundaries on the level of empathy communicated or expressed may need to be 'fine tuned' in Personal Consultancy as we move between the different stages of working that the model implies. Empathy can be seen as a 'way of being' and a communication skill (Egan, 1994). When we talk about 'fine tuning' empathy we are referring to it as a communication skill. It is not our intention to suggest that practitioners moderate the amount of empathy they experience for their client, simply that they should exercise caution when communicating empathy – and that sometimes it is useful to be selective. There are times when a client might benefit from the 'empathy dial' being turned up high and there are times when it is more appropriate to keep the level low. For example, a new client may not be prepared for experiencing high levels of mutual emotional understanding. The communication of accurate empathy can elicit raw emotion on a level the client may not have anticipated. If trust is not yet fully established it might be difficult for the practitioner to contain the session and for the client to feel safe. A sense of vulnerability associated with the expression and experience of difficult feelings could have a detrimental effect on the future of the relationship thereby compromising potential positive outcomes. We concur with Egan (1994) who asserts:

> Since empathy is a kind of intimacy, too much empathy too soon can inhibit rather than facilitate helping. Warmth, closeness and empathy are not goals in themselves … If empathy, or too much empathy too soon, stands in the way of this goal (to help clients clarify their problems), then it should be avoided.

We propose, therefore, a flexible approach to communicating empathy depending on the stage we are working in at a given time. However, we caution that it would be too simplistic to assume that the more 'therapeutic' type work within Personal Consultancy will require higher levels of empathy than the 'coaching'. We think that it is possible to be as empathic with someone when they are excited and working dynamically as it is when working with the same person experiencing emotional pain or trauma (which is not to suggest that excitement is only attributed to coaching or pain to therapy). We would propose then that managing the boundaries in relation to empathy is more akin to tuning in to a particular flavour of emotion and communicating this in a way that is appropriate at the time. In the Generating stage, the client may value the practitioner's empathy for feelings of hope and enthusiasm and feel the alliance strengthened as a result. On the other hand, feelings of current frustration alluded to at such points may be noted in passing, but with the empathy dial turned down relatively low, so as not to shift the work out of Generating if that is where the energy is focused at the time. (If these feelings haven't been discussed before, they may, of course, be explored in a subsequent listening stage or it may be necessary to move back into the Rebalancing stage.)

Agreement on the goals of coach–therapy or Personal Consultancy

When working as a Personal Consultant or integrative coach–therapist it is perhaps even more important that both practitioner and client (and any third party such as an organisation that may have commissioned the work) are on the same page in terms of what they are working towards and what they would like to have achieved once the work is over. It is possible and even likely that the client will have behavioural or performance type goals as well as therapeutic goals and that successful attainment of one goal may impact or depend upon achieving or addressing the other. For example, a client may want to achieve promotion at work yet be insecure due to childhood abuse and the beliefs they hold about themselves as a result. They may need to unpack their feelings around the abuse and explore and address any negative self-beliefs before they are free to move on to work on the more proactive goals associated with their career. On the other hand, a certain amount of work towards career goals may help to empower them to work on the difficult and painful issue of abuse. It may also be possible to work on both issues concurrently depending on the client's preferences and what seems most appropriate at the time. The relationship of this to the concept of 'boundaries' may not seem obvious, but we would suggest that many practitioners are likely to have asked themselves at times 'Is this what we are supposed to be working on?', and have some doubts about whether they are working within the boundaries of their contract with the client. The important thing is to keep track of where the client is in terms of what they want to achieve because things can change, other priorities can take over once the work has started, and the relationship between different types of goals can change. So, not only start with the end in mind but keep the end in mind. It is important to not fall into the trap of assuming that the practitioner always knows what the client wants. Personal Consultants need to listen carefully to their clients and keep in mind how the work they are doing relates to the client's goals. If this is not clear, or if the client appears to be pursuing a different direction, it may be helpful to discuss this. The client may indeed have got in touch with a new goal and it would be useful for this to be shared. On the other hand, they may just have become sidetracked, or be going off on a tangent. They may not communicate either of these possibilities fully (if they are not asked) until they are completing evaluation forms at the end and by then it will be too late!

Agreement on the tasks

This is about what the work will consist of and what needs to be done by client and practitioner both within the sessions and outside of the sessions in order to achieve established goals. The tasks within the sessions could include elements such as the client agreeing to be as open as is comfortably possible and the practitioner agreeing to listen carefully, check understanding, explain any techniques they think might be useful and explicitly point out any changes in boundaries. This brings up the important boundary of 'informed consent'. It is of course very important that any approaches or techniques that are suggested are only implemented and used with the client's full understanding and agreement. Aside from the ethical dimension, this matters because clients will disengage if they don't feel comfortable with an approach. Research informs us that outcomes are more likely to be successful if the client understands, feels comfortable and ultimately 'buys in' to any approach or technique that is used (Duncan et al., 2010). Timing and pacing are part of the tasks and responsibilities of the practitioner. Perhaps if the client moves too quickly they may feel overwhelmed; too slowly and they might not feel sufficiently stretched. It is important to recognise what the client's optimal pace is early on, but also keep alert in this respect because the pace may change, for example, when doing practical and proactive type work in the Generating stage and when dealing with deeper issues in the Rebalancing stage. Once again, it is important to keep track of the tasks and where practitioner and client both feel they are, in terms of what is being done and whether it is working or not. It may be necessary to ask such evaluation questions and discuss them because, as aspirations and goals shift throughout the course of the work, so too do the tasks.

The practitioner also needs to consider how much they direct the process at this point, or where the boundary lies in terms of offering direction. It is important to recognise that there are often decisions to be made on the spectrum from being very client-centred to being very directive in terms of process, but that these extremes do not represent a simple binary choice. In between being completely directive and completely client-led, there is a whole range of ways of working with the client to discuss and share responsibility for the goals and tasks of the work. It is important to keep this boundary in mind, and when appropriate have questions such as direction discussed and addressed collaboratively. In a sense this is all 'grist for the mill'. A client may come for Personal Consultancy expecting the practitioner to direct the process, ask questions, provide structure, identify problems, provide insight, set homework tasks, etc., and anticipate taking a passive role as a result. Another client might arrive at sessions and launch into a monologue expecting the practitioner to listen and follow wherever they lead without offering much in the way of intervention or direction. In each of these cases, an open and collaborative exploration of the goals of the work, and discussion of the tasks involved in working towards those goals, should help both parties negotiate a way of working which is more likely to be helpful, and where each knows what to expect of the other.

Agreement on the views taken of the client's issues

This is about developing a shared understanding of the client's issues and furthermore about developing a shared understanding of how the client understands their issues. It is important that the practitioner sees the issues from the client's perspective and this means understanding the issues from the cognitive, emotional and experiential viewpoint of the client. As well as the specifics of their goals, problems, narratives, etc., the practitioner also needs to become skilled at listening for the client's existing 'conceptual frameworks' – what models or theories (however informal, implicit or unacknowledged) they are using to understand themselves, their issues and the process of change. We would see an important boundary existing between working with a view of the client's issues that is clear and familiar to them and working with views that might be clear to the practitioner (from a particular theory or model) but are not clear to the client. Recognising that boundary is important because in most cases best prospect for positive change lies in staying with views that make sense to the client or are at least a good fit with their existing views (Duncan et al., 2010). For example, cognitive behavioural techniques are more likely to be effective with clients who already conceptualise their issues in terms of the ways their negative thoughts or beliefs influence their feelings and behaviour; psychodynamic approaches are more likely to be effective with clients who sense that there is a connection between an issue they are struggling to make sense of in the present and some significant but not fully processed experience in their past. It may, however, be the case that at times exploring a different view with the client can be experienced as a positive challenge, a new perspective, and that a new insight or possibility can fall into place as a result. An example of this might be helping a client to analyse a particular interaction in Transactional Analysis terms, if this has not been familiar to them previously. We suggest that it is important to recognise that, in shifting to such a view, a boundary has been crossed and the client's collaboration needs to be engaged in order to maintain the best possible alliance.

Personal Consultants also need to be aware that many clients can be more comfortable working in one stage than another and may, for example, have different ways of conceptualising their aspirations and goals on one hand and past pain and trauma on the other. It does not automatically follow that, because a client has worked seemingly easily in the Rebalancing stage, they will find future focused work in the Generating stage as comfortable. This may in part be due to the different views they take of concepts such as 'pain' and 'hope', as in the case study example below. As a result, the practitioner needs to be particularly sensitive to potential shifts in perception and 'views taken' when working in different stages.

Brian

Brian has had a fair amount of therapy in the past and his experience has led him to believe that exploring past pain helps him to develop insight into himself, self-awareness and an understanding of his feelings and responses in the present. He has found the process both cathartic and helpful. At the same time throughout life he has found that, when he has attached hope to a particular aspiration or ambition and invested energy in it, he has been disappointed or things have gone badly wrong. As a result he has developed a strong resistance to putting himself through this again. His view is that having a goal is unlikely to work out for him, and will probably end in disappointment or disaster. However, Brian is aware that if he wants to move beyond his current sense of being stuck and going nowhere he needs to undertake some future-oriented work. He engaged in Personal Consultancy explicitly because he wanted to be able to explore his aspirations but made it clear in initial contracting that this would be difficult for him and would need to be done in a non-threatening way. He initially worked comfortably in the Rebalancing stage but found any movement into the Generating stage frightening. It was important to explore this with Brian – to have a clear shared appreciation of his existing framework for making sense of his relationship to the world and the process of change. As a result, it was possible to work with Brian in the Generating stage by exploring his hopes and aspirations very broadly at first. This involved avoiding a focus on any particular explicit goals, which would have led him to become anxious and disengage from the work. Part of Brian's 'model' was that any opportunities for positive change would present themselves as and when – trying to 'force' things would lead to failure and disappointment – so it was important to acknowledge this in the work. The extent to which assumptions like this were to be challenged was also part of the ongoing collaborative discussion about the goals and tasks of the work.

It remains important though for practitioners to continue to clarify their understanding throughout the course of the work because things can 'fall down' due to an inaccurate or clumsy understanding of how the client views their issues. This can be done through tentative use of empathy and probing, for example 'Let me just explain how I think you see this … Have I got that right?'

We need to keep track of the above elements of the 'working alliance' so that there is clarity and understanding between practitioner and client and both remain on the same page in terms of the empathic bond, aims, tasks and how the issues are conceptualised. This needs to be an ongoing and evolving process and requires collaboration between both parties. We suggest that the working alliance provides a more effective and sophisticated way of implementing *meaningful* boundaries (in terms of what the practitioner and client can expect from each other within the relationship) as opposed to merely learning that we should be clear about time, length of session, location, etc. It locates more subtle boundaries within a framework where their purpose is clear, because it is linked to key elements of the alliance and thereby the process of successful work.

Contracting

Contracting is an important part of setting and maintaining boundaries in a coaching or therapy relationship. It enables the client to be clear about what they are being offered, what might be expected of them and what they might expect from the practitioner. When offering Personal Consultancy or an integrative coach–therapy approach it is probably even more important. So what do we need to consider?

The first thing to think about is how the practitioner receives the referral and therefore consider what the client already knows about Personal Consultancy or integrative coach–therapy. Have they sought a Personal Consultant because this is what they are specifically looking for? Or have they presented themselves initially as a coaching or a counselling client?

If they have specifically sought an approach that integrates coaching and therapy then they have probably made an informed choice, likely to be based on the fact that they see their issues as falling into the realm of both disciplines. It is also possible that even if they don't think they have 'therapy' issues to address they might prefer a coaching practitioner with a therapy background, because they may see that as enhancing the work. In the same way we have had therapy clients who liked the fact that we are experienced and qualified coaches and sometimes see that as something of a bonus, opening up the expectation of a more dynamic and proactive approach.

On the other hand we also see clients whose initial request has been for either a 'pure' coaching or 'pure' therapy approach. However, our experience has demonstrated that individuals rarely fall clearly into one domain and often, as the work progresses, it can be appropriate and even necessary to move the work into a different stage than we originally agreed. This means it is necessary to renegotiate the contract in order to approach the work in an integrative coach–therapy way.

When contracting for Personal Consultancy it is important that the client understands what this means. This can involve a verbal explanation and rationale for this approach but it may also be useful to direct them to some written materials – which could be a brief section on the practitioner's website or a leaflet that they can take home and digest later. Written material can be helpful because many clients come to a first session with a high level of anxiety or excitement so it may not always be easy for them to take everything in or fully comprehend the ramifications of what the consultant is proposing. Later, when they are less likely to feel pressured by the situation (or the practitioner), they are able to look at the offerings in a more rational and objective way and make decisions accordingly. So, assuming the client has read up on the approach and wants to proceed, what might be included in a Personal Consultancy contract that wouldn't be seen in a coaching or therapy contract?

It is important to mention at this point that all practitioners approach contracting in different ways. Similarly, Personal Consultants and integrative coach–therapists will each develop an approach to this that is unique to them. However, working across a coach–therapy continuum can involve working in very different ways and this does need to be acknowledged at the outset because the stages will *feel* different to the client. For example, the Rebalancing stage may involve much in-depth probing and reflective work such as resolving internal conflicts, exploring past experiences and developing insight into thought processes and irrational beliefs. As we noted earlier, this work is often slower in pace. On the other hand the generating stage will focus on positive change, setting goals and implementing action plans, utilising strengths and developing more appropriate thoughts and beliefs. This work is frequently faster in pace, more energised and often very dynamic.

The boundaries of the work may well need to be different when in different stages and, again, this needs to be explained during initial contracting. For example, when working therapeutically it may be necessary to see each other weekly simply because the nature of the work is more intensive. During this period we usually discourage contact between sessions, so that the client has sufficient time to process what is emerging. However, when working in the Generating stage it may be preferable to see each other less often (maybe fortnightly or monthly) but for longer (perhaps an hour and a half or longer depending on the context). Many practitioners have some contact between sessions during this stage (often using e-mail) because this helps to maintain momentum and commitment to goals and action plans. All of this needs to be understood and agreed by the client at the beginning otherwise the boundaries will seem blurred due to lack of clarity, which could create confusion or even insecurity. We think that it is fine to be flexible with the boundaries in the way that we describe as long as:

• the client knows where they are at the outset and at any given time during the course of the work;

- they understand the purpose and rationale behind any change in boundaries;
- you have their informed consent.

When practitioners contract with 'pure' coaching or therapy clients it is probably important to mention that they also sometimes work as a Personal Consultant and they should explain what that involves. This is not to suggest that they plan to direct the work towards integrative coach–therapy but it merely flags up that therapy work may influence the coaching and vice versa. It is also helpful to offer a brief explanation that it is not unusual for clients to come with one issue and end up wanting to address something else, and that this will be discussed in more detail down the line if it happens. A brief conversation in this respect at the outset simply lets the client know something about orientation and background, and how being dually trained may impact on the way a practitioner works. It also prepares them for any changes that may arise as things unfold. If this does happen then it will be necessary – at the time – to have a more detailed discussion about what else might be offered, taking into account the points made above. When doing this, as when suggesting anything different from what has been contracted for, it is important that clients fully understand and are able to give informed consent without feeling pressure or coercion.

Assessment

Practitioners have a varied approach to assessment. We respect this and don't want to be prescriptive in what we recommend. For example, some therapists will not undertake a formal assessment at all because they don't want to develop preconceived ideas or assumptions about the client that may get in the way later or contaminate the work. On the other hand, other practitioners take assessment very seriously indeed and use the opportunity to gather as much information as possible, because they see the assessment process as being useful in helping to direct the work and believe it allows for better management of risk. We don't take a stance on this and think practitioners need to consider and choose for themselves how they approach the issue. In fact one of us is in favour of detailed assessments and the other doesn't do assessments at all. However, practitioners who are trained in both disciplines (coaching and therapy) often ask us how we approach assessment given that the process can be quite different for coaching clients and therapy clients. The bottom line is that practitioners are advised to align the approach to Personal Consultancy assessments with that of their therapy assessments. The work is likely to touch on therapeutic issues and therefore potential risks need to be managed with Personal Consultancy clients in the same way as in therapy.

So, for those in favour of a fairly detailed therapeutic assessment, what might need to be included? Mental health issues past and present, suicide attempts and ideation, medication, experience of violence, substance misuse issues past and present, etc. could all be seen as important. It is also important to have details of the client's GP, or any other professional they are connected to, because if, for example, there is a need to break confidentiality, then it is necessary to know who to talk to. Ideally, this will be a living and breathing document (as opposed to a tick box/form filling exercise) that evolves over time and can help not only with managing risk but also with flagging up issues for the practitioner and client that may be useful to work with.

In addition, most coaching practitioners have questionnaires that they give their clients before the work starts which are designed to produce a snapshot of the client's current picture and issues, how they see themselves, their strengths, resources, environment, hindering factors, etc. The purpose of this is to raise insight and encourage motivation as well as to be a starting point in developing aims for the work. Tools and techniques such as these are as useful within the Personal Consultancy model as in coaching. This will be discussed in more detail in Chapter 9.

Contracting with organisations

Contracting with organisations is always more complex and how it is carried out often depends on what they are looking for from the practitioner(s). It will usually entail an umbrella agreement between both parties about the nature of the work, practicalities, remuneration, who is responsible for what, etc. It will also include how much information or feedback (if any), and to whom, will be divulged about the content of the work. It is this last point that needs to be dealt with sensitively when a third party (such as an employer) is involved because there can sometimes be dilemmas around *who* the client is – the employer who has commissioned the work and is paying, or the client the practitioner will be working with face to face. Usually it is a combination of both. The practitioner needs to negotiate, clarify and agree with all stakeholders at the outset any responsibility around giving feedback and sharing information, to prevent confusion later on, and so that the client is clear about any limits to confidentiality. For example, it may simply include having to report back to the organisation *if* the client has attended the sessions, with a financial penalty to the client if they don't. On the other end of the spectrum, the organisation may have clear objectives about what they are looking for from the coaching side. Examples might include working with a new senior executive to help them to develop 'gravitas' or improve their communication or leadership/ management skills. The extent to which an organisation wants feedback about the coaching and to what degree the aims and objectives are being achieved can vary from organisation to organisation. The ways that they might measure the success of the intervention will also differ. However, clarity and 'buy in' from all concerned is vital at the outset about *what* can be communicated, by *whom* and at *what* stages of the process.

It may be necessary to explain to the organisation that the rationale for including a therapeutic element is to allow the client to explore patterns and behaviours from the past (for example) that may be getting in the way of achieving optimum performance and that this element of the work really should be off limits in terms of feedback. We know that many practitioners have been hesitant in the past about offering a 'therapeutic' intervention to organisations as they are worried it might lose them potential contracts. Perhaps they see the corporate world as wanting something altogether crisper and with a business edge. That may be true but we think it depends on *how* it is presented. Practitioners who are clear and professional in their presentation (retaining a crisp business edge) and give a convincing rationale for choice of approach have every chance for success. We have noticed more recently that we have gained corporate coaching contracts *because* of the therapeutic element to our work, not in spite of it.

In conclusion, it has to be remembered that we are all individuals and have different approaches to therapy, coaching, coach–therapy and boundaries. It almost goes without saying that the boundary containing the work and the boundary between the different stages will be somewhat different with every practitioner depending on therapy and coach orientation, preferred ways of working, the client's preferences and issues and the context of work. Also different will be the extent to which the practitioner directs the process and the movement between stages. Some practitioners will use the Personal Consultancy model in a way that is very responsive to where they see the client as being, whereas others will be more directive in encouraging movement from one stage to another. In this chapter we have tried to cover some issues that we think are important and identify some guiding principles for safe, ethical and meaningful boundary management. We respect that there will be various ways that Personal Consultants will apply boundaries within their practice. The bottom line though has to be that however practitioners apply boundaries within Personal Consultancy work it is important to be clear and collaborative with the client throughout.

Chapter 8

The process

Case studies to illustrate the kinds of issues that can arise when working with the Personal Consultancy framework

Our intention within this book has been to explain what Personal Consultancy is and why we think it is a useful framework for integrating disciplines such as counselling, therapy and coaching. We have discussed how this framework can be applied to practice in a wide range of contexts. Of course, there could never be a real substitute for observing practice. When we teach Personal Consultancy we demonstrate the application of the Personal Consultancy framework or some of its aspects using volunteers so there is an opportunity to witness the kind of issues that can arise for the client and the practitioner when moving from one stage to another.

For the same reason, we have chosen to introduce two of our clients Margery and Katie in the hope that this will provide a flavour of the kind of work that might be done when working as a Personal Consultant. Margery's case study provides an in-depth insight into a first session and Katie's offers an overview of Personal Consultancy work that continued for about nine months.

Margery – a first session

Margery worked within a governmental department that was undergoing some major restructuring as a result of new governmental policy. To cope with this staff had been offered coaching and given a selection of coaches' profiles to choose from. She said that she had selected her coach on the basis of wanting a therapeutic element (in addition to the coaching) as she recognised that she was experiencing extreme stress and anxiety due to uncertainty around her professional future in the short term. She also had unresolved issues from her childhood in Nigeria that had surfaced. She wanted to work on these issues in addition to developing a plan about what to do regarding her career. Having read the profiles of the available coaches and the approaches they used she thought that the Personal Consultancy model best suited her needs.

The contract with the organisation meant that the content of the sessions were completely confidential and there was no stipulation about what clients should be focusing on. The practitioner's responsibility to the organisation was merely to report if clients did not turn up to sessions as all staff had agreed to the possibility of a financial penalty if this happened. Three sessions of one and a half hours in length were to be negotiated over a three month period. Margery chose to see me at my home where I have a small private practice for two days of the week. Questionnaires and evaluations were completed both before the sessions commenced and after they were completed in order to measure efficacy, chart progress made in specific areas (chosen by the client) and offer some direction for the future.

During the first session Margery spent quite a long time telling her story and describing how the different issues interweaved and impacted on each other. In this first stage of the Personal Consultancy framework (Authentic Listening) my responses were fairly minimal as I wanted to give genuine attention as well as give her space to express herself emotionally and cognitively and establish trust and rapport. I paid particular attention on a perceptual level to slight incongruities about what she said and how she behaved in particular around her work/life balance. She was adamant that she wanted to find a role that fitted around her family commitments (a husband and three daughters) as she stated they were her priority. However, her body language and facial expression communicated that this might not be the whole truth. Similarly, the focus on her cognitive communication (her thought processes and beliefs) revealed quite a deep-seated belief around the value she placed on herself both at home and at work. This was compounded by her behaviour in the session with the practitioner, initially at least choosing to take on a somewhat subservient role by constantly checking if she was doing things right: 'Am I rambling? Am I making sense to you? I don't want to waste your time.' She appeared to be doing her best to behave like a good client.

Despite there being many things that could be challenged, it was more important in this stage to allow her to talk and see where that would take her. Any intervention from me would have determined a direction that may or may not have been right for her. Also this 'listening time' gave me the opportunity to get a clearer grasp of her situation on a variety of levels. I heard her assessment of what was happening in real practical terms and was able to balance that alongside her perceptions, cognitions and behaviours and really understand how she viewed the world. In terms of the practitioner dimension of the Personal Consultancy model I was very much at the 'being' end of the axis. In telling her story in the early stages of the relationship Margery was at the 'existing patterns' end of the client axis. As far as the relationship axis went we were somewhere between 'depth' and 'surface', occasionally dipping deeper as Margery appeared to 'test' the waters of how much she could trust me.

After about half an hour there was a natural shift into the second stage (Rebalancing) of the Personal Consultancy model. This followed a long pause when Margery looked at me and said, 'That's more or less it ... What do you think?' I responded that I could see there was a lot going on for her and she seemed to be wrestling with some difficult emotions (fear and feeling trapped) in relation to the uncertainty at work which had brought up anxieties related to her childhood. I compared these emotions to her response on the assessment questionnaire to the question 'Why have you chosen coaching at this time?': 'With the changes I seem to be "caged in" – fear of facing challenges and more changes and frightened that I am not progressing career-wise'.

This allowed us to explore her story at a deeper level, looking at the feelings she had expressed earlier in the session (verbally and non-verbally) as well as what had been communicated in the initial questionnaire. Fear seemed to be the overriding emotion (and may have masked other less powerful emotions) – fear of the unknown, fear of challenge, fear of taking risks, fear of unsettling her family and fear of not ever reaching her full potential. I observed that the fear seemed 'all pervading' and wondered what living with the fear had been like for her. She talked about her support networks: immediate family at home; family members in Nigeria (mother, sister, brothers); colleagues and friends at work; and friends at her local church. Being valued by those she cared about had helped her to cope. I tentatively reminded her that she had described herself as 'strong' on the initial questionnaire and wondered how much she thought that was true. She replied that she thought it was, stating that her mother always described her as 'strong and capable' and she still identified with that. She said that she had endured great difficulties as a child growing up in Nigeria and had developed her strength in response to this adversity but she moved quickly on and seemed uncomfortable.

I said gently, 'I'm getting a strong sense that there are things you don't really want to talk about ... at the moment.'

She nodded her head and was very still for a few moments and then said, 'It's hard to equate the feelings of fear to feelings of strength.'

I said that I understood. 'I can see that it must be confusing at times and maybe even adds to the anxieties that you have talked about because perhaps with such conflicting emotions you start to lose sense of who you really are?'

She nodded her head quickly. 'That's exactly it! I know that I'm strong but I'm paralysed with fear and end up not knowing what to do for the best'.

During this exchange our relationship moved further into depth on the relationship axis (perhaps due to the communication of empathy) although I felt some reticence and anxiety from Margery that she didn't want to go too deep at this point. On the client axis she was exploring her 'existing patterns' but had communicated that she was thinking about what to 'do' which was an indication that she perhaps was preoccupied with 'emerging patterns' despite not knowing what they might be. As the practitioner, I was still a way along the 'being with' mode but was thinking that for the rest of this (first) session it might be useful for now to see if she wanted to move into a more 'active' mode. This was based on her reluctance to venture much deeper and because she had communicated some practical aims in her questionnaire that I thought would be helpful to discuss at this point so that we could be clear about what our overall aims were, what she was hoping to get out of our sessions, and how I might best be able to help.

I commented that we had about 35 minutes left and wondered how she felt about moving into a more proactive stage (Generating) for the reasons stated above. I stated clearly that this was her choice and that we could return to more therapeutic type work if it seemed appropriate in subsequent sessions. She agreed that she would like to do that. She said it had been very helpful to talk about her emotions and fears and tell her story, but she would appreciate coming away from the session with something tangible in terms of what she wanted, and perhaps what next to do regarding her career situation. As she talked, I returned to the first stage of Authentic Listening to ensure that I was giving real *attention and to check whether her verbal responses matched with her body language and whether we had made the right choice in terms of the direction of our work at that time.*

We returned to her questionnaire as she had stated that she hoped coaching would help her to take the first step to overcome her fears and unlock her potential to maximise her performance and achieve her potential. I said that these were very clear aims and used a laddering technique to elicit meaning and purpose around these (see Chapter 9).

I asked, 'What would it mean to you if you are able to do this – override your fears and be able to be the best that you can be?'

She thought for a while. 'Well, I guess it would mean that I'd be performing well at work ... I'd perform better during this restructuring. You know, job applications, interviews.'

'That's great,' I said. 'What will it mean to you though if you're actually able to do that – enhance your performance, approach the recruitment process in a positive and confident way?'

'It would be liberating!' she said.

'Liberating! That's a strong word', I said, smiling and reflecting back the positivity and strength she had communicated in that one word. 'If you were liberated, what would that mean to you? How would you be feeling?'

She didn't hesitate. 'I'd be calm, capable and confident,' she said.

I communicated to her that I thought this was really significant because she had recognised and described what I saw as her 'higher order' goals. Her behavioural goals were to improve performance and get to grips with her fears, but it was really important that she understood her true purpose of achieving this. Feeling calm, capable and confident was actually what Margery was really *aiming for. This was exciting because it provided focus to the work and also made it real in terms of what the purpose was.*

We then considered how we (in the sessions) and she (outside the sessions) might start to put that in practice. She said that in subsequent sessions she would like to work on ways to minimise or remove her fears and/or at least put them into context. I agreed that this was something we could definitely do and wondered if she had actually already started to do that in some small way given she was now communicating her view of the fear as something that could be addressed – as opposed to something that was completely outside her control. I asked her what had helped her to feel calm, confident and in control in the past.

'Just doing it and telling myself I can do it and reminding myself that I've overcome fear before ... and communicating more with those close to me so that I hear them when they tell me I'm strong – rather than isolating myself.'

I suggested that perhaps she knew the answers to this issue better than I did and she laughed. I asked if this was something she might put into practice before our next session. I also asked if there was anything on a practical level (in terms of job searches, applications, etc.) that she thought might help get the ball rolling in a more specific way. She said that she had signed up for some job searches, but hadn't read through what had been sent. I wondered how it would feel if she actually started doing this.

'Absolutely great,' she said. 'Once I get started I think I'll feel much more positive about the process.'

I wondered what she might do to maintain momentum and she said that she would agree a plan with her line manager that she would work on job applications for an hour every day at an agreed time. She said that having a contract like that in place would help to keep her on track and make her feel supported.

During the Generating stage of the Personal Consultancy model I moved into being more active and was much further along the 'doing with' mode. Margery seemed to edge herself slightly away from her 'existing patterns' and with encouragement moved further towards her 'emerging pattern'. The relationship axis moved nearer the surface as we considered what her tangible aims and goals were and what she might do in the first instance to achieve them. Her perceptions had changed too as she was starting to see that her situation, although difficult, was a challenge that she could overcome. On a cognitive level she was starting to think and believe that her fears could be addressed, and her behaviour in the session was much more relaxed and cheerful. She had also recognised what she could do on a behavioural level and how that might impact on her thought processes and her feelings.

With about five minutes left I suggested we review the session and consider any insights that had come to the fore, how she was feeling currently compared with when we had started, and think about the direction we might want the work to take.

She indicated that it had been cathartic for her. She was able to unload some confused and chaotic thoughts. Voicing her fears had actually helped her to put them into some perspective although she said that she still wanted to do some work around the origins of these. She said that she had been able to reconnect to her strength, be clearer about what she was aiming for and that she had the makings of a plan to go way with.

The review was particularly important because it helped to ensure that I had an accurate picture of how she was seeing her issues, goals and any strategies – and that we were still on the 'same page'. It was important that the process remain collaborative so that any future direction made sense to her in terms of what she wanted to achieve from our time together. This accuracy of understanding helped to engage and communicate a deeper level of empathy. I felt I understood the nuances of her experiencing better as a result of this return to 'Authentic Listening' for the final minutes of the session. I believe that this helped to consolidate the relationship which provided the foundation for some significant transformative work in later sessions.

Katie – an overview of the work

Katie was 27. She was referred from a colleague for counselling and had chosen a practitioner who also had coaching experience and qualifications. She had recently moved to London from a rural part of Scotland with her boyfriend. The initial issues she presented with were to do with her current relationship (her partner had had drug problems in the past that he had overcome but had some physical and mental health problems relating to that). She also wanted to be able to understand and manage feelings of anger that had been a problem most of her adult life. During the first session it was also apparent she wanted to work on her career. Until she came to London she had worked as a care worker in a residential home. She had good qualifications to degree level but had spent a couple of years travelling and jobs locally had been quite limited in opportunities. At this point we talked about what she was hoping to get out of the therapy and she shared that she wanted to feel better in relation to her problems and difficulties, but she also wanted to get moving on her career. She actually saw the two facets as being interconnected. Katie was already talking about a way of being helped that sounded similar to an integrative coach–therapy approach. Consequently, after some discussion, the contract was renegotiated to suit the Personal Consultancy approach. She agreed that she would like to work on the therapeutic and coaching issues in parallel and chose to attend weekly sessions for one hour.

Because some of the sessions at least might include both a therapeutic type intervention (Rebalancing) and coaching (Generating) it was important to be clear about expectations and boundaries. We agreed that any contact between sessions would be related to the coaching (in the first instance she would send me her CV). Clarity about movement between the different stages of the Personal Consultancy model was particularly important given that the boundaries were different. It was also important to return to Authentic Listening to ensure that any change in direction taken was appropriate and a collaborative choice.

Katie initially chose to explore her feelings on anger as well as work on her career. She said she liked to focus on the two issues alongside each other because she felt that in that way she would not get overwhelmed and could manage the therapeutic exploration at a pace she could cope with. She was also very practical and the work initially undertaken in the Generating stage brought very immediate results in terms of identifying a clear goal. She excelled at Maths and wanted to get a job as a banker, so she developed a clear plan to achieve this. The work she did in the Generating stage helped to raise her self-esteem and the focused attention she received in the Authentic Listening stage helped to cement the practitioner–client relationship and establish trust. Both were vital in helping her navigate the more difficult work in the Rebalancing stage.

In the third session Katie revealed that she had been sexually abused by her father when she was twelve. Her father had since died and her feelings towards him were ambivalent and confused. On the one hand she loved him and had always seen him as a source of support and encouragement as in other ways he had been a good father. He had held the family together (she had two older sisters) after her mother left when Katie was ten. On the other hand, as she had grown older she had realised that what he had done was wrong and that he had 'robbed her of something very important'. Things were further complicated because since his death she had experienced feelings of loss and she also knew that she would never have the opportunity to discuss the abuse with him. She felt as if he had condemned her to carry this knowledge and the feelings associated with it for the rest of her life. In addition she felt 'enormous guilt' for her part in this. She felt dirty and shameful because of the 'special' attention her father had paid her and because she had felt arousal during his advances.

I was very conscious that Katie only wanted to explore this in 'bite-sized' chunks and that she wanted to control the pace of the process. Otherwise she would feel unsafe. A session would typically start on the 'surface' end of the relationship axis (a small talk about what she had been doing in the past week) and then we would move tentatively into Authentic Listening and/or Rebalancing depending on what was being communicated. At this point in the session the relationship would progress quite quickly towards the 'depth' end of the axis. As she was exploring the abuse and the thoughts and feelings (past and present), it seemed very important that she controlled the level of depth that we were working at and she could cope with. I was very aware of the transference and counter-transference within our relationship. It seemed at times that she saw me in a 'parental' role. In response to this I experienced very strong feelings around wanting to nurture and care for her. Even between sessions I would find myself fantasising about inviting her round to a family dinner ... I felt that transference needed to be acknowledged and worked through and that I needed robust supervision to ensure that I was managing the boundaries appropriately. This was obviously of supreme importance given that the parent she had trusted and loved had transgressed the boundaries of their relationship so badly. From me she required someone warm, accepting and non-judgemental but who also clarified and held the boundaries of this relationship.

During this time whilst Katie explored her 'existing patterns' I remained mostly around the 'being with' end of the practitioner axis. She perhaps spent three sessions working on the abuse so that she could make better sense of it. However, it became clear during these sessions that it would be easier for her to reach acceptance at an affective level about what had actually happened (the abuse) than it would be for the part she thought *she had played in the abuse – and associated emotions. This became our focus for future sessions.*

Katie experienced high degrees of self-disgust and revulsion as she thought that it was her fault her father had singled her out and she believed she must have encouraged him. She felt particular shame because she had 'enjoyed' his attentions and had experienced sexual arousal. My ultimate aim was to help her integrate her experience to a level that she could accept – but to do that it was necessary to first separate her current self from the girl she had been at twelve. I encouraged her to explore the abuse from a position of detachment because she was too embroiled to realistically understand her own role. I therefore worked concurrently with the 'current day Katie' and suggested she refer to 'twelve-year-old Katie' in the third person. I also was very honest about my own opinions (and those of society in general) about what a twelve-year-old child might be able to consent to. This element of the work took some time. I used the ABC model from REBT (Neenan and Dryden, 2000) to help dispute Katie's core beliefs about her role in the abuse:

'You say you believe that twelve-year-old Katie was responsible because she encouraged her father. How much power does a twelve-year-old have compared to an adult, especially her father who has ultimate power over her? How capable are twelve-year-old children at making decisions that might impact and affect their whole life?'

This was difficult work. Katie could accept on a cognitive level that her father had abused his power but on an affective level she still believed that she was to blame. I encouraged her to weigh the evidence in support of her belief. My challenges were gentle yet firm and delivered in a 'drip, drip' way. Katie needed to work things out at her own pace.

A couple of sessions later she told me that she had been on the tube and seen a twelve-year-old schoolgirl with her school bags. Katie said, 'She looked so young, so innocent and so completely vulnerable – I realised how powerless she would be – physically and emotionally – compared with an adult man.'

This was a breakthrough moment because it meant that Katie could actually start to reframe her beliefs. She was ultimately able to integrate, accept and provide nurture for 'twelve-year-old Katie'.

This freed Katie up to focus properly on other issues. She still wanted to work on her relationship but was able to do so from a place of self-confidence. In addition she was keen to advance her career. The plan we had developed in earlier sessions had succeeded to the point of gaining several interviews, but each time she had been unsuccessful. The effective integration of 'twelve-year-old Katie' with 'current day Katie' though resulted in an increase of resilience in the face of these failures. Her anger had dissipated and she felt in control of her life. This meant she became more pragmatic about job interviews as opposed to the anxiety she had experienced in the past when she had thought, 'I'm a fake and people will see through me – they will see how rotten I am.'

Katie was eventually offered two jobs in a field that is actually difficult to get into! She still sometimes found herself slipping into her old belief systems when stressed but had learned to recognise this and knew how to challenge herself.

The work we did in the last part of the Generating stage was dynamic and inspiring both for Katie and for me. She moved along the client axis into 'emerging patterns' and as the practitioner I was 'doing' more with her in terms of using techniques and tools in order to help her develop a plan to achieve her goal. This included helping her to explore, own and enhance existing strengths and resources as well discovering strengths and talents that she had been previously unaware of. This helped her prepare a better CV and perform more confidently in interviews. There were hiccups along the way and we moved into the Supporting stage, which helped consolidate the work that we had done and overcome obstacles as they arose. This involved help on occasions to challenge negative thoughts and beliefs about herself which resurfaced from time to time. There were still problems within her relationship – her partner's health problems were serious and ongoing – but she reaffirmed her commitment to the relationship whilst acknowledging that it was going to be difficult.

At times also we moved back into Authentic Listening and Rebalancing stages, for example on her father's birthday and the anniversary of his death. She finally recognised that it was important (for her) 'to accept the bad alongside the good', and that it was appropriate to feel loss for the parent she had loved and lost but who had also caused her great pain. This final insight meant that Katie could move forward with her life, her relationship and her new job without the shackles imposed on her in her childhood.

We hope that these case studies have been as illuminating for the reader as they were for us as practitioners. We think that 'witnessing' a session or parts of sessions can provide insights into the kind of decisions clients and practitioners might need to make when moving through the stages and along dimensions of the model. Of course, a practitioner from another therapy orientation might have used the model differently. Similarly, someone else may have chosen different coaching techniques. This is what makes the model flexible and unique to every practitioner. It also allows for individual creativity meaning that the framework should match client and practitioner preferences and not the other way around. This would enable Personal Consultancy practice to be congruent and real as opposed to being mechanical and rigid.

The bottom line (as in all coaching or therapy practice) is that the work should be collaborative throughout. The client needs to be able to make choices when appropriate about the direction of the process, and there needs to be agreement on goals, tasks and any other concepts, techniques or approaches that are incorporated. For this reason it is essential that the practitioner understands how the client views the world, their issues and the *process* by which they understand their issues (see Chapter 7).

Chapter 9

Integrating other concepts, techniques and processes

Introduction

Our intention in this chapter is to demonstrate the flexibility of the Personal Consultancy model and illustrate how it can be used by practitioners from a range of therapeutic backgrounds and orientations. It allows professionals to work in the rebalancing stage exactly as they would when doing their therapy work – whether they see themselves as purist, integrative or eclectic. In the same way, it is not necessary to adapt an individual style of coaching to suit the Generating stage. Because of this the model can be used in an authentic way.

However, Personal Consultancy does provide an opportunity to integrate other concepts, techniques and processes if practitioners choose to. We have witnessed this occurring quite naturally during practice of skills on our training programmes. Because people come to us from a variety of therapeutic and coaching backgrounds with different types and levels of training and experience there is often a richness of knowledge and skills that can be shared. The extent to which practitioners choose to develop their practice in this way is of course a personal choice, but we encourage people to try out different things as long as concepts, techniques or approaches that are integrated into the practitioner's version of the Personal Consultancy model fit with their values and philosophies.

As integrative practitioners, promoting an overarching integrative model, we encourage professionals to have an open mind about ways of working because in this way they continue to grow and develop as does the field. However, we also recognise that confidence and belief in a chosen approach (and being able to communicate this to the client) is important for successful outcomes (Duncan et al., 2010). So the integrating of other concepts, approaches and techniques should be balanced with the practitioner's confidence in how they practise the Personal Consultancy model and their ability to be able to incorporate it in an authentic way.

We have chosen some concepts, approaches and techniques here to illustrate how they might be integrated into the Personal Consultancy framework and at what stages we think they might best fit. Of course, every practitioner will have a different idea about what fits where and it is more important that the practitioner feels comfortable with their own version of the Personal Consultancy model than trying to fit a process into a stage that doesn't feel quite right to them. Similarly we have chosen a mere selection of processes, approaches, concepts and techniques that resonate with us. This is by no means exhaustive but simply intended to provide some examples of the ways that other approaches and techniques can be integrated effectively.

Rebalancing

The shift from authentic listening to rebalancing often happens very naturally. The client has communicated their experience and at a certain point (different for all clients) they turn to the practitioner for a sign about what might happen next. During the listening stage the practitioner's focus has been on the client. They have been listening and observing so that they understand the nuances of what has been communicated and also, in order to build rapport, engage the client's trust and build the foundation of a solid relationship upon which everything else can safely be built. Movement into the rebalancing stage involves clarifying aspects of the story that may have seemed unclear, confused or sometimes contradictory. It allows the practitioner to tentatively test their perception of how the client views the world and reinforce the empathic bond verbally by demonstrating understanding as well as looking for clues for strengths and resources the client may have overlooked.

Depending on what has emerged from the authentic listening stage and the first part of the rebalancing stage there are a number of conceptual frameworks or techniques that may be used if appropriate.

Malan's triangle of insight

In the rebalancing stage there are various ways that a practitioner might try to help the client make connections between current and past experiences, feelings, thoughts or behaviours. Insights raised into 'patterns' can be very useful because it helps the client to look at the experience from a wider perspective. This can be a precursor to the client taking responsibility for the part they might have played and are perhaps still playing that has led to the state of events. It is hard to adopt and maintain a 'poor me' attitude when there is evidence that something has been happening time and again.

Malan's (1979) triangle of insight is particularly useful because of its simplicity and the focus on parallels between relationships – 'in here' with the practitioner, 'out there' in the present and 'back then' in the past. It is likely that patterns learned by the client in the past are being played out in the present and will also be repeated in the client–practitioner relationship. This is a very good fit with the dimensions of the Personal Consultancy model because it explicitly allows the practitioner to focus on the relationship between themselves and the client (relationship axis) and it also encourages the client to think about their existing patterns (see Figure 9.1).

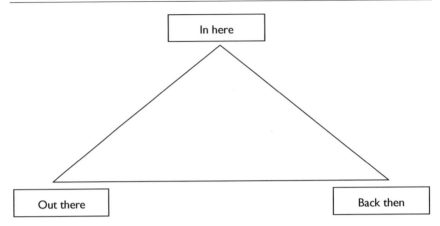

Figure 9.1 Malan's triangle of insight

The practitioner can use the triangle as a guide to help the client identify connections and parallels between two or all of the sets of experience. For example, a client who exhibits impatience with the practitioner '*in here*' may well be doing the same '*out there*' and may start to see that they have a history of doing so – '*back then*'. It may also be that a client who has experienced panic and anxiety in certain contexts '*back then*' and '*out there*' may choose the safe space '*in here*' with the practitioner to practise a new way of managing this. In this way, the relationship '*in here*' can provide opportunities for understanding experimentation and learning that the client can take '*out there*'.

Self-concept

The rebalancing stage is the ideal time to help the client develop an enhanced understanding of themselves. Insights raised at this point can be illuminating for the client and often have an immediate impact about how they feel about themselves. This raised self-awareness can also be particularly useful when moving forward into the generating stage. Self-concept work as outlined here (adapted from Rogers, 2003) allows the client to explore and integrate who they think they are (self-concept) with who they would like to be and/or think they should be (ideal self), and who they really are (real self).

Figures 9.2 and 9.3 illustrate that the greater the degree of congruence between self concept, ideal self and real self, the more fully functioning a person is (Figure 9.3). However, when there is incongruence between these versions of the self the person is likely to be less fully functioning (Figure 9.2) and experience higher levels of anxiety and/or depression.

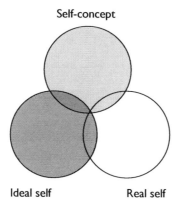

Figure 9.2 Model of self: impaired functioning

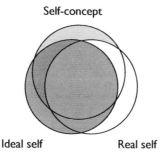

Figure 9.3 Model of self: fully functioning

Sometimes there may be a high degree of congruence between two of the versions of self but not with the third. For example the way a person really is *(real self)* would correlate to how they see themselves *(self-concept)* but not with how they would like to be or think that they should be *(ideal self)*. The circles in the diagram would adjust accordingly.

There are various ways of helping the client to raise awareness about self. However, an interesting and quite dynamic way of doing this is by using the following exercise.

Using a pen and paper, invite the client to:

- List the qualities of someone they like or admire. This can be someone they know, a historical figure or even a character in a book or a film .
- Describe their own qualities from the point of view of someone who knows them well and likes them. (If done as part of a 'homework' task the client could ask someone to do this for them).
- Describe their own qualities.

The first bullet point will generate aspects of the ideal self, the second aspects of the real self and the third of the self-concept. Once complete, the information gathered can be pulled together to show where there is congruence and where not. This can be useful because the client gets indications of any disparities; it also gives them access to parts of themselves (thoughts, behaviours, feelings, responses) that other people may notice but which they themselves have missed. This may help them understand why sometimes they may have acted in ways that have surprised them or haven't fitted with how they see themselves. For example, someone who sees themselves as being calm yet has lost their temper may discover that someone close to them describes them as 'feisty' or 'irritable'. When incorporating feedback from others it is necessary to bear in mind of course that they may sometimes be wrong or even biased. The views of others, therefore, are helpful when trying to discover the 'real self' but not always correct. Raised awareness and subsequent adjustment of their self-concept can then lead to exploration of the contexts where anger was expressed, how they actually feel about it and choices they may or may not make in response to this.

Erikson's psychosocial stages of development

Erik Erikson's theory of psychosocial development is an elegant conceptual framework around identity, personality and the life stages at which these develop. As such, this fits well into the rebalancing stage of the Personal Consultancy model because it specifically focuses upon the client's existing patterns (the client dimension) and helps them to understand how they were developed and at which life stage. This focus raises client awareness about their behavioural patterns, personality and identity, as well as about their impact on the present. In addition to helping them understand themselves it can also be useful for understanding others and for managing and dealing with conflict.

In brief, Erikson (1968) believed that personality develops in a series of stages throughout life. His theory (developed from field research with Native Americans) asserts that people go through eight 'psychosocial crisis stages' which significantly affect each person's development and personality. Each stage is manifested as a conflict or dilemma between two opposing emotional forces that should be successfully negotiated in order to achieve balance. Unsuccessful completion can mean that people develop a tendency towards one or other of the opposing forces, which can lead to recurring emotional, psychological or behavioural problems in later life. For example, an infant who experienced trauma in early life such as the loss of a parent may not have developed an appropriate balance between trust and mistrust. They may tend towards one or the other leading to obvious problems. Similarly, unsuccessful experiences at the industry vs. inferiority stage (between five and twelve) can lead to a tendency towards being overly focused on work and/ or learning or apathy and uselessness.

In the Rebalancing stage the practitioner can help the client revisit stages that have not been adequately worked through or where balance hasn't been achieved so that this can be redressed and the client can hopefully move forward, free from emotional 'baggage'.

The practitioner might encourage the client to explore how decisions, patterns of behaviour and/or coping strategies made sense or seemed rational or necessary at the time but have persisted to a point where they are no longer useful. For example, the teenager who used self-deprecation and criticism to deflect disapproval from others may discover that what worked well as a coping strategy for an adolescent may be something of a hindrance when they are in their thirties. Additionally, the practitioner may encourage a client with trust issues to think about how this manifests and consider what might need to happen for things to be better. It may be useful to explore what assumptions are being made in order to 'deeply trust' or 'deeply mistrust' and to what extent they are valid now. What did it feel like back in the time when this was an issue (when perhaps they didn't get fed and experienced neglect) and how might things be different now? What is the client's ideal about being able to trust and what might be involved in taking that risk? The practitioner may encourage the trust within the client–practitioner relationship as a safe starting point to developing relationships that include a healthy balance of trust and caution (see Table 9.1).

Generating

Movement into the Generating stage usually follows a period back in the Authentic Listening stage. By this time the client hopefully will have gained greater understanding of their existing patterns, and developed new insights and shifts in perception. They will have spent time in the Authentic Listening stage assimilating this knowledge and coming to terms with different ways of thinking and perceiving things. Of course, there will be some clients who don't require or want to work in the Rebalancing stage because they may arrive with clear ideas of an area they want to move forward with. They may even have a clear goal or an action plan and require help in working out how best to achieve the goal or implement or sustain the plan or with contingencies. In this case the work will start in Authentic Listening but then move into Generating once the practitioner and client agree that they know enough of the story and are ready to move on.

Goal setting

Setting and achieving goals with the purpose of effecting positive change is perhaps synonymous with the activity of coaching, and to some extent counselling. We do not intend to be prescriptive as to how the practitioner does this. For that reason, there is space and flexibility within the structure of the Personal Consultancy framework for individual practitioners to select (if they choose to) the approach or model that resonates most for them. The GROW model (Alexander, 2010) is possibly one of the best known goal-oriented models in the coaching arena. It provides a simple framework for practitioners and clients to identify

Table 9.1 Erikson's stages of psychosocial development

Stage	Crisis	Important Events	Conclusion
Infancy (birth to 18 months)	Trust vs. Mistrust	Feeding	Children need to develop a sense of trust that caregivers will meet their basic needs and provide nurture, love, reliability, care, and affection. Without this a child might grow up with a basic mistrust of the world.
Early Childhood (2 to 3 years)	Autonomy vs. Shame and Doubt	Toilet Training	Toddlers need to develop a sense of independence and personal control over physical skills. Success leads to feelings of autonomy, failure results in feelings of shame and doubt about their abilities.
Preschool (3 to 5 years)	Initiative vs. Guilt	Exploration	Pre-schoolers need to begin asserting control and power over the environment and start to use their own initiative. Success in this stage leads to a sense of purpose. Children who try to exert too much power develop guilt about their needs, wants and desires.
School Age (6 to 11 years)	Industry vs. Inferiority	School	Throughout school years, children need to cope with new social and academic demands and develop confidence through learning. Success leads to a sense of competence, whilst failure may result in an inferiority complex.
Adolescence (12 to 18 years)	Identity vs. Role Confusion	Social Relationships	Teens need to develop a sense of self and personal identity and they become concerned with how they seem to others. Success leads to an ability to stay true themselves and know who they are whilst failure leads to role confusion.
Young Adulthood (19 to 40 years)	Intimacy vs. Isolation	Relationships	Young adults need to form intimate, loving relationships with other people. Success leads to strong relationships, whilst failure results in feelings of loneliness and isolation.
Middle Adulthood (40 to 65 years)	Generativity vs. Stagnation	Work and Parenthood	Adults need to create or nurture things, by having children or making a contribution to society that benefits other people. Success leads to feelings of usefulness and accomplishment, whilst failure results in feelings of stagnation.
Maturity (65 to death)	Integrity vs. Despair	Reflection on Life	Senior citizens need to look back on life and feel a sense of fulfilment. Success at this stage leads to feelings of integrity and wisdom, whilst failure leads to regret, bitterness, and despair.

goals and targets, assess the reality of their current situation, suggest options for possible courses of action and demonstrate willpower to commit to them. However, as one of us has argued elsewhere, GROW and the like seem too basic to deal with the complexity of client motivation (Jinks and Dexter, 2012). We agree with Clutterbuck (2010) that the danger of models such as these are that practice becomes mechanistic, critical clues are overlooked and the practitioner can fall into the trap of letting their agenda supersede that of the clients.

Goal setting is important because if a person knows what they are aiming for they are more focused on how they go about achieving it. To use a dartboard as a metaphor – more darts will hit the board if we know where it is than if we are throwing blind. We may hit the dartboard but success depends on luck and every failed attempt leads to a reduction in confidence and motivation. On the other hand when we are clear about what we are aiming for we are better placed to come up with strategies that will eventually result in a 'bull's eye'. Careful and systematic action plans with the goal in clear sight lead to motivation and confidence being sustained and increased.

It is vital that a client has full ownership of their goals and that they have not been imposed by a third party. When working within a contract that includes a third party (such as an organisation) the practitioner needs to be clear about whether organisational goals are aligned and fit with the client's values. It is also important that the goal holds meaning and purpose for the client. We will explore this in more detail later in the chapter.

Stage 2 of Egan's Skilled Helper model

We consider Egan's (2010) Skilled Helper model to be one of the more sophisticated goal-oriented models. The model is sometimes criticised for being mechanistic, but this may be the case only if it is practised without due attention to its subtleties. We see the second stage of the Skilled Helper model as being a good fit for the Generating stage of the Personal Consultancy framework. The three tasks within stage 2 (the preferred future) provide explicit focus around generating a broad range of possibilities for a better future, making choices from the range of possibilities and developing goals, and helping the client test their commitment to the choices they have made or goals they have established. We appreciate the versatility and flexibility of this stage of the Skilled Helper model. In particular it lends itself to incorporating other concepts, approaches, tools and techniques as we will demonstrate later in this chapter (see Figure 9.4).

Task 1	Task 2	Task 3
Help clients discover possibilities for a better future	Help clients move from possibilities to choices and craft and shape their goals	Help clients commit themselves

Figure 9.4 Egan's Skilled Helper model: stage 2

Task 1

Effective goal setting requires skill, knowledge, experience and sophistication in application. Perhaps the task that is most overlooked (or rushed through) is helping clients to explore possibilities for a better future (task 1). We agree with White and Epston (1990) that dialogues which generate a landscape of dreams, hopes, aspirations and values and develop a client's vision of how they really might like things to be and think beyond the horizon are ultimately more valuable in helping people move forward than the mechanics of specific goals and action plans. After all, it is from this material that the goal will be ultimately shaped. It is therefore important to help the client refine their ideas with detail. Detail helps to give ideas a reality that aids the client to engage with future-focused thinking. The practitioner needs to be very sensitive to how the client views their world at this point. Some clients embrace the opportunity to work with dreams, hopes and aspirations and find it very energising and inspiring, whereas others shy away. Some clients may respond to 'How might it be if it were perfect?' but others can only manage to think about how it might be if things were a *little* bit better, so language used needs to reflect the client's preferences.

There are several ways to generate possibilities and ideas. Sometimes a future-focused dialogue can help the client build a clear picture that starts to really resonate. The practitioner can use prompts such as:

- 'In this perfect/better/slightly better future … what are you doing – or not doing?'
- 'What are you thinking – or not thinking?'
- 'Who are you with – who is no longer there?'
- 'How are you feeling and what does that mean?'
- 'What are your hopes?'
- 'How are others responding to you?'
- 'How does this impact on the other areas of your life?'
- 'How does the problem seem if you are managing it in this way?'
- 'What would it be like if you developed the opportunity/project/relationship in this way?'
- 'Who do you know that might have done that?'

Other options include use of creative techniques such as painting or drawing. This can be particularly effective for clients who are cautious, reticent or struggle to verbalise feelings. It is also a valuable way of encouraging clients to explore their future in some detail. As one of us proposed elsewhere:

We want practitioners to have the abilities to help clients develop their vision or dream. In contrast to a child's painting, where the sky is at the top and the sea at the bottom, the sea and sky need to meet. In other words – don't sketch it; paint it properly and with detail. Client and coach are then in a position to look at the real meaning of a goal in the context of a bigger picture

(Jinks and Dexter 2012).

Task 2

Egan (2010) describes task 2 as innovation – turning possibilities into a practical programme for change. Here the client is encouraged to design, shape and hone their goal from the material elicited in task 1. Practitioners can help them to do this by encouraging them to think of what they would like or need in terms of an outcome, solution or accomplishment. This needs to be clear and specific rather than general and broad. Coming back to the dartboard metaphor, if the client doesn't know exactly *where* the dartboard is they are unlikely to hit it. Similarly, if they are unclear about exactly *what* the goal is they won't know when/if they achieve it. Acronyms such as SMART have become embedded in coach language and clearly have their uses in encouraging specificity:

S – Specific. Ensuring that the goal is clear and concise.
M – Measurable. Encouraging the client to think of ways to be able to measure progress and to know when they have achieved the goal.
A – Appropriate. Helping the client to decide if the goal is challenging enough to stretch the client and worthwhile enough in terms of reward and what it might cost them.
R – Realistic. Helping the client to consider if the goal is achievable in terms of how much power, control and resources they might have to make it happen.
T – Time frame. Setting a time frame by which time the goal will be achieved. This should be close enough in time to maintain motivation and far enough away to be realistically achievable.

(Adapted from Dexter et al., 2011)

There is a danger that techniques such as SMART can sometimes be applied in a superficial and mechanistic way. When refining and shaping goals the client (not the technique) needs to be in the forefront of the practitioner's mind so that questions are adapted to reflect what the practitioner has already learned about the client in the Authentic Listening and Rebalancing stages of the Personal Consultancy model. For example, 'I remember you said that things didn't work out last time because you didn't factor in enough time. What might be a better time scale for this?' is likely to engage the client more than 'What sort of time scale do you need to achieve this?'

When used with purpose, intentionality and sensitivity the client is likely to be really engaged rather than simply 'going through the motions' and then can genuinely become focused about exactly what it is they want to achieve.

Task 3

The value of exploring a client's commitment to the goal cannot be overestimated. It is important that they really understand what it will cost them to achieve it as well as considering the ways in which their life will be better. For example, when buying a television we might be very clear what the benefits might be but we also need to know how much it costs and if we are prepared to pay that amount. If the price of the television is too high it may mean we can't afford the holiday we were planning. If losing the holiday is an appropriate trade off for gaining the television, then we would go ahead and purchase it, but if not we would need to think again … It is better to encourage the client to explore the full ramifications of their goal at this stage because they still can choose another goal if the cost is too high. Failure to achieve the goal will of course leave the client feeling demotivated and disempowered. Much better to decide to buy a cheaper television in the store than to realise when it is home and fixed on the wall that the price was too high.

Goal laddering

As demonstrated in the section on crafting and shaping goals, coaches and counsellors are familiar with helping the client shape a goal into something crisp and more specific. This task is all about crafting the material generated earlier into something concrete and tangible that the client can focus upon. However, we think it is equally significant, if not more, to be thorough about what is *really* wanted from the outcome or accomplishment (the goal) and related behaviour (strategy). What is perhaps most important in fact is the value and meaning attached to achieving the goal.

The goal ladder can be used to help the client by moving down from the goal to develop strategies, action plans and behavioural activities that will be a pathway to achieving an identified goal. However, the client can also be encouraged to move up the ladder so that they can properly understand what achieving the goal will *mean* to them in terms of value. The practitioner asks the client, 'If you could achieve this … what would it mean to you?' until they reach a point that they have expressed meaning in terms of a value or emotion. For example, 'It would mean I would be at peace.'

We refer to this as a 'higher goal' or aspiration. It is very important that the client connects with what achieving the goal will ultimately mean because we suggest that actually this is what they *really* want or need – to be secure, vibrant or fulfilled, for example. Recognising higher goals can be liberating because a client will often realise that even if they do not achieve this (being secure, vibrant or fulfilled) through the goal they have chosen (perhaps they do not get the position at work that they were aiming for or are unable to mend a broken relationship) there will be other ways to achieve their aspirations (see Figure 9.5).

Higher goals or aspirations

Overarching goal expressed as value, emotion, meaning or purpose

Q: If you were to achieve that what would it really mean?

R: I'd feel secure, fulfilled, a success – at peace

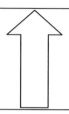

Broader goals or aims

More ambitious

Q: How might things be different overall if you achieve that?

R: We'd have more money, could visit family in …, I'd be doing the thing I trained for

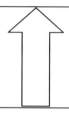

Goals

Q: What are you hoping to achieve?

R: I want to get a job as an Actuary

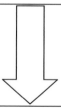

Strategies

A pathway or means to achieve something else

Q: What sort of things might you do?

R: I'd revamp my CV, contact agencies by phone, get to know key people, brush up on interview skills etc.

Figure 9.5 The goal ladder

Cost–benefit analysis

Cost–benefit analysis is a useful tool to help a client establish commitment to their goal because it helps them see at a glance and in some detail the benefits of achieving the goal but also what it will cost. A simple table, divided in two with the goal at the top, allows them to list these. Having done this the client is often able to see easily whether the goal is worthwhile or not. It is sometimes more complicated and in those cases it may be useful to score the cost or benefit (between 1 and 10) in terms of how powerful each benefit and cost is. Ultimately, the client makes a decision about whether to move forward with the goal based on the total quantity of benefits compared with the costs and how they stack up against each other in terms of how powerful they are. For example, a client who has initially chosen a goal to achieve a Masters level qualification may have identified a number of *benefits* as to how life will be better if they achieve this. However, if one of the costs means compromising valuable time spent with their young family they may consider this too powerful a cost – even when stacked up against all of the tempting benefits. If it is clear that the cost is too high then more exploration is needed around what might be a more suitable goal.

Other techniques and interventions

The nature of the Generating stage means that there are a wide range of interventions and techniques that can be applied. Other useful examples might be: role play, visualisation, empty chair work, assertiveness training, SWOT and PESTLE analysis, strengths spotting, homework tasks, behavioural experiments, brainstorming, action planning, forcefield analysis, relaxation and mindfulness techniques to name a few.

Supporting

This stage is primarily about 'being with' the client so the range of techniques available is limited. When obstacles occur it may involve implementing contingency plans that were established during the Generating stage. For example, a client experiencing a problem with an overbearing manager (that seems to be a barrier to them progressing in the way they had planned) may return to strengthen work that was done in the Generating stage. It may be useful to recall a previously identified strength about being an 'effective communicator', for example. This can be empowering at a time when they might have been experiencing a lack of confidence. They would then be in a better position to explore what might need to happen to be able to confidently and clearly communicate the situation with their boss. In order to do this, perhaps they will need to refresh their knowledge and skills around assertiveness.

On the other hand, perhaps a contingency plan developed in the Generating stage had been to develop a list of resources that might help if/when this sort of obstacle presents. Returning to a list of resources that was put together at a time when the client was feeling confident and purposeful may help them connect with more powerful and positive feelings and therefore feel more relaxed about tackling the problem. In addition, the list of resources may identify support systems that might help the client realise that they don't necessarily need to manage this problem in isolation.

Approaching obstacles this way can encourage a client to see that there are different options available to them. Managing a problem or obstacle effectively if and when it occurs is a valuable lesson for the client in that they learn 'all is not lost' after all and they can be more confident about doing this another time. Learning to no longer fear obstacles and problems can be liberating and reinforce confidence and belief in their own abilities.

Balance

Sometimes the Supporting stage is about helping the client to balance perception of their world. For example, a client who becomes over focused with the myriad of problems that are surfacing at work to the detriment of other areas of their lives may very quickly become disillusioned, disempowered or even distressed. They can fall into the trap of thinking that they need to apply all their energy into solving the problems which can result in them feeling consumed by them. This is rarely effective.

The practitioner is in a unique place to help the client bring back into the foreground other parts of their lives that have been neglected. Explicitly encouraging dialogue about the holiday they were planning, a book they were reading or a triathalon they were going to enter is a way of reminding the client of another *important* part of themselves. Encouraging them to go home in time to cook a nice meal or see a film and switch off from work may actually help to replenish energy levels that have been drained in the workplace. Contracting with them to take their lunch away from the workplace so they get some time to think is likely to result in them feeling calmer and more in control. This increases the likelihood that they will then be able to address the problems at work more effectively. Dialogues such as the ones described may also occur in the Rebalancing or Generating stages since they can involve the practitioner taking on a more proactive role. However, the location of any technique integrated depends on the practitioner's interpretation of the Personal Consultancy framework.

Conclusion

In a chapter this size it has been impossible to do justice to the range of concepts, approaches and techniques that would be a 'good fit' with the various stages of the Personal Consultancy framework. There are also some approaches that probably straddle the different stages. For example, REBT's ABC model (Neenan and Dryden, 2000) can be located both in the Rebalancing and the Generating stages.

It could be said that insights raised around 'irrational beliefs' match well with work relating to the client's existing patterns in the Rebalancing stage. However, 'disputing' and developing of new beliefs are more in tune with emerging patterns in the Generating stage. Similarly, conceptual models such as the Cycle of Change (Prochaska, 2004) may be used as another way of locating where the client is in relation to the changes they would like to make. If they see themselves as being in the 'pre-contemplation stage' of that model, for example, then some exploration in the Rebalancing stage may be needed. If they are in the 'contemplation or planning stages', then they may be ready to start thinking about what they actually want and develop goals in the Generating stage.

We promote the integration of other concepts, approaches and techniques if and when they enhance the practice and are relevant to the client and their issue(s). Any approach or technique needs to make sense to both and will only work effectively when incorporated authentically.

Part II

Context and application

Guest contributors

Chapter 10

Should we offer Personal Consultancy?

An exploratory dialogue between practitioner and organisation

Jayne Hildreth and Siobhan Dunleavy

Introduction

This chapter offers a unique window into the experience of an integrative coach–therapist introducing the concept of Personal Consultancy to an organisation that in the beginning didn't even know of its existence. It sets out a dialogue using the questions that were raised by the business manager representing the organisation, and demonstrates how, through responses to these questions, a sophisticated understanding was gained around what Personal Consultancy was, where it sat in relation to the other services that were already on offer, how it might be introduced and to whom it could be applied. It concludes with an overview of where the organisation currently is and how it sees itself moving forward with this approach.

To begin we thought it would be helpful to offer some background to our co-writing of this piece in order to offer some insight into our specific interest and perspective in relation to the Personal Consultancy model.

Jayne is a practitioner and works as an associate at My Possible Self Ltd (MPS), which is a social enterprise offering counselling and coaching to individuals and groups in a variety of contexts and settings. She is dually qualified, having a background in counselling and a Masters in Personal and Corporate Coaching.

Jayne had participated in some research around the Personal Consultancy model in 2009 which sparked her interest and raised questions about her practice. Having initially seen the disciplines as poles apart, increasingly Jayne started to view things differently. She had the knowledge and expertise of the two disciplines and was feeling frustrated working within either purely a counselling or coaching contract when faced with clients who she felt would have really benefited from the range of her expertise.

Siobhan is the business manager at MPS and has been coordinating the Employee Assistance Programmes (EAPs) as well as the training and coaching which MPS provides to multinational companies for the past year.

Jayne brought awareness of the integrative approach to MPS and there initiated a dialogue around the practical aspects of introducing and integrating Personal Consultancy into an organisation where a contract already existed providing counselling and coaching as separate entities.

When invited to write this chapter we discussed how best to communicate what we had learned from this joint voyage of discovery. We wondered what would be most useful to convey to the reader about Personal Consultancy provision within an organisational setting. We wanted it to be relevant to the practitioner and also from a marketing perspective. Many questions had arisen from our very early discussions (and continue to do so) about working in this way and how MPS might include Personal Consultancy as an additional offering. We decided that we would share the dialogue we had and a brief description of the journey in the hope that it brings the progress we have made so far to life. This is not a transcription but a distillation of a number of conversations that took place on the subject.

The dialogue

SIOBHAN: *What is Personal Consultancy?*

JAYNE: *It is a model or framework for integrating the disciplines of coaching and therapy ...*

Initially the questions began in relation to Siobhan's need to understand what was meant by integrating the disciplines of coaching and therapy and in particular what the term Personal Consultant encompassed. It was vital that Siobhan developed an in-depth understanding about this before being able to make a decision about offering this as a service. She needed to consider how well it fitted with MPS's organisational vision and values, and she needed to have the confidence to be able to promote it. If MPS chose to offer coach–therapy integration under the umbrella of their services it would communicate an acceptance and alliance with this way of working whilst still in its infancy. On the one hand this could be seen as an opportunity to lead the way, but it could also have been something of a risk.

There was some confusion for Siobhan having heard the terms Personal Consultancy and Integrative coach–therapy approach.

SIOBHAN: *Which then is the term that practitioners would choose to use?*

JAYNE: *This is a question that has been asked of me previously and of course it is impossible for me to speak for others but from my own personal experience I use the terms interchangeably. It depends on where I am and who I am talking to as not everyone always understands what is meant by the term Personal Consultant or appreciates the terminology. In addition, for me it is significant to highlight that when using the term Personal Consultant I use it to convey that I am using the Personal Consultancy model as a specific framework for integrating my practice of coaching and therapy. There are others available for this purpose and as we have seen with the development of counselling and coaching models I believe we will see more created and adapted. I am also certain that as things develop in the area of integration, practitioners will feel more able and comfortable to adopt new terms that better describe their practice. Inevitably the marketplace will become accustomed to hearing the use of such terms and will develop a clearer understanding of what they mean. The practice of integrating the disciplines will become more widely accepted and commonplace as a third way of working.*

SIOBHAN: *How many people are currently working in this way?*

JAYNE: *It's impossible for me to give an accurate and definite answer to this, but as director and co-founder of the Association of Integrative Coach–Therapy Professionals (AICTP) I can say that in the first 12 months of opening a new LinkedIn discussion/special interest group in excess of four hundred members have joined and are active in emerging discussions around safe and ethical practice. Prior to this, whilst involved with BACP Coaching Division I had attended discussion groups and conferences and it was apparent that there were many therapists out there that coach, some with additional coaching qualifications and some not. It seemed that the emergence of these new professional organisations for practitioners was beginning to allow practitioners to talk more honestly and openly about their practice. They were beginning to feel validated and safe to acknowledge that, not only did they work with the two disciplines separately, but that an integration of the two felt more authentic and true to their roots, experience and expertise. They talked about 'coming out of the closet'. Back then, increasingly, I had to question if it was possible for me to go into a room with a client to coach, and leave the therapist outside. There were elements of myself as a therapist that I considered an important part of me and to try to deny them felt inauthentic, dishonest and quite frankly uncomfortable. As a practitioner I see myself as having a human encounter with a client and to deny part of myself felt wrong.*

SIOBHAN: *If practitioners were coming out of the closet that surely could only be advantageous for the development and professionalisation of this way of working and effective governance?*

JAYNE: *I absolutely see this as advantageous, not least because by bringing it into the open there is an embracing and ownership of what practitioners are doing behind those closed doors. This is essential, at least in part to ensure that we are working safely and ethically. Additionally, it offers the opportunity for people to talk about how they do it, raise questions and have discussions about 'best practice'. This inevitably offers opportunities for learning and development for individual practitioners, as well as adding to the body of knowledge around this new discipline, enabling growth and excellence in the field. It encourages more conscious consideration of what we are doing and why, along with greater clarity about the process of contracting and what is being offered. This allows us to develop intentionality and skill around the movement between disciplines and fosters increased self-awareness. Also if we are practising 'in the closet' we surely communicate that there is something to hide, which does nothing for the promotion and development of this way of working. It seemed that it was timely to be able to acknowledge and own our thoughts and beliefs about working in this way; and to have the courage to stand up and embrace it. I have to say that, for me, when involved in the original piece of research, it felt very radical to be even thinking in this way.*

SIOBHAN: *As far as qualifications go, what would an organisation be looking for – who is qualified to do it?*

This was a really important question for MPS when considering whether to offer a Personal Consultancy approach, because they needed to ensure that the organisation's identity, status and professionalism were protected.

JAYNE: *Practitioners need to demonstrate that they have a sound therapeutic background with some additional coach training, as well as some training around integration. I believe they should ideally be a member of an organisation that has clear guidelines and support for the work they are doing. They should also have a clinical supervisor who is able to understand, support and challenge this particular way of working, in order to ensure safe and ethical practice.*

A natural follow-on question then emerged around training and what is currently available for those who would want to increase their knowledge and skills.

SIOBHAN: *Is there any training out there at the moment?*

JAYNE: *Training is very limited at present. There are a couple of private organisations that I am aware of, only one of which is specifically offering the Personal Consultancy model for integration. In addition the University of East London is poised to start a postgraduate certificate programme, which is the first of its kind. So, whilst it is very early days, these are very exciting times. I think that, by choosing to offer this programme, the University is clearly making a statement about how they view the future – with coach–therapy integration emerging, they have taken the decision to try to lead the way.*

SIOBHAN: *One concern I had was whether someone might come for this approach who really wanted counselling but didn't want to say?*

JAYNE: *I think that that may well happen. However, I personally don't feel that there is anything particularly problematic about that. My thinking is that, if someone is able to access a service and engage with a practitioner who is suitably qualified, then during the assessment period there is an opportunity for discussion around what the client wants from the outset. It may be that the starting balance swings more to the therapeutic end and then shifts as the work progresses.*

SIOBHAN: *If that was the case would you always then be aiming to bring it back to the coaching?*

JAYNE: *For me it would be in response to what the client needed and when. I don't think that, to engage in this process, a client would need to be signing up and saying that they wanted to spend 50 per cent of the time in each discipline, for example. It doesn't work like that. In my experience, when a client presents, we often don't know exactly what might happen and what might be most useful as the work progresses. What we can do, however, is give the client choice about interventions, emphasis and direction as things unfold, and of course this type of collaborative approach would have been discussed in the initial assessment and contracting. So I might actually say to my client, 'It seems here there are two ways we could go ... ' and then usually follow the client's lead.*

SIOBHAN: *If you are saying that you are led by client need, how then does this fit with a company requesting that the work ties in with company objectives?*

JAYNE: *That is something that would be discussed, negotiated and agreed with the coachee on starting and when contracting for that piece of work. We would still be working towards company objectives and it may be that some of the therapeutic work enables those to be met. Because in my experience it may be that something underlying is a barrier to the client successfully achieving and maintaining change.*

Being client led isn't just about accepting any choice they might make at face value. It is necessary to discuss choices, and being led by client need may sometimes mean that it is necessary to challenge them to stretch their thinking, or refer back to the original aims and goals for the work. It may also be that there is a need to acknowledge avoidance and possible collusion. This is all done with intentionality to fit with the client's needs, as well as company objectives.

MPS provide EAP contracts that generally offer six sessions, which raised the following question.

SIOBHAN: *As far as session times go, we work to six sessions. With this kind of work would you need longer?*

JAYNE: *The way I see it is that you do the best you can within the contract you have. The focus for my work is around what can realistically be achieved in the time I have with the client, and again this would be discussed from the outset. I believe significant work can happen whether all you have is one session or twelve.*

SIOBHAN: This leads me to think of the contract. How would we contract with the organisation, and with the individual, to work in this way?

JAYNE: Generally I find organisations will require a contract in the same way as you do for your workplace counselling and coaching. This contract would need to cover all aspects that a therapeutic contract would, for example around risk and confidentiality, as well as anything that you identify as missing that is covered on the one you use for coaching. In addition I think it is good practice to include some provision for extension of the work if deemed necessary, by negotiation with the organisation. In my work, I do a very comprehensive verbal contract at the beginning of the work to allow me to explain what is meant by this way of working, and the subtleties around boundaries. This will involve discussion of areas such as regularity and length of sessions, contact between sessions and also pace. It is essential to share information fully and appropriately with your client so that they have a detailed understanding of what they are contracting for. I see contracting as an ongoing process, which continues throughout the work, so it would be something that was be revisited when deemed necessary either by myself or my client. Of course, this would also need to fit within the boundaries of the organisational contract that was purchasing the service.

SIOBHAN: With regard to contact between sessions, how does that work and how do you manage that as things change?

JAYNE: As part of the contracting process discussions about boundaries will have taken place, so already the client will be anticipating change along the way. When the work is in progress I will be communicating very clearly what my expectations are as well as inviting the client to be part of this. If we are working more at the coaching end of the spectrum, for example, I will perhaps be asking the client to e-mail me with some work in between sessions. For me it comes back to clarity and transparency. If it felt like the boundary had been crossed I would discuss this with the client in the same way as if I were either coaching or counselling.

SIOBHAN: So, with regard to assessment, who can you work with in this way, or is it appropriate for everybody?

JAYNE: Well my feeling is that, given the approach straddles both disciplines it is, at least potentially, open and appropriate for anyone. This way of working simply allows us to respond to the need of the client. Contracting to work as an integrative coach–therapist enables me to draw on all of my skills and expertise in response to what is needed when. For example it may be that a client chooses this way of working and then ends up doing very little work at the therapeutic end of the spectrum as it hasn't felt relevant. Of course, that is fine. As I said, it is about being able, within the contract, to respond to what a client needs, or wants. I have no expectations as to what a client does in a session, I may make suggestions highlighting choices, but ultimately it lies with them.

SIOBHAN: *Hearing your response to that makes me think about this next question, which is something that has been raised with one of our corporate clients. Who would make the decision around who to refer for this approach? Would it be HR?*

JAYNE: *My feeling is that it should be the client, where possible, that perhaps they have the bio of coaches on offer and make a decision based on that. Otherwise it may appear that some sort of judgement was being made about the coachee with regard to their need, perhaps about something being 'wrong' with them that needed fixing. In my opinion it is always of benefit for a client to feel they have choice – which allows for a greater level of engagement with the process, ending with more positive results. However, remember that working in this way simply allows movement where needed or wanted so if a client came who didn't want to work in this way, then I would offer a pure coaching intervention. For me the frustration is being in a position where I am not able to work with something because it hasn't been contracted for. This way, we have the option, because often on presentation we are not sure what will surface.*

It was apparent through this conversation that Siobhan was gaining a far greater understanding.

SIOBHAN: *The more I understand it, the more it makes sense that HR wouldn't be making the decision. Now, what I am not understanding is some of the resistance I have experienced from both organisations and other practitioners.*

JAYNE: *Of course, without speaking to individuals personally it would be impossible to know exactly what any resistance might be about. However, in my experience it often tends to be around a lack of knowledge and full understanding.*

Although Siobhan herself had not been resistant to the introduction of working in this way, I could certainly identify a shift in her thinking whilst engaged in the process of our dialogue.

JAYNE: *It's possible that other practitioners may feel a little threatened, perhaps not only from lack of knowledge of this way of working, but also through exclusion and fear of potentially losing work in what is already a challenging market.*

SIOBHAN: *I imagine that counsellors may raise objections to this approach, more than other coaches perhaps, although I may be wrong. They may fear losing work and also fear that counselling issues are not going to be dealt with in enough depth if a 2 in 1 approach is used?*

JAYNE: *To be honest I imagine it could be either, perhaps for different reasons. For counsellors you make the point that there could be questions around working in enough depth, and truthfully whenever asked this sort of question I feel I have to say, well how much depth is enough and how do we know that? The Personal Consultancy model allows the client to go into as much depth as the client appears to need using the depth–surface axis, which is an element of the framework. From my perspective, it goes back to what I was saying about using the allocated time in a way that offers the client the best potential outcome that is in line with what they and the organisation want, if that is part of the contract.*

Siobhan at this point was very keen to be able to promote this as a service offered from MPS. This led to her thinking about it from a marketing perspective.

SIOBHAN: *How might we market this approach to a big corporate client? Specifically, the organisation we pitched to recently seemed very interested in the approach, because they saw the lack of psychological understanding (as they called it) amongst their previous coaches to have been a disadvantage. They had never had anything like it there and I think, as a business, having this as a Unique Selling Point is brilliant for us.*

JAYNE: *Whilst I am certainly no marketing expert, I think that when dealing with the corporate world one of the things we can do is be mindful of our language and adapt it accordingly; so, for example, I avoid the term 'counselling' as I am aware of the preconceptions this can bring. In this arena, I believe this is where the term Personal Consultant fits very well as it is language they understand and can relate to.*

SIOBHAN: *I agree, because unfortunately for some within organisations there is still a stigma around being seen to 'come for counselling', so it would definitely be beneficial to be aware of the terminology used and adapt it accordingly. Which raises another point: might it be useful to come up with some additional material for our existing corporate clients?*

JAYNE: *Yes, absolutely. It goes back to understanding. How can someone make an informed choice without the information? It is our role to communicate Personal Consultancy in a way that fits with their needs and uses language that is acceptable to them, that they understand. Also, it could perhaps be useful to include a couple of case studies, so that they are able to grasp the application and the benefits.*

Whilst considering marketing, the next question was significant to follow on with, given that the fees at MPS currently differ for counselling and coaching.

SIOBHAN: *How would it be charged out then? Is it the same as coaching or more, because I suppose I would understand if that were the case?*

JAYNE: *This is an interesting question and one I am certain we will see a great deal of discussion around. I personally charge out at my usual coaching rate, but I am also mindful that practitioners who have invested in training in both areas may view it differently and charge it out at a more specialist rate. It will therefore depend on the individual practitioner when working independently. As an organisation it will be in relation to how you view it as a service and I suppose you'll attach a fee that feels appropriate, in the same way as you do for all of your services.*

SIOBHAN: *Piloting the approach with a percentage of new coachees coming through would also be beneficial, and asking for feedback at the end of the process. Would this be in line with confidentiality guidelines for the coachee?*

JAYNE: *This would depend on exactly what feedback you would be looking for and from whom. I see nothing wrong with asking for feedback from the coachee, if they understand at the outset exactly what would be required of them. It would be essential for them to be able to opt out from being part of the pilot if they choose to, without it stopping them accessing support. I also think it would be good practice, as is in the case in research, that participants have the right to withdraw at any time if they so wish. So, provided it was put together in this way, I think this could be of great benefit in terms of marketing the service using their feedback, and providing an opportunity to write about the findings, which would add to the body of knowledge. I also think that using this kind of evaluative process can be really helpful to the client, because focusing in detail on their process and outcomes can often serve to reinforce the benefits for them.*

SIOBHAN: *From a more practical angle, what about notes and storage of them?*

JAYNE: *The notes need to be treated using the same guidelines you currently follow for counselling notes. However, my expectation is that those guidelines also include your coaching notes. I know as an organisation you separate the notes so I would recommend that you put them in with the counselling notes but, if you prefer, they could be stored in a separate cabinet.*

SIOBHAN: *And what about insurance to work in this way?*

JAYNE: *As an independent practitioner I was originally covered to work as a therapist and a coach. When I began to work in an integrative way I contacted my insurers to ascertain I was covered to do this. They were perfectly happy; however, I would recommend you encourage all of your associates to do the same to ensure adequate cover.*

Conclusion

JAYNE: Taking part in this process has been an incredibly valuable experience for me as an integrative coach–therapy practitioner. It has challenged me to consider questions that I hadn't thought of from an organisational perspective, and in addition has further cemented my understanding of working in this way. For example, when contracting with clients it has reinforced my thinking around having a formal contract and in addition engaging the coachee in the process of verbal contracting. This not only communicates to the client a clarity about what they might expect in our work together, but also that there is something very empowering for them in having the opportunity for discussion and negotiation. In many ways I feel I now have a greater confidence with my knowledge base, because it feels it has been tested somewhat. I feel more prepared when promoting myself as a Personal Consultant, and far more comfortable and competent to answer any questions that might come my way.

SIOBHAN: Discussing all of the above with Jayne has really helped me to answer any queries I had around the approach. Personally, I am really enthusiastic about using the Personal Consultancy model going forward. When pitching for new contracts with organisations I aim to put Personal Consultancy at the forefront of the services we offer and feel confident now, following Jayne's responses, of being able to answer any questions about how it will work in practice, as well as the advantages of using the approach. I see the Personal Consultancy model working particularly well with an organisation we are about to begin working with that provides remote clinical monitoring to those with long-term chronic illnesses. The aim is to bolt on a health coaching programme to the existing packages they already provide. Integrative practitioners would be a natural fit for this type of work.

It's early days but the feedback we have received so far for the approach has been excellent. It has been incorporated into the existing coaching programme without any issues and has been warmly received. I feel certain that organisations will continue to use the approach in addition to the coaching and EAP programmes they already have with us. With potential new clients we will suggest piloting the approach to demonstrate the benefits, and I am really excited to see how the approach works in a health coaching environment. We hope we have done some justice to the subject matter, offering learning and raising discussion and debate, particularly given our passion for this way of working.

Chapter 11

Below the surface

An integrative approach to leadership coaching

Linda Aspey

Introduction

Like many practitioners of my era who were trained as counsellors and therapists some years ago, in my case in the early 1990s, I find myself now with a variety of training and experience in personal, professional and organisational development and a number of roles including consultant, executive coach, trainer, mediator, facilitator and coach supervisor. Many development practitioners are by nature drawn to variety and new learning, and will have encountered along their journey many theories, models, approaches and role models. Some or even all of these will have informed and developed their way of working into what can be a fairly eclectic mix.

As has been explored in earlier chapters, many find it difficult to draw a *consistent and definitive distinction* between, in particular, coaching and counselling or therapy. Practices are changing all the time, perhaps in response to the way people's lives and external realities are changing in so many ways; 'holding the space' and enabling growth through a relationship is now not only the stuff of counselling – it's become a critical part of the coaching relationship. Interacting at depth or on the surface within any session is normal as thoughts and feelings ebb and flow; ideas and practices from both spheres of counselling and coaching influence each other. Yet the ethical frameworks of our professional bodies, for example BACP (2013b), alert us to consider that 'the existence of a dual relationship with a client is seldom neutral and can have a powerful beneficial or detrimental impact that may not always be easily foreseeable'. So when we increasingly find ourselves with dual role dilemmas, how do we best handle them? The debate around differentiation will no doubt continue for some time; however, this quote from Ernesto Spinelli (2010), sums up my views perfectly:

> While all manner of distinctions have been made with regard to the differences between the two professions, all are problematic and open to any number of counter-examples and argument. The divergences proposed rest on the implicit assumption of a unified, if imaginary, type of coaching as well as a unified, if imaginary, type of therapy.

Extensive research indicates that in a similar type of relationships to coaching – e.g. counselling (Rogers, 2008), trainee counsellor learning (Smith, 2011) and counselling supervision (Bambling and King, 2000) – relationships themselves have a strong impact on the effectiveness of the client's or learner's development. Indeed they may be even more important than the theories or tools that practitioners choose to use.

So within the coaching relationship I only bring in various tools and techniques if I truly think they will meet a particular need; my focus is on the relationship. 'Managed eclecticism' is a term coined by Clutterbuck (2012) which he sees as 'an intelligent, sensitive ability to select a broad approach, and within that approach, appropriate tools and techniques, which meet the particular needs of a particular client at a particular time'. This is probably the best way to describe how I aspire for my practice as an integrative coach to be.

I believe that integrative practice does not negate the need for coaching without therapeutic content (e.g. skills or performance coaching) or therapy without coaching content (e.g. processing complex trauma). However, as my practice is largely in the area of leadership coaching, I draw on all elements of my background in the work and refer on when the issue is not something we should work on in the broader context of leadership coaching. I am not offering longer-term reparative psychotherapy, but clients and their lives are complex and it seems counterproductive to turn a client away or refer them on because they don't slot neatly into the mould of a perfect coaching client. Naturally, we will assess what is needed before we work together and if coaching is not the best solution for them we will soon know.

Stigma towards therapy

In my experience many executives feel uncomfortable about asking for emotional or psychological support if it is labelled as counselling or therapy, yet they can do so more easily when it's part of their coaching. Despite, in recent years, the growth of goal-oriented approaches to counselling, in particular Solution Focused Brief Therapy (de Shazer and Berg, 1988), many still view any kind of talking therapy as a long-drawn-out, painful, expensive and even self-indulgent way of dealing with life's problems, and coaching as a much more pleasant and energising option. Perhaps this is partly because in recent years the term 'therapy' has become a 'catch all' for any kind of psychological intervention, including psychoanalysis, which some find daunting. I am reminded of the film *Annie Hall* (Allen, 1977) in which Woody Allen plays the neurotic Alvey Singer. At one point in the film Annie is astonished to discover that Alvey has been seeing an analyst for 'just' fifteen years. Alvey responds, 'Yeah, I'm gonna give him one more year, and then I'm goin' to Lourdes.'

I have written elsewhere of a vivid encounter some twenty years ago with stigma towards counselling in the executive context (Aspey, 2010). When asked if I would do some 'one-to-one training' with a highly stressed executive who was failing to meet tough and unrelenting targets, going through a divorce and at risk of 'derailing', I asked if they had considered counselling for him. This was greeted with genuine horror and protest that he's 'not mentally ill!' The client felt the same, yet showed clear signs of depression. Having considered the situation in supervision, I worked with him for three months, offering him time to talk, using various stress management tools, helping him to develop self-insight and the ability to think more clearly without the fog of stress. I subsequently discovered that other colleagues of mine were working in similar ways and calling it executive coaching.

Perhaps we're moving away from the stigma. Research conducted by the British Association of Counselling and Psychotherapy (BACP, 2010) shows that attitudes are changing with 91 per cent of respondents agreeing that 'It is more acceptable to talk about emotional problems than it was in the past.' However, I wonder what this research would have shown if it had been conducted solely on senior executives? I suspect it would have been quite different and that it is still not completely acceptable to talk about emotional problems if you're a senior executive – particularly a male one.

An integrative approach to executive coaching

As a tool for integration, the Personal Consultancy framework offers not a new approach but a way to map, understand and be clear about the work I'm doing with my clients, with the dimensions of relationship, the client and practitioner at the core. 'Being with' and 'doing with' the client offers me a helpful way to think about what is happening as we move through the various stages of Authentic Listening, Rebalancing, Generating and Supporting. These help the client to move from existing patterns to new ones; I have also found it has provided me and the coaches whom I supervise with greater clarity. When combined with a systemic mindset – which I particularly need as I work in organisational contexts – it offers a way of engaging clients in work at multiple levels, if they so choose.

My coaching practice focuses on developing the capability of middle and senior managers and organisational leaders who have responsibility for the current and future success of an organisation. I don't personally make a distinction between executive and leadership coaching because most executives have some form of leadership role and many leaders benefit from revisiting executive and management skills. The coaching often involves supporting my clients to become more self-aware in order to carry out their leadership role more effectively and to behave in ways that followers can believe in and aspire to. My aim is to facilitate my clients' personal and/or professional development *and* to help them to resolve their internal conflicts and problems. In executive work most clients tend to come to coaching for the former, and for some it evolves into the latter, at varying levels. This may go back and forth; it depends on where the client wants to go. Some present internal conflict and crisis immediately; with others they surface later in the coaching relationship; and some choose their coaching to be at surface level only. Some, already highly successful in their careers, want to explore or revisit their values and find deeper meaning and purpose as leaders.

An integrative approach offers us the opportunity to work on a number of levels if the client wishes, not just deeply or just on the surface. Their journey towards achieving their potential as a leader – or maintaining their success – can be challenging for them in a number of ways that involve issues of confidence, self-esteem, relationship with self, the family of origin, the overuse of defence processes, fear of derailment. All these, and more, often surface in the coaching relationship. Ignoring or rushing past them in the service of coaching goals is I believe doing a disservice to the client, to their longer-term development and may even run counter to positive and sustainable change.

So, like most practitioners, I have developed my own ways of working, in my case holding these as the primary tasks of executive and leadership coaching in mind:

- developing self-understanding and self-management skills (including building self-confidence, questioning erroneous and limiting assumptions, managing anxiety, building resilience and becoming more reflective);
- understanding and managing others (including being a trusted leader and role model who can manage others' anxieties and help them to achieve their potential);
- developing their awareness of the wider systems in which they operate (having a strategic mindset, knowing what their own role and purpose is, and how their values and behaviours are impacted by and impact upon these systems); and
- developing their ability to think clearly and act decisively (often in the face of masses of information or, conversely, with little information).

I typically work with executives for six to twelve sessions, with session length varying from one to two and a half hours, depending on their needs, preference and learning style. I have worked with some clients for several years at particular points in their career. New clients are usually referred by their HR director, or come as a result of a recommendation by my clients, or as part of a wider leadership development programme sponsored by their employer – my corporate client. Prior to meeting them I send some information about executive coaching and what it entails, and a little about my background and approach. Most will look me up on the internet and I will do the same of them, as well as do some company research if the organisation is a new client. We will then meet before contracting for a full coaching engagement to discuss what they would like to achieve from the coaching. The session sometimes involves the use of questionnaires that encourage them to reflect on a number of areas. The practical nature of these early processes usually opens a window for them to start thinking about themselves, their challenges and their hopes in a new way. This meeting enables them to think more about whether or not they really want coaching and, if so, what they want from it.

It enables us to consider if I am the right coach, if coaching is the right intervention, and what the best way of working will be to achieve their objectives. Where it's relevant I ask their reasons for selecting me as their potential coach – stated reasons vary from knowing someone I've worked with through to the particular sector experience I have. It is rare that someone tells me I've been chosen because of my therapy training unless they are clearly in crisis. Some have not read my profile until the last minute and, when they do, express some hesitation that I am a therapist. I tell them that we can work at depth or not, or somewhere in the middle, and that the way that I work is informed by a number of trainings, including my therapy training. I also tell them that if we make any significant shifts in the way we work, I will ensure this is what they want before we proceed in any new direction. This generally helps with clarity and reassures them that they won't be spending 15 years in analysis with me!

Naturally, not all clients find it easy to 'be themselves' within the coaching relationship – trust needs to be earned for vulnerability to be shown and the client's defences cannot and should not be dismantled without good reason. Some may have been referred for coaching, some may have self-selected, some may not want to be there, some do. So from the first point of contact with the client and beyond I aim to be mindful of possible unconscious factors within the client, the relationship and within myself, including defence processes, transference and my own counter-transference, as I would do if the contract was for therapy.

Once we have agreed to work together, we agree frequency of sessions, where we'll meet, cancellation or postponement terms, the confidentiality framework (including any organisational reporting requirements and 3-way meetings – more often for middle management than senior level), intersession support and contact, and evaluation. Invoicing arrangements are usually discussed with their sponsor or HRD. At an appropriate time during the coaching contract I may collect, with their agreement, anonymous 360 feedback. I may also use some psychometric profiling or other assessment tools to identify their strengths and highlight areas for development. This and any other data will inform the coaching objectives and success measures, and, wherever possible, we'll link these to their own and the organisation's objectives. The most senior executives' objectives may be less performance-driven and more linked to leadership style, meaning and purpose, or sometimes simply having time to think because they don't get it anywhere else. And again, if the task is crisis management, some of these processes such as 360 feedback or profiling may not be suitable, at least not at the early stages, until equilibrium has been restored and that may take some time. The case below will illustrate some of the points I discussed above.

Janine

Janine was a newly hired CEO in a fast moving digital business. She was referred by the HR Director who had quickly noticed the fast pace of her life and the long hours that Janine was putting in. She offered to find her an executive coach, to which Janine agreed. At the pre-coaching session Janine told me her main goals were to learn to handle stress more effectively, develop a good relationship with her board and put a plan in place to take the company into new markets; 360 feedback wasn't appropriate as she was new to the company. She saw it as a very straightforward matter and spent the first full session talking through various aspects of these three areas. I focused on the Personal Consultancy dimension of 'being with' – she clearly wanted to move forward quickly and to tick off each item as if on a meeting agenda. She spoke at speed and at 'surface' even when she spoke about her stress levels, and when I ventured, several times, to encourage her to slow down a little towards a more reflective style, she dismissed the suggestion with a smile and a wave of her hand. I chose not to voice my observations too soon. At the second session three weeks later she told me that all was not well at the company. It had come to light that serious fraud had been taking place for some time in an area of the business; one of her key directors had been arrested and suspended. Within the next few days a number of other issues had surfaced, from a staff member raising a grievance against a senior manager through to several suppliers complaining about non-payment of invoices. Each issue meant a series of difficult conversations with her new colleagues. Again I focused on 'being with' so she could think through the issues herself, which she did, very productively but still at great speed. When we moved into 'doing with' we discussed strategies for her to manage the various situations and juggle the workload, and she decided to allocate some of her responsibilities to her senior management team whilst she tackled these critical issues. At the next meeting she told me she had managed to get on top of things sufficiently to perform well at her first board meeting, but this took her several evenings and weekends to prepare for. Then she'd had another blow – a significant data breach that affected 50,000 customers and which was reported in the trade press. Each event put more and more pressure on her. She tearfully confided that she felt way out of her depth. She had never expected anything like these recent events, nor encountered anything like it in her career. She had so wanted this job but now felt unsupported and 'conned' by the board. She 'hadn't got round' to allocating some of her responsibilities to her senior management team, and her partner kept urging her to leave saying the company was toxic – maybe he was right but she didn't want to give up just yet.

I could feel her disappointment, anger, frustration and internal conflict. Had I moved into a coaching or 'doing with mindset' at this stage of the session I may have begun to ask her what she thought her options were. Instead, I continued to give her my undivided attention whilst she wept. She continued to talk, dabbing her eyes, and began to realise that she had encountered a situation like this before – at the age of 22 in her first management role. She'd just been promoted to managing people, yet a week later was required to lay off twenty people and reorganise a department. With no training in dealing with this kind of situation, she'd struggled. Frightened to ask for help, she battled on until she became ill, and eventually took over two weeks off work. She told them and herself that she had 'flu' but she now reflected that it was probably stress. Having come to this realisation, she went even further. As a child, her parents worked long hours in their own shop so she became the primary carer for her disabled sister. Between her school work (she was massively bright and academically ambitious) and her caring duties, she'd not had much time to develop friends so had grown up feeling 'different'. As she relaxed further into talking and the stories unfolded, she began to make sense of them and how they linked to her current situation. I continued to give attention, to 'be with'. She began to see more clearly what needed to be done – ask the board for support, share more of the burden with her management team, take a more systematic and strategic approach to the issues, and balance work and rest time better. Janine had moved herself into the Rebalancing and Generating phase, with new awareness of how hard she could drive herself, an understanding of what she'd been assuming on a number of levels, and how difficult asking for help had been for her.

The case for a unifying framework in executive coaching

Whilst 'managed eclecticism' is a useful way to identify how some of us work pluralistically and relatively flexibly, the integrative approach poses the practitioner several potential challenges:

- First, we could be so busy in thinking about and introducing, however sensitively, various models, tools and techniques to the client in the intended service of their development that the quality of our attention on them can be compromised (Aspey, 2010).
- Second, like many of my peers, I've undergone various trainings and have bookshelves groaning with many read and just as many as yet unread books, in my case linked to a personal promise of a six-month reading sabbatical which may never materialise. Added to that are the journals, magazines, blogs and training courses all wanting to grab our attention. It would be all too easy to bombard our heads and our clients with the latest and most exciting ideas and unless we are working within a unifying framework we may be in danger of 'unsystematic eclecticism' (Grant, 2011a). As de Haan and Blass (2007) point out: 'coaches work very intuitively because they rarely if ever give a rationale for the great diversity of ways in which they coach … in short, coaching will remain a largely intuitive area of work until it can be demonstrated conclusively what works in what circumstances'. I believe this also means we may not always know which intuitively selected interventions are the most effective because we may not use them consistently enough to say they are tried and tested.
- Third, integration poses a potential challenge for accessing and using supervision. Whilst the so-called 'third way' of integration is still in its infancy, finding a supervisor who is adequately experienced in both executive

coaching and therapy and who supports working this way is not that easy. I have found that having a unifying framework to hold in mind during supervision – both my own and when I am the supervisor – can be just as useful as it is in coaching. It helps us to navigate our way together through this relatively new territory.

There are other challenges explored much more fully in this book including the management of boundaries and the ethics of working integratively, so I would now like to explore the Personal Consultancy model in more detail as relevant to my own integrative approach.

Dimensions of the Personal Consultancy model in executive coaching

Working at depth

Wherever you go, there you are is the title of the book by Jon Kabat-Zinn (2004) about developing mindfulness. The phrase also reminds me that, despite many people believing they have a work persona and a personal life persona, it is not always possible to keep them separate – we bring our whole selves to our work. And understanding this self – past, present and potential – is key to an integrative approach. Whilst some coaches have concerns about 'digging around' in their client's past, we cannot escape the fact that people's formative years and experiences have shaped them and made them into the people they are today. The client may have positive experiences and beliefs they have forgotten that can serve them well if they resurface when times are challenging. They may have deeply held self-limiting assumptions that are holding them back, for example 'I'm not up to this', and may invest huge amounts of emotional energy in keeping the lid on – which is energy that could be better spent creating a transformational vision. I sometimes encounter what has been called 'Imposter Syndrome' (Clance and Imes, 1978) where people are unable to internalise their accomplishments, despite all evidence to the contrary, and have an underlying fear that they don't really deserve to be where they are, that it is all a fluke and that one day they will be uncovered as an impostor.

If my clients are to develop their capacity to initiate and manage change, tolerate ambiguity, deal with others' uncertainties, think clearly, stay calm under fire, 'fly low and fly high', be willing to make decisions that may or may not work out and anything else that organisations expect (sometimes unrealistically) of their leaders, I believe self-understanding is vitally important. They need to be able to question – from a stance of self-kindness not critical judgement – old and existing behaviours and patterns and decide if they'd like to make a shift to new ones – and how they might do this. Acknowledging the aspects that are influenced by the past and knowing 'hot buttons' puts them in a position of greater strength when trying to make changes. Also, helping them to gain an understanding of their journey in getting to where they are today, perhaps because of or in spite of the challenges they've faced, can be remarkably uplifting. As mentioned earlier, at some point in the coaching we may have some data about their past and current situation including their goals. However, I am always careful at this stage not to jump into interpreting their answers or offering solutions because 'working at depth' is only possible and effective if we spend enough time in the coaching on 'being with'.

'Being with': listening and supporting

'Being with the client' and 'doing with the client' immediately speaks to me of two different energies. My particular way of 'being with' is based upon Nancy Kline's Thinking Environment™ (Kline, 1998). This holds that 'the quality of everything we do depends on the thinking we do first' (ibid.) and that we do our finest thinking when someone actually *helps* us to think. It is built around what Kline calls the *Ten Components* at the heart of which is sustained and seamless Attention, along with Ease, Equality, Encouragement, Appreciation, Diversity, Information, Feelings, Place and 'Incisive Questions'™ (questions that challenge limiting assumptions that may be untrue but which the client often lives as true). Each of these components has its own meaning and significance in the Thinking Environment. The framework was originally developed in the 1970s from Kline's observations in education and later in leadership development. Interestingly it has seen a surge in interest in recent years in the executive coaching space. Perhaps this is because executives are now bombarded with so much information and so many decisions to make that they have little time and space for thinking. They have more meetings, more papers to read, more calls on their time, more people to manage, more complexity to make sense of and more technology to contend with than at any time in the history of mankind.

The 'authentic listening' described within the Personal Consultancy model is at the heart of the Thinking Environment – listening with interest and fascination to what the client is saying and expectantly to what they might say next, not interrupting but encouraging, allowing the full and free expression of feelings and thoughts, giving sustained attention of such quality that it stimulates thinking. It means trusting that the client will be able to think for themselves, gain their own 'aha' moments, generate their own strategies and solutions, and set their own goals, with our support.

Typically in a coaching session I will spend at least 70 per cent of the time focusing on giving attention, after asking them a simple question, 'What would you like to think about, and what are your thoughts?' I will not interrupt or ask another question until I am sure that the client has gone to the edge of their own thinking, aided by my attention. 'Just' doing this appears to enable the client to self-coach. They will ask their own questions aloud, 'Do I really think that?', handle their own assumptions 'Now I've said it, I can see it's not true. Of course I know how to handle this', make their own links 'I wonder if I'm more like my boss than I realise?' and more. This way of 'being with' seems to create such a level of safety that the client can access thoughts and feelings previously unknown to them, or even an 'unthought known' (Bollas, 1987) – 'known' at a preconscious level but not yet made conscious. Thereby they can appropriately release their feelings and self-generate new ways forward, often with minimal verbal prompting from the coach. So in the Thinking Environment clients seem able to work both at depth and at surface as they feel the need to.

Kline suggests the need for three 'streams' of Attention to enable this level of self-coaching:

1   *To content* – what the client is actually saying;
2   *To response* – what that content might invoke in us;
3   *To The Thinking Environment* – holding all the Ten Components in our awareness.

To provide the best conditions for the client to think at their best and generate ideas the coach must balance these three streams.

Limbic resonance (Lewis et al., 2001) is a term coined to describe empathic harmony arising from the limbic system of the brain when people are attuned to each others' internal states. These and other advances in neuroscience and coaching (Rock and Page, 2009) show us that being with people in a particular way quietens the amygdala (two small areas in the limbic brain responsible for triggering the fight, flight or freeze responses) and creates feelings of safety, trust and attachment, generating 'approach' hormones such as dopamine and serotonin. These appear to make it possible to fully explore our thinking *and* generate new thoughts because we are unhindered by fear.

In executive coaching there appears to be a great deal of learning and development that arises from the relationship itself. Clients will often cite examples of how they have recreated some of the positive elements of our coaching relationship in their interactions with others. This might be as simple as 'listening more', 'not jumping to conclusions' or asking others 'what else do you think?' before jumping in and offering their own views.

'Doing with': Rebalancing and Generating

As I have written about elsewhere (Aspey, 2012), some see coaching as 'more driven, more upbeat and more of a two-way dialogue than counselling', so more questions are asked than in counselling. I am certainly aware of being more optimistic and focused in coaching than I am in counselling, but I believe that 'being with' the client is the thing which is of greatest value, not the number of questions we ask. For example, 'being with' Janine and giving her space to express herself enabled her to move herself into the Rebalancing stage to locate and resolve internal conflicts. And this may vary from session to session – some sessions have more 'doing' than 'being', others vice versa. It depends on the client's preferred focus at the time. We must though when Rebalancing and Generating not lose sight of 'being with' entirely – it helps me to think of 'being with' as a constant note played throughout a piece of music whilst a melody plays around it. In Thinking Environment work we never completely stop that note.

The 'doing with' phase can move the work into a more directive, proactive, focused and goal-oriented mode. Here we can offer additional insights or fresh perspectives for the client, or help them to examine the origins and triggers of unwanted behaviours. Like us all, executives have highs and lows, good days and bad days, failures and successes. However, executives and their actions are usually more visible and the price of failure higher. The workplace can be highly anxiety-provoking – a place where we have to prove ourselves, gain acceptance or handle rejection, win or lose, survive or die. Executive derailment is often the result of a client's attempts to regain control, but in so doing they have either demonstrated behaviours that damaged others or their own reputation, or the situation has generated so much stress that they have had a 'meltdown'. It is natural that anxiety can show up in people's behaviours and reactions. For some, the coaching relationship is one of the few where they can safely discuss personal and professional anxieties and their triumphs, without fear of being chastised or judged, accused of playing politics or of blowing their own trumpet when they celebrate their successes. On that note, being seen to be successful is often as important as the success itself and, as a result, many clients don't share their work concerns at home for fear of worrying their family or disappointing them, and this can be a heavy burden to carry alone.

Effective rebalancing at the perceptual, cognitive, affective or behavioural domains can sometimes be aided by sharing our thoughts with the client, with their permission. For example, asking if you can offer some feedback, or a gentle yet direct challenge to something they've just said, or draw a diagram to illustrate a model that may help to further their own thinking or offer a different perspective for them to consider. We can ask what more they would like to achieve in the session and work on the new goals, underneath which are likely to be more assumptions that are holding them back. In the Thinking Environment we think of it as a Spectrum of Independence (Aspey, 2013) with the client's independent thinking at one end and the coach giving direction at the other. When we cease giving the client sustained attention, ask questions or offer an idea or challenge, we naturally move into a more directive mode. This can be necessary and very useful when used sparingly and with care. This is probably the time when the coach needs to be most aware of the urge to throw the latest and greatest management and leadership ideas, hot off the press, to the client!

Using the Thinking Environment can be extremely powerful, as reported by one of my colleagues in supervision when she first used it with one of her new executive coaching clients:

> He told me he came to coaching thinking that I would give him advice, come up with suggestions and tell him the best ways to do things. It's a badge of

honour in that company to have an executive coach and he thought he'd better get value for money! He told me later he was probably expecting to be taught something new. It did happen but not at all in the way he'd thought it would. He said that just by talking to me about his role, his relationship with his boss, even how difficult his school years had been after his father died, and how much he still missed him, he felt more relaxed. Like sharing the load really; he'd never thought that much about what made him tick. And, as he was talking about these things, he was learning, and thinking about his own reactions to what had happened in the past and what was happening now at work. It was a surprisingly powerful experience. He said he felt really invigorated at the end of the session, not at all judged, just supported. And it was really quite unexpected.

In this chapter I have outlined my particular way of working integratively and why. Integration has been happening for some time and I believe that, whatever we call the work we do with clients, we remain mindful of at least four essentials: the needs of the client, the context in which they live and work, the contract we agree with them and our level of competence in addressing their needs – not just those that present at first meeting but those which may emerge during the course of the relationship.

Helping executives on their journey from old, unwanted patterns of feeling, thinking and being to new, desired and liberating ones is one of the most rewarding jobs in the world. In my view having the Personal Consultancy model is a significant step towards building a new understanding of integrative practice and all that it can offer.

Personal Consultancy with young people

'Are we bothered?'

Carolyn Mumby

Introduction

As front line services for young people disappear or face great threat, discussing the need for a new integrative framework for counselling and coaching with adolescents may on the face of it appear be the modern day equivalent of 'fiddling while Rome burns'. To adapt Catherine Tate's ubiquitous teenage Lauren phrase, 'Are we bothered?' But as resources for supporting young people dwindle, and are targeted on those in highest need, it is more important than ever that we identify new, innovative, efficient, cost-effective and swift responses that can support all young people as they develop and change.

This chapter will describe some of the dynamics and features of adolescence and the importance of providing integrated and accessible services to support young people through the transition to adulthood. It will also suggest that there is a need for young people to have access to a coaching approach. In some cases this is already happening, as many young people's counsellors are of necessity more proactive in their approach, albeit often under the radar and perhaps not always to the extent that would be most effective. Finally, it will examine the Personal Consultancy model and explore how the integrated framework offered can contain and support the fluctuating focus of adolescent experience, and the challenges of early adulthood; and, in addition, how it provides within one relationship both restorative and proactive support that is highly effective for matching the needs of a range of young people.

> At no other phase of the life cycle are the pressures of finding oneself and the threat of losing oneself so closely allied.
>
> (Erikson, 1968)

Young people between the ages of about 11 and 25 are negotiating a time of intense growth, and rapid change towards a potentially exciting, potentially unnerving and uncertain future. They are beginning to move away from the freedoms (within careful constraints) of their childhood, towards the autonomies, opportunities and responsibilities of adulthood. If they have lacked a secure attachment in their early years, and/or face particular difficulties and struggle to find good enough support networks in their current situation, this journey is even more perilous and the outcome potentially more doubtful (Wingfield, 2008). As well as a journey we can see adolescence as a kind of 'dance' involving risk and resilience, in rapidly transforming bodies within which emotions may swing wildly at times, and constructs are tested and reshaped. The adolescent brain also appears to be flexible and responsive and is undergoing significant remodelling, with more frequently used circuits becoming insulated to increase the speed and efficiency of the transmission of messages. As Sercombe (2010) states, 'this begins with the deep structures of the brain that are more fundamental for survival, including the circuits for social relationship, and moves forward to embrace the parts of the brain that are associated with conscious thinking and reasoning'.

The brain seems to rewire along the principle of 'use it or lose it' and during this life-stage there may be increased vulnerability to negative experiences and enhanced receptivity to the positive. Risk and resilience factors arise within the individual in terms of temperament and aptitude, within families and the wider community (Coleman and Hagell, 2007), which may be very supportive for some young people and sadly lacking or even threatening for others. In early adolescence the young person may experience greater freedom: to walk around alone, or with friends, texting, talking, hanging out – a time of excitement and risk taking. At the same time there is an expectation that they will take on some heavier burdens – the fearful weight of their school bags symbolising all they have to carry, to remember, to bear. Peer groups may be sources of support, encouragement, elation, but also of denigration and attack. Young people are leaving things behind, coming to terms with, facing up to and deciding things. Yet, in this time of intense flux, they are also required to individuate and belong, and to lay down the foundations of their future through education training and employment.

Under one roof

Given the complexity of this transition to adulthood and the need for access to early intervention so that potential risk is mediated and any resilience supported and built on, it is not surprising that young people themselves have shown a preference for services that can offer them a holistic response, preferably under one roof:

> Young people have a lot of problems and it is easier for them to walk into a place that deals with young people. … It is good to come to just one place where they sort everything out. I wouldn't want to keep explaining my situation over and over again, it is just too difficult and upsetting.
>
> (20-year-old male; Kenrick and Lee, 2010).

The Mental Health Foundation carried out extensive research and discovered that young people wanted 'services to practise holistically and offer a diverse range of support to meet young people's mental health, emotional well-being and practical needs' (Garcia et al., 2007).

YIACS – an integrated approach

In response to the multiple needs of young people, Youth Access represents a network of 200 young people's information, advice, counselling and support services (YIACS). YIACS nationwide have for some time recognised the importance of providing integrated services which offer both therapeutic holding for those in distress and supportive interventions for those at risk and which hold optimism and practical support for the potential of young people, from the beginning of puberty through to young adulthood. Through interventions such as counselling and other psychological therapies, advice work, health clinics, community education and personal support, YIACS offer a unique combination of early intervention, prevention and crisis intervention for young people:

> Open to all young people, YIACS offer a universal access point to targeted and specialist services, supporting young people across a diverse range of issues that are frequently inter-related:
> * social welfare issues e.g. benefits, housing, debt, employment
> * mental and emotional health issues e.g. depression, low self-esteem, self-harm, family problems and stress
> * wider personal and health issues e.g. relationships, sexual health, drugs and alcohol, healthy eating
> * practical issues e.g. careers, money management, independent living skills
> (Kenrick and Lee, 2010).

YIACS have been identified as particularly important for 16- to 25-year-olds since this young adult group face specific issues associated with the transition from adolescence to adulthood and is at risk of falling though the gaps between children's and adult provision (Social Exclusion Unit, 2005).

A proactive counselling approach

Counselling services for young people usually draw on the services of counsellors trained in generic adult counselling. Their skills include the ability to listen carefully and with depth, bringing attitudes of empathy, acceptance, of positive regard and respect for the client's world and agenda. Counsellors provide reflection and holding which enables the client to work out what they think, experience what they feel and see what they do and what they might do differently. However, counselling services for young people have developed in significantly different ways to address the need for a more proactive approach in adolescence. Experience has shown that there is more the counsellor needs to bring if they are to optimise the support for young people. Youth Access offers specialised training to help develop counsellor knowledge and skills to meet this need. Young people respond to a flexible and responsive approach. A young person may typically come for counselling feeling desperate and then a week later present as relatively confident and carefree (or the other way around!). Both positions may be in some way true for them, as with adults. However, young people's sense of themselves and view of their situation may be more easily influenced and change more rapidly and dramatically.

Erik Erikson (1950) in his theory of life stages says the task in adolescence is to resolve identity and direction and negotiate role confusion – to be yourself and to share this with others. For children, development mostly depends on 'what is done to us', whereas in adolescence development depends on 'what we do'. Adolescence is a state of active transition to independence; this move can be supported by a more proactive approach (Mumby, 2011).

Proactive counselling is a term used by Geldard and Geldard (2010) to describe a process with its foundations in existential philosophy and constructivist thinking. This foundation supports the process of young people reflecting on and learning from their experiences, and underpins the testing and revising of constructs – an important part of adolescence. The approach includes symbolic, creative, cognitive-behavioural and psycho-educational strategies. Having these options enables the counsellor to move further to meet a young person by joining with some adolescent communication processes (including the need for diversion and greater transparency, and showing more of themselves without compromising the therapeutic framework).

The importance of developing a good enough attachment

This listening, respectful adult may be the first and only experience a young person has had so far of being heard. This can be startling and uncomfortable and something they need to get used to. It may threaten angry defences involuntarily erected against the terror of vulnerability if they have been subject to violence in their childhood (Batmanghelidjh, 2009). They may want to flee from and reject, or alternatively sink everything into and cling to this new relationship. More vulnerable young people, who would benefit from an experience of deeper attachment, may need to come for a long time. This way, time can be spent building this relationship, sometimes in ordinary ways, getting to know each other, checking each other out, experiencing the security of the keen but non-intrusive interest of a supportive adult, before they are able to address the deeper wounds they bring from disrupted or dangerous childhoods.

Alternatively for other young people one session may be enough to put their mind at rest, to understand and perhaps resolve their problem. They may not see the point of further meetings – they are 'over it' now, they want to move on. Milner and Bateman (2011) 'found that children may not wish to, or feel unable to, explore the reasons why they are struggling, but do wish to change things'.

Other young people move back and forth between a deeper exploration of past problems and a focus on the here and now, or on how they want to do things differently in the future. Geldard and Geldard (2010) talk about the importance of proactive counsellors making use of adolescent communication processes, which may contain a significant amount of what adults can perceive as digression:

> Because young people are continually revising their constructs they are often trying to grapple with many differing thoughts and ideas at the same time … by digressing they are able to deal with new thoughts without putting them on hold.

Geldard and Geldard (2010) go on to emphasise that,

> Digression also has a very useful function in allowing a young person to move away from something that is very troubling for them. By changing the topic they can stop talking about issues which are emotionally disturbing and instead talk about less troubling things. They may then return to talking about the emotionally troubling issues after having a period of time during which the conversation has been less intense.

It is my experience that this 'digression' from working at depth can happen, not just within a session but also over a longer period of time. Young people can benefit from having opportunities to consolidate the work done at a deeper level by working for a time on more practical or immediate issues, or spending time in activities that are enjoyable. This makes the therapeutic process more digestible, more manageable and can strengthen the relationship of trust between themselves and the counsellor before returning to working at depth again.

Coaching young people – a missed opportunity?

In my experience of training qualified counsellors I have found that many counsellors who are working in schools, sometimes without any previous experience of working in young people's centres, have begun to find their way to a more proactive way of working. They have found that this is necessary in order to build the relationship with young people, to find creative ways to help them express their feelings, identify the changes they wish to make and to support them to reach their goals. For some counsellors it has been almost a 'guilty secret'. They have a sense that they have somehow wandered from the path of the 'pure' counselling approach. Working proactively in the ways described means that many of these counsellors are using approaches commonly used in coaching, though coaching itself as a distinct activity seems to be rarely offered to young people either in the setting of YIACS or within schools.

YIACS services vary according to local need, being free, independent and confidential services; and they offer a range of young person-centred interventions, taking a holistic approach to meeting multiple and complex needs. In these services multi-disciplinary teams provide 'wrap around' support. Access routes are flexible and include drop-in sessions, with an open door policy that means young people can self-refer and become acquainted with the different types of service on offer in an informal atmosphere. They may initially walk through the door for information or to join a group of volunteers, yet may later choose to go through a 'connecting door' to access counselling in an organisation with which they have built up some familiarity and trust. Alternatively they may be referred for counselling, and then be introduced to other services within the organisation, such as opportunities to volunteer or to get information or advice, which focus on making their way in the wider world.

Many YIACS fully understand the need for a central flow in the organisation. They see that although different professionals are trained to do different things, it is important that key people understand something about *all* of the different services from signposting, advice work, sexual health, support groups, volunteering opportunities, youth work and counselling. They form a central hub of knowledge and can enable the professionals to signpost from one service to another. Other YIACS have, perhaps unwittingly, drifted into having a more isolated counselling service. The boundaries designed to keep the young person safe and facilitate the therapeutic alliance become a 'mysterious wall', outside of which not much is really known, and within which the counsellor looks inward into the world of the young person. However, they may fail to recognise that just outside there are currencies available which might help build up the young person's resources and confidence; or practical support which could enable young people to feel better equipped for dealing with their situation.

I have supervised counsellors who, fresh from diplomas without any modules focused on working specifically with young people, continue to look for the pathology of the young person. Perhaps what may be needed is proper advice about benefits, or an opportunity to make friends, actively build on their strengths, learn some new skills, or to find out their options in terms of housing or education.

Young people can become labelled through an unbalanced focus on only their problems, which is why a key principle of Youth Access Counselling Assessment standards is the emphasis on seeking also to acknowledge skills and strengths.

Strengthening neural pathways

Recent developments in MRI scanning have developed our understanding about the plasticity of the brain, and that experience can change aspects of its structures. This ability to remodel appears to be particularly pronounced in adolescence as young people's brains are still in development. A particular change is occurring in what Siegel and Bryson (2012) refer to as the 'upstairs brain' – the function that enables coordination of behaviour, directing attention, recognising consequences of actions and planning future tasks. Siegel describes how experiences create physical structures in the brain, 'When neurons fire together, they grow new connections between them. Over time, the connections that result from firing lead to "rewiring" in the brain.'

If we provide young people with the support to learn and practise problem solving, decision-making, planning and experimenting with and testing solutions, we can help them build and strengthen neural pathways and contribute to resilience and life-skills. This is easier to do if we have built a relationship of trust with a young person.

Neuroscience and coaching expert Paul Brown sees trust as an essential attachment emotion and suggests that it influences the brain and increases our ability to face difficulties. Because of this he recommends that coaches look at Bowlby's attachment theory: 'Coaching clients continually present with their past. Ignoring this is like architects not bothering about foundations' (Brown, 2013).

It is my view that we need a model of intervention that can help young people recognise and explore the foundations upon which they are trying to build. An intervention that would strengthen them so that they are more secure and content and enable them to build upwards and outwards so they can learn to aspire to and achieve greater things.

Personal Consultancy – the missing link?

As we have seen, proactive counselling for young people already embraces aspects of what can also be found in coaching approaches. Similarly, BACP (2013b) acknowledge that whilst coaching is 'characterised by interventions which are more likely to be developmental in nature' and 'counselling may be characterised by interventions which are more likely to be reparative in nature' that 'a number of existing therapeutic approaches ... can more or less explicitly be seen as encompassing both therapeutic and developmental components within a single framework'. In the same document BACP also states:

> Clients' needs, and ways of meeting them, need to be considered as part of a dynamic process. For example, coaching may surface issues of a deeper psychological nature. Conversely, the recovery of psychological balance through counselling may enable progression to a more developmental focus.
> (BACP, 2013b).

Could an integrated approach such as Personal Consultancy be the missing link in young people's support services? This approach allows the practitioner to respond to their fluctuations in confidence and optimism. It acknowledges both the need for nurture and holding, and the importance of honouring their sense of buoyancy and possibility, explicitly making a space to explore their aspirations and support them to develop realistic and ambitious ways forward.

Such a framework keeps the faith with both the 'threat of losing oneself' and the 'pressure to find oneself' and provides a space to address both. It does not seek to split the reparative and the restorative from the aspiration and ongoing developmental needs of young people. With such an approach, at the point of referral, we could hold sight of the young person in a more holistic way and as a result avoid seeking to channel them into services according to whether we perceive them as distressed or capable of greater things. Just as some young people might enter a YIAC through one 'door' and then access other services once they are familiar and comfortable in the setting, other young people might enter Personal Consultancy through the door marked 'coaching'. Boys and young men may perceive this as more acceptable than counselling, which can carry a stigma or an expectation of something more medical and serious. As trust builds the young person is able to reveal more of themselves and is therefore more likely to be able to shift, if needed, into the restorative work of rebalancing, traditionally associated with counselling. At the same time, this model gives us a place to locate some of the proactive counselling interventions and to explicitly use them in the service of going forward. By the same token, when they face further challenges, or slips, they have the option and the relationship, which can enable them to revisit past themes, and re-orientate themselves once again. Healing is not necessarily a linear process. As adults, if we have undertaken any kind of deeper self-reflection we will be familiar with this reprise of particular themes or stumbling blocks, sometimes coming back to that 'same old chestnut'. If we have the self-compassion, which may develop through a positive helping relationship with someone who will listen with acceptance, we might dig a little deeper or gain a little more insight yet.

Adapting the Personal Consultancy model to communicate with young people

Writing in *BACP Counselling Children and Young People* (CCYP) journal (Mumby, 2011) I explored how the language in the Personal Consultancy model might be adapted to make the process more explicit and relevant for young people. I also wanted to offer guidance to practitioners and help them recognise the changing focus of the work, reflecting the changeability inherent in adolescence. The framework is concerned with both 'being' and 'doing', and includes a respectful exploration of where the young person is at *now*, as well as an overt interest in helping them identify where they want to get to. It emphasises that a primary process throughout is that of being listened to. It acknowledges the need to find a sense of emotional, cognitive and behavioural balance. This can support a collaborative approach to managing risk, which perhaps has in the past, or threatens now, to destabilise the young person. At the same time it explicitly enables a focus on building resilience and is supportive of positive risk taking and experimentation, which allows the young person to grow and determine their own way forward. The framework recognises that ongoing support enables change, both internal and external, to be absorbed and maintained.

Being heard

'Authentic listening' sets out the part of the process which is both the beginning and the ongoing experience of working with a Personal Consultant and enables the young person to 'get heard'. Younger young people especially may be more used to being told what to do and what not to do by adults, rather than being listened to for their own story and their own view. Being heard can in itself be a powerful healing and motivating experience. It may take time for the young person to open up, or a great deal may come pouring out at once. It may take time for the young people to begin to really hear themselves, to tune in to their own thoughts, feelings and impulses. This part of the process may involve working creatively with the young person encouraging them to draw or paint feelings and getting a fuller picture of their situation using genograms or life-lines, or life-space diagrams. This stage increases awareness both in the young person and the practitioner of 'what is'. Listening permeates every aspect of the Personal Consultancy model and is important for allowing the 'what has been, what is and what could be' to emerge.

Finding your balance

The focus on listening is of course ubiquitous in young people's counselling, as is the second quadrant 'Rebalancing' – providing space to identify and explore emotions; to look at patterns of thought and behaviour which may be causing or sustaining stuck places, or undesirable and unresolved conflict in the young person's internal self or in their relationships with others. 'Find your balance' may be something that makes better sense to young people. Part of this process is to identify what the young person is already doing well. Solution Focused approaches can be useful here.

Young people may be living in difficulties not of their own making or in situations they do not yet have the power to change. Having this understood and acknowledged may contribute to resilience. Exploring strategies for coping, until they have enough autonomy to leave or make the changes they would like to make, is important. For some young people, getting to this stage may be all they need.

Moving forward

The third quadrant moves us into coaching territory. 'Generating' can be expressed as 'move on' or 'move forward'. This may involve using visualisation, exploring options, making decisions, forming goals and testing solutions. For some young people this will also be a move away from previous patterns, and previously unquestioned habits, which may have become damaging. This space for generating ideas and trying out new ways of behaving may involve taking calculated risks that move a young person out of their comfort zone. The consequences of this can be empowering to a young person because as Sercombe (2010) asserts, 'We find that when young people face risks, and face them down, they change. They are afterwards more "mature", more balanced, more effective agents, more thoughtful.' To have a focus on generating offers an essential opportunity, not only repairing what has become damaged but actively strengthening resilience.

Supporting

When first thinking about adapting the language of the model for young people I thought the fourth phase 'Supporting' might be better expressed as 'Keep Going'. My thoughts were that this stage is to do with momentum, and the practitioner is engaged in giving support to navigate difficulties and maintain motivation. In that sense it is about going forward. However, revisiting this more recently I think that to phrase it this way doesn't stay true to the dimension of 'being', and from an attachment perspective doesn't accurately communicate the importance of being able to return to 'holding', the safety of a supportive and accepting adult. This support from the Personal Consultant, or coach–therapist, can also be strengthened by the young person identifying friends, family members, youth workers, teachers and/or mentors who can offer further holding or encouragement. Identifying other sources of support adds to the developing autonomy of the young person. A fundamental aspect of resilience is our ability to support ourselves. From the trust developed in the relationship, where the young person is offered generative listening, they can begin to develop greater compassion for themselves. When they are able to be less self-judgemental and more self-supportive they are more likely to face and work through their difficulties. There is a great deal that we can learn from mindfulness here: 'Mindfulness is awareness, cultivated by paying attention in a sustained and particular way: on purpose, in the present moment, and non-judgmentally' (Kabat-Zinn, 2012).

This creates space to rebalance and to reorientate. Recent studies claim that mindfulness

> has been shown to reduce stress, anxiety, reactivity and bad behaviour, improve sleep and self-esteem, and bring about greater calmness, relaxation, the ability to manage behaviour and emotions, self-awareness and empathy … It can help young people pay greater attention, be more focused, think in more innovative ways, use existing knowledge more effectively, improve working memory, and enhance planning, problem solving and reasoning skills.
>
> (Weare, 2012).

The skills of mindfulness can be taught to young people, within the Personal Consultancy approach, as they respond well both to the idea of finding ways to access more calm, and also to freeing up their potential (Burnett, 2009). So it is with the importance of this process in mind that I reverted in my own thinking to the original name of 'Supporting' for this phase. The practitioner supports the embedding of the learning, and supports the young person as they experiment with change. In this phase there can be a search for, and validation of, other forms of support – an overt recognition that we all need various supportive relationships as we move through life. Finally, 'Supporting' works for me because it acknowledges the need for self-support and self-compassion, which I see as the essential bedrock for young people and adults to move forward in life.

Issues

It is important that practitioners offering approaches are clear what they are doing, are equipped to provide it and are professionally supported and accountable. The beauty of services 'under one roof' is that it provides the opportunity to maintain the clarity and boundaries of distinct professions alongside the ability to refer easily to other services within the project, and it delivers flexibility of response to offer a more holistic service in one place. Coaching as a profession has rarely been represented within children's and young people's services and I believe offering standalone coaching may not be enough, particularly where young people are vulnerable and still finding their feet. Personal Consultancy is able to offer coaching as *part of* a coherent way forward, generating ideas and developing goals and action plans and building on the resilience identified – but this is complimented by the inclusion of more therapeutic type interventions.

Conclusion

At the time of writing support services for young people have been badly hit by the results of the economic downturn and consequent cuts to services in the statutory and voluntary sectors. Those remaining are in a state of uncertainty as wider public sector and NHS reforms reshape structures and organisational delivery models. The voluntary sector is often the home of innovation and can produce creative and more immediate responses to changing needs. However, innovative developments are harder to pick up due to fast dwindling resources. The paths towards the autonomy and accountability of adulthood are ill defined as we face an economic crisis, a dismantling of the signposts and an unravelling of the safety nets provided to help young people negotiate their way forward. Even for those with the stamps of social capital, qualifications, connections and experience in their passports, the journey is not assured, the destination not certain.

Economic pressure notwithstanding, our society cannot stand back and allow the vast potential of the young person – their fresh perspective, determination, energy and focus, their passion, sense of fairness and creativity – to wither on the vine. I believe that offering a coaching approach, within the Personal Consultancy framework, and alongside other targeted and specialist YIAC services, would provide an innovative way forward that does not demand a complete restructuring of services. This would nurture the potential and meet the changing needs of today's young people. It is an opportunity to strengthen our offer and strengthen our support, both to face the threats and meet the exciting challenges of adolescence.

Chapter 13

Personal Consultancy with addictions

Ann Collins

Introduction

Building on the previous chapters' exploration of the Personal Consultancy (PC) framework, this chapter will examine its application within the area of addiction of women in the probationary service. Whilst the term addiction can convey a plethora of meanings and interpretations, its essence for the purpose of this chapter can be encapsulated by Toates, (2004) description that addiction is the 'compulsive use of psychoactive drugs which illicit a psychological effect'. The most commonly used psychoactive drugs, according to Atkinson et al. (1990), include: depressants (alcohol, barbiturates, minor tranquilisers); opiates (heroin, morphine); stimulants (amphetamines, cocaine, nicotine, caffeine); hallucinogens (LSD); cannabis (marijuana, hashish). These drugs affect behaviour and consciousnesses and act in a specific biochemical way on the brain. With repeated use they result in physical and psychological dependency. Working with addiction involves not only dealing with the dependency but also addressing this in tandem with the underlying reasons that instigated the misuse.

This chapter first describes the clients' environment and background. It then proceeds by describing how the PC model is applied in this specific setting through the use of two case studies. The intention is to demonstrate the model's flexibility to suit the variety of clients' circumstances whilst working with them in their weekly sessions. Finally, it will summarise the ways in which PC can be beneficial and some themes for further exploration.

Environment and background of clients

The PC framework will be considered here in the context of working with women who have been referred to an approved hostel by the probation service. Depending on the conditions of their licence or order, the women may be on remand or awaiting sentence. The hostel accommodates up to 22 women, who spend between a few weeks and six months living there, until they are moved to permanent accommodation or to prison. During their stay, the women work on developing their self-efficacy and on adopting behaviours likely to reduce their incidences of reoffending. The women are subject to restrictions about the times they can leave the hostel, and failure to comply with this, or any other transgressions, can result in them being recalled to prison.

The women within the hostel have a diverse set of education and social backgrounds, which may include:

- relationship problems directly contributing to their criminality;
- histories of violence and abuse making them victims as well as offenders;
- substance misuse problems that make their lives more chaotic;
- histories of harming themselves; and
- mental health problems that have often been undiagnosed and/or untreated.

Living in the hostel as an alternative to prison can be difficult as the women are in closer proximity to each other and this can lead to a variety of altercations. The hostel is supported by 15 members of staff including a manager who is a qualified probation officer, two deputy managers and a substance misuse worker.

A condition of their stay is that the women have to attend a compulsory programme, which may include working with the substance misuse worker if relevant. The programme consists of group workshops run over a six-week period covering topics which include: relationships, domestic abuse, safety and communication. Residents have the opportunity of receiving individual coaching/ counselling which is not a condition of their stay at the hostel. As this service is not an adjunct to the hostel or the probationary service, the women see it as a safe environment that provides objective support. Whilst most women attend of their own volition, some are encouraged to do so through the support of their key worker who is assigned to them throughout their stay at the hostel.

Most of the women have never previously had counselling. A few have experienced a small number of sessions, generally limited as a result of moving between prisons during the course of their sentence. This is common practice within the prison service and tends to reduce the longer-term effectiveness of counselling in prisons. In contrast, as women stay for longer periods of time at the hostel, the interventions can be consistently sustained, which seems to increase the likelihood of achieving meaningful personal change.

Contextualising the Personal Consultancy model within this environment

Whilst the previous section provides a brief background to the clients' environment, we also need to be aware that the clients are individuals who have a multitude of personal issues and are often on anti-psychotic, anti-depressant or other medications. The combination of factors can add a huge amount of complexity and challenge the support that can realistically be provided to these clients. Notwithstanding this, however, results are achieved, largely as a result of working collaboratively and focusing on the client's needs.

In the formative stages, the first critical step (focusing on the 'Personal') side is to understand the client and build trust, which has usually been virtually non-existent throughout these women's lives. Even within the hostel, trust levels with other residents can be problematic and relationships volatile, often adding to or triggering the very issues the women are already struggling to manage. The development of the relationship and interaction in the 'Personal' side focuses on the depth axis of the PC model and is crucial to developing a working alliance. The critical attributes for working with these women include those outlined by Jinks and Popovic (2011): being genuine, reliable and trustworthy, acting with acceptance and respect, and having integrity. Other important attributes would include flexibility, confidence, warmth, interest and openness. Building this collaborative base therefore assimilates the three dimensions of the PC framework: the client, the practitioner or consultant, and the relationship, which will be explored in more detail later in the chapter.

While the women's length of stay in the hostel varies, as mentioned earlier, they generally have some indication of the likely timescale, making it easier to negotiate the focus for their sessions. So, for example, women with an 8-week stay may focus on interpersonal communication and assertion, whereas those with a 24-week stay may focus on deeper issues such dealing with abuse and/or abusive relationships.

Being clear about the focus and what can be achieved is carefully managed in the contracting stage and throughout the process to ensure as much as possible that work on issues is complete or in a safe place for the client when the sessions end. Despite the time constraints, working along the depth axis and focusing on the intra-personal world of the client is achievable. Understanding the underlying issues also facilitates more substantial work at the surface level, which will usually encompass the women's experiences within the hostel. (Life in the hostel frequently raises issues that need addressing in their sessions.) Supporting clients from a practitioner or consultant perspective (vertical axis) requires both a non-directive and directive style that will oscillate depending on the client's needs.

The Personal Consultancy model in practice

Focusing on two case studies, this section will demonstrate how PC operates within this environment. The client's progress is tracked using the Clinical Outcomes in Routine Evaluation (CORE) system which measures:

- subjective well-being;
- problem symptoms, such as anxiety depression, physical and trauma;
- functioning, which includes coping with situations and setbacks, close relationships and social relationships;
- risk and harm to self and others.

In addition, an assessment questionnaire measures their interpersonal and communication style, team interaction and personal effectiveness. This is filled in by both residents and their key workers, before and after their sessions, to track their interpersonal progress. Contracting with the clients maintains all the ethical and confidentiality provisions of working as a coach and/or therapist and the women with substance-abuse issues commit to not attending sessions intoxicated. Only on three occasions, with the two different clients discussed here, were the weekly sessions terminated because the client was intoxicated, and in each case they returned clear the following week.

Case studies

The case studies described here are of women seen in the hostel who, as with most of the others, can be considered victims themselves. Many have histories of sexual, physical and emotional abuse by members and/or friends of their own families, or by partners. Whilst coping with the affects of abuse is difficult enough, Sanderson (2008) identifies that often the relational difficulties that ensue in dealing with the betrayal of trust and the distortion of perception can be as traumatising as the abuse itself. The assertion is that these women resort to substance abuse to disassociate from their emotional pain and memories. Sanderson supports this view citing research that confirms a strong association between childhood sexual abuse (CSA) and substance abuse.

Using the PC framework with clients in this environment will highlight the fluidity of boundaries between counselling and coaching in response to the issues they present weekly. In order to provide sufficient insight and depth, the cases described in the following sections specify certain aspects of the issues worked on during sessions, though not all the issues in their totality. For the purposes of anonymity and confidentiality clients' names and certain personal details have been changed.

Lucy

Lucy, a 20-year-old woman, did time for burglary and was in the hostel for two months before being moved to a drug rehab centre. She presented with unresolved issues following the death of her dad a year earlier. Her narrative included her mum leaving home when she was 4 years old, at which time she was left with her dad. When she was 7 he started to touch her inappropriately and she was raped by him at the age of 13, which then continued to occur for a number of years. She described the isolation and loneliness she experienced during this time and the way it led to her becoming rebellious and taking heroin.

As a result, she was in and out of care for the remainder of her teenage years. Research supports the view that addiction often has a direct correlation with family background, and that poor parental and family functioning, exhibited through a deficiency in parental supervision, rejection, separation and conflict, often increases the likelihood of substance abuse (Nurco et al., 1997).

At 17, and still using heroin, Lucy became pregnant. With her daughter she then resided with her boyfriend's mother. In order to support her and her boyfriend's habit, Lucy became involved in petty crime, burglary and prostitution. When she came to the hostel she had been prescribed methadone and had been off heroin for a year. She had also been diagnosed with a borderline personality disorder and prescribed anti-psychotics, but she had no suicidal or self-harming tendencies. The DSM-IV classification of borderline personality disorder encompassed the existence of an antisocial personality disorder, owing to Lucy's general conduct coupled with the extent of her substance abuse.

The application of the Personal Consultancy model

In her initial sessions Lucy talked rapidly, maintained minimal eye contact and her body was hunched over as she sat in her chair. Her concentration levels wavered, owing to the influence of her medication and disturbed sleep patterns, such that her third session was terminated after 20 minutes. Working with Lucy within the 'Personal' side of the model highlighted crucially that her dad's death was the catalyst for her being overwhelmed by past unresolved issues. She described having limited interaction with others in the hostel and, whilst outwardly loud and aggressive, inwardly she had low self-esteem issues which prevented her communicating effectively with both staff and residents.

Staying within the 'Personal' framework, the interaction maintained a controlled level of depth which allowed an understanding of Lucy's inner world and provided a context for understanding the existing patterns in her life. Through the process of disclosure it became apparent that Lucy's issues were complex and that many required longer-term support. However, having a safe environment without prejudgements or assumptions enabled Lucy to begin processing her emotions and cognitions and gain greater insights into herself as a person. Authentic listening (stage one) was crucial in building the relationship with Lucy as she had little trust in people and found it difficult to talk about what had happened to her. Meanwhile, the 'Consultancy' side explored what could realistically be contracted to work on in seven sessions. The other areas requiring longer-term support were highlighted for her to address in her future counselling at the rehab centre (to which she was being automatically transferred following her stay at the hostel).

The areas agreed upon for the focus of her PC sessions were the difficulties Lucy had in her social interactions with everyone in the hostel. This was a specific and immediate need as her aggressive outbursts with staff and residents at the hostel had the potential to result in her being recalled to jail. This would also mean that she would not be able to go to rehab to work on her longer-term addiction and psychological issues. During the course of her sessions Lucy learnt to become more self-aware and to assert herself respectfully with others. Within stage two of the process (Rebalancing), Lucy began to identify her past behaviours and ways of coping which were being triggered through her interaction with others. Working in stage two did not negate stage one (Authentic Listening) – this just continued in parallel throughout the process. Lucy gradually began to share the experiences she had most dreaded talking about, whereas in the past she had inhibited them from surfacing by taking drugs. This disclosure was a crucial step for Lucy – staying with something that was uncomfortable for her emotionally but necessary to come to terms with and understand the underlying reasons for her addiction to heroin.

The relationship (depth axis) with Lucy included staying within her world but enabling a surface focus to occur using a cognitive behavioural approach. Lucy was able to capture her existing patterns of behaviour, thinking and emotions that were not working and to begin to identify in what ways they could change. Specifically, using a cognitive behavioural approach was facilitated through the SPACE circular diagram (Edgerton and Palmer, 2005) which represents:

S – the social context the client is operating in;
P – physiology;
A – actions or behaviours;
C – cognitions;
E – emotions.

Through this process Lucy identified how her core belief of worthlessness influenced her thinking and how she felt. She saw how the impact of methadone, her lack of sleep and not eating properly contributed and affected her behaviour and reactions.

Lucy's interpersonal difficulties with others highlighted her social anxiety, stemming from a fear of not really knowing how to behave appropriately in social situations. In stage three (Generating), use of the cognitive behavioural approach enabled Lucy to understand how her assumptions and thinking impacted on her reactions to situations and people and to begin to explore alternatives. A major block for Lucy to overcome was changing the negative perceptions of staff, who saw her as difficult and non-communicative. She was supported (stage four) in developing confidence and identifying the staff to whom she felt comfortable to talk. By engaging in regular communication with them, she enabled them to understand and support her, particularly on the days she found things difficult to deal with.

Other areas worked on with Lucy were her tiredness, along with the effects of methadone which she had been taking for the last year. Lucy began to keep a diary of her energy levels and to identify the patterns when her energy dropped making her more prone to behaving aggressively. Working within stage three and four (Generating/Supporting) Lucy saw how her broken sleep patterns and poor eating habits contributed to her tiredness. Aside from attending the hostel workshops, Lucy had no structure to her day and rarely exercised, adding to her general levels of lethargy. Generating solutions to manage her days/weeks more effectively, Lucy devised a plan which included taking her medication at night instead of in the morning. The increased energy this gave her was noticeable as she became more alert in her sessions, and through incremental steps became more confident that she could personally change and make her life different. Lucy was also shown relaxation techniques which would help her to develop new ways to self-sooth rather than relying on drugs, as was the case previously.

Lucy attended all seven sessions and was able to share the unimaginable pain she had suppressed most of her life in a controlled safe environment. The surface work focused on her positively communicating and asserting herself. This was evident in her subsequent sessions: instead of a slouching position she sat upright in her chair; she was able to hold eye contact; and her speech became more relaxed and less agitated than it had been. CBT's psycho-educational approach enabled Lucy to identify patterns of behaviour in relationships, such as in a friendship she had with another resident to whom Lucy gave money and time generously but never had it reciprocated. She recognised how she gave everything to preserve her need for acceptance by others. Whilst her interactions with others were still a challenge, Lucy started to become more aware of herself with others, which was appreciated by staff and reflected in her post self-assessment questionnaire. At a deeper level Lucy learnt about the underlying causes of her addiction, which helped prepare her for the move to rehab and achieve her personal objective of not being recalled to prison.

In summary, the work with Lucy demonstrated the value of the coaching and counselling disciplines interweaving with each other whilst simultaneously demonstrating effective work in the different stages of the Personal Consultancy model and integration of the other approaches, processes and theories. All this helped Lucy to make significant steps towards self-awareness and change. At the beginning, Lucy's CORE scores were at a moderate to severe level of distress. When she completed her seven sessions she was in a healthy functioning position. Whilst Lucy had a long way to go, she stated that being at the hostel and having her sessions had helped her take responsibility for herself and her issues for the first time.

Alice

Alice, a 45-year-old educated woman, was in the hostel pending her court case over the death of her partner. Alice had two teenage children (who lived with her ex-husband) whom she had not seen for two years. She and her sister had been sexually abused by her father from the age of 7 to 15. Whilst closer to her mother, she described this relationship as non-emotional and distant. Horne (2001) suggests that a child whose parents do not respond to their growing sense of agency will have a limited capacity to integrate this into their developing self. The detachment Alice experienced from her parents may have resulted in Alice struggling, as she developed, to integrate her damaged body and mind into her changing ego so that she eventually found solace through alcohol. This would seem to support Horne's perspective.

Alice had few friends and was quite introverted. By her early twenties she had met a man whose family were close family friends and was married to him for 11 years before they divorced. After her children were born, intimacy was practically non-existent and their relationship changed to a functional relationship of two people living together. Many years later, Alice's husband disclosed that he was a transsexual (though she thought he was gay but could never admit it), which provided her with some indication of why their relationship had changed. She described how her husband projected an impression externally of how much he loved and cared for her, but at home he was cold, manipulative and non-emotional. From an early age, Alice had learnt to disassociate from her feelings, which Mollon (1993 as cited in Sanderson, 2008, p.182) identifies as being able to apply a self-hypnotic assertion, 'I am not here; this is not happening to me; I am not this body.'

After divorcing, Alice's drinking increased and she ended up in rehab, where she met her partner, Dave. He was addicted to alcohol and diagnosed with paranoid schizophrenia, and when drunk became aggressive and abusive towards her. One day following one of their many arguments, Dave fell backwards out of the caravan in which they lived. Alice saw nothing unusual in this as he often fell over, so left him and went to the pub. When she returned, Dave was alive but groggy. They both went to sleep but unfortunately he never woke up and died as a result of head injuries sustained in the fall.

Alice turned up to all the sessions clear of alcohol, but by her own admission she was drinking a few times during the week. Alice was not on any medication and there were no other mental health issues identified or suicidal and self-harm risks associated with her. Her CORE score indicated that she was moderately distressed, which was largely affected by her impending court case.

The application of the Personal Consultancy model

Within the 'Personal' framework the interaction focused primarily on the depth axis – establishing the relationship and the process of authentic listening (stage one) in order to understand what was going on for Alice. This provided insights, links and connections to how Alice coped with her situation. For example, it identified what Nijenhuis et al. (1998 as cited in Sanderson, 2008, p.186) describe as 'freezing', whereby Alice tried to stop feeling and avoid being hurt again by using painting as a psychological escape. However, Alice's paintings were also a way of communicating her feelings, and using this in the sessions became a different medium for exploring her internal conflicts, which in turn helped develop her emotional literacy.

Within the 'Consultancy' phase, when agreeing the areas of focus for her nine sessions, Alice aspired to reconcile with her past and find strategies to cope with her upcoming court case. Switching back to the 'Personal' phase the relationship developed within the mode of 'being with the client' (vertical axis) when Alice explored how, within her relationships, she could not rely on anyone to support her emotional needs. Even when she had confronted and confided in her mother about her father, her mother had dismissed it and blamed her. Alice had also confronted her father and it was only after the third attempt that he finally accepted what he had done and apologised, confirming that it was not a conjecture on her part.

In stages one and two (Authentic Listening and Rebalancing) Alice explored the abuse and examined the loss associated with this: that of herself, her life's expectations, her marriage, her partner and now potentially her freedom. Assessing this from a psychoanalytic perspective and interacting on the depth axis, Alice described her 'voice being locked within' so that it strangled her ability to communicate and be heard by her parents, her husband and more recently the solicitor taking her case. Alice explored her internal conflicts and developed awareness of her ego (the mediator with the external world) being fractured, which negated the adaptive development of her self-representation and resulted in a defensive ego function.

Working with Alice on this did enable her experience of the abuse to become integrated, as described by Sanderson (2008), through understanding her current mental state and activities at a higher level of conscious awareness. By developing her emotional literacy using adaptive reflections (i.e. the address – 'I' or 'you'; sound or seem; the qualifier – 'a bit' or 'very'; the feeling – 'angry' or 'sad') she was enabled to identify her own emotions, as well as those of others, as part of her work outside the sessions. This became a critical part of the work with Alice and one of the strategies for dealing with her preparation for her court case. The work in the 'surface' interaction and stages three and four (Generating and Supporting) enabled Alice to learn to project herself assertively and communicate with emotion (rather than detachment) about what had happened the day her partner died.

Continuing the work in stages three and four allowed a range of areas to be addressed including her drinking. Using a cognitive behavioural approach similar to that used in Lucy's case, Alice was able to identify where her cognitive patterns supported her negative self-belief (she does not deserve anything) and where alcohol was her behavioural response to suppress her feelings. In stage three (Generating) achievable goals were set to reduce the number of drinks in a week so as to build her confidence in being able to stop completely. During the course of her nine sessions, barring one occasion, Alice maintained her goal of drinking only two vodka shorts every two days. She attended her weekly AA sessions and got further support from the substance abuse worker in between her sessions. Through the use of mindfulness techniques she learnt how to relax and divert her rumination patterns that contributed to her drinking. In addition she continued to use her painting as a means of self-expression for her emotions and feelings.

In her concluding ninth session, Alice recognised that she was personally better equipped to deal with her court case, even though she was anxious about it. She had experienced the sessions as awakening her senses and described feeling more movement within her. Alice's CORE scores supported this: they had moved from being moderately anxious to mildly anxious. Addressing her past helped Alice to work through her feelings of guilt and shame, to find acceptance of what had happened and that she had used alcohol to numb her senses in order to cope. Feeling a greater sense of conscious awareness, she recognised that further work was needed and she was more confident in continuing to get help. Meeting Alice a few weeks later following her trial, she reported that the case had gone in her favour and she believed she had the opportunity to restart her life and rebuild the relationship with her children.

Conclusion

This chapter demonstrates that the PC framework can be applied in complex cases and initiate the process of change with clients. It also recognises that working integratively with clients such as these requires a high level of experience and skills. Notwithstanding this, what these case studies provide is a succinct precis of how the Personal Consultancy framework enables working with clients with addictions in a way that brings together approaches traditionally associated with therapy and coaching. An important factor in working integratively is being transparent with clients, which in the case of PC is facilitated by being cognisant of where the work is within the model at any given time. This allows the transition between coaching and counselling modes to have a natural flow within the sessions. This flow is maintained through a continual feedback loop which ensures that client's needs are met whilst simultaneously maintaining a safe and ethical way of working with these vulnerable women.

It was possible to use the Personal Consultancy model in this environment, at least in part, because each client had support in between their sessions, from their substance misuse workers and key workers, as well as other staff. This is not to suggest that what has been outlined here could be applied across all situations, although some aspects could be put to good use, particularly regarding the discontinuation or reduction of drink/drugs. As in a lot of cases once clients fully understand the reason for their addiction, they can, with the right support, work towards recovery by developing new ways of behaving to counteract the old patterns that lead them to misuse. Incumbent in this premise is setting realistic goals with clients and accepting that at times they may go astray. The supporting stage of the Personal Consultancy model is particularly useful in such circumstances to help the client maintain positive change and to help them stay (or get back) 'on track'. It is recognised that this is a valuable part of the work as many of these clients have behaviour that is ingrained and it can take time to help the client modify conditioned behaviours.

While the pros and cons of this chapter might be debated from either a purist counselling or coaching perspective, what has been portrayed here supports the notion that working with the Personal Consultancy framework can help the client in achieving their objectives. By contrast, operating within a purely remedial counselling approach or practical coaching stance may reduce the benefits available from working across both disciplines. In addition, the style of approach used in either or both disciplines could be debated (e.g. person-centred, psychodynamic, cognitive behavioural, existential). Which (if any) is more effective is likely to depend on the training, orientation and experience of the practitioner and the client's needs and preferences. Whilst not in any way undermining the work of either coaching or counselling or the various approaches that might be used, this chapter has attempted to illustrate that working within an integrative framework can encompass a variety of skills, experiences and techniques by providing a more inclusive but concrete way of working at the 'depth' and 'surface' levels with clients.

This account does not in any sense claim to offer a definitive view, but it attempts to build and create case evidence that might stimulate debate, which is critical to pushing the boundaries of how and where the Personal Consultancy framework can be applied, enhanced and developed. Working within such an integrative framework is relatively new and further work is needed to develop the areas of supervision, training, accreditation, ethical principles and so forth. However, what these case studies show is that a coach–therapist can operate without the rigid restrictions of working within pre-defined coaching and counselling domains. Conversely, it is important to assert that working within an integrated framework may have its own constraints, as one size may not fit all situations or clients. It is appreciated that the coach–therapist needs to be aware of their own limitations in experience, skills and knowledge and be able to refer clients if necessary.

A delineation between coaching and counselling exists associated with the journey each discipline has taken so far, but it should be recognised that working in an integrative way between disciplines has the potential to combine the benefits that both approaches can provide, it is not inherently misaligned given the extensive common ground, and it can be worthy of consideration if we want to move forward.

Chapter 14

Comparing existential perspectives on integration with Personal Consultancy

Yannick Jacob

Introduction

For many years existential psychotherapists – such as van Deurzen (1997), Yalom (1980) or the practitioners cited in Cooper's (2003) overview of the variety of existential approaches to therapy – have engaged with clients struggling to cope with life's challenges. It seems that, more often than other approaches to therapy, they have incorporated, within the overarching framework of existentialism, aspects of different disciplines such as humanistic psychology (Bugenthal, 1978) or psycho-analysis (Frankl, 1984). More recently, an increasing number of coaches started to recognise the relevance of existential themes to their clients' agendas and they adopted existential thought and philosophy into their work in executive coaching (e.g. Hanaway, 2012; or Joplin, 2012), in career coaching (Pullinger, 2012), decision-making models (LeBon and Arnaud, 2012) and in combination with many other approaches such as Cognitive Behaviour Therapy (Mirea, 2012), Neuro-Linguistic Programming (Reed, 2012), Mindfulness (Nanda, 2012), Transactional Analysis (Lewis, 2012) as well as in conjunction with psychometric assessment tools such as the Myers–Briggs type indicator of personality (Pringle, 2012). These practitioners believe that existential philosophy 'can add depth and breadth to any form of coaching' (van Deurzen and Hanaway, 2012, p.xvi).

Working one-to-one with clients from an existential perspective involves working with 'human lived existence' (Cooper, 2003). Coaches and therapists, together with clients, create an exploratory space that facilitates a better understanding of how the individual experiences living which helps them identify and understand the paradoxes and challenges that life presents. This is a process in which clients are likely to discover their values and what is important to them, become aware of their perception of how the world works, their possibilities in life and freedom of choice, and discover what they can and cannot change, which encourages them to take responsibility and engage in life as it presents itself more fully. Existential practitioners therefore often work along the whole spectrum of human experience. They embark on a journey with each client, which at times may be facilitated by a therapist and at times by a coach. This chapter will explore the integration of coaching and therapy from an existential perspective. By examining similarities and differences of an existential approach to both practices, it will be evaluated to which degree existentialism, as a wider framework, can be utilised for such integration. Furthermore, inferences will be made with regards to its compatibility with the Personal Consultancy framework.

Setting the stage: an existential perspective on human existence

Existential practitioners acknowledge that all human beings share certain existential givens as a result of merely being alive and being in the world with others. These givens are often paradoxes or conflicts between two ends of a polarity. Anxiety arises when we are faced with the dilemmas of our existential givens: we are free to but also condemned to choose, whereas every choice excludes many other possibilities; we naturally try to create or search for meaning and purpose in a world that seems to lack an overarching meaning of life; we are frequently reminded of our mortality (through illness, danger, birthdays or bereavement) and feel both motivated and paralysed by this awareness; we cherish and fear uncertainty; and we recognise the need for being with others and at the same time we are aware that ultimately we can never know anybody as well as they know themselves.

Not surprisingly, many people try to avoid these paradoxes in order to make their lives easier, more comfortable and more bearable. Sartre (1956 [1943]) termed this mode of being 'living in bad faith'. Arguably, avoidance and denial are effective defence mechanisms and can make us feel better on the surface, but facing our existential truths is inevitable during our lifetime as they surface regularly and cannot be permanently ignored. While these encounters may have undesirable consequences, such as anxiety, depressive episodes or paralysis when having to make a choice, from an existential perspective they are not necessarily signs of pathology. Furthermore, these existential givens are universal and apply to all people, regardless of culture, age, social class or education. The concern with the questions of what makes us human and how to live life fully in the face of its givens makes existential thought a universal philosophy.

Working existentially with clients

When working existentially with clients, the phenomenological method is paramount to the exploration process and allows the practitioner to understand, unpack and reflect back what the client brings into the relationship, which can, in turn, facilitate learning, discovery and self-awareness. This process provides a strong foundation from which the client feels able to engage with life and its inevitable struggles, make difficult decisions, find direction and purpose, and live more fully and authentically.

The relationship between client and practitioner is the core component of facilitating lasting change. The practitioner needs to constantly evaluate and shift their mode of practice as the client goes through phases of questioning and recreating meaning, struggling to cope with his or her personal dilemmas, making concrete plans to face them, resenting and accepting certain givens in his or her life and so on. For this purpose, client and practitioner create a space together within which clients can safely doubt, ponder, reflect and understand their lives better. What this space (or what happens within it) is called – coaching, therapy or counselling – is merely a matter of definition, and, as I will argue in the following part, each can be applied within an existential framework.

Existential coaching and existential psychotherapy

With an ever growing number of approaches defining psychotherapy has become difficult. For similar reasons it is also hard to define coaching (Stober and Grant, 2006b). There are countless approaches to therapy and it has become increasingly difficult to find what they all have in common. Coaching also is difficult to define (ibid.). While there is little doubt that niche markets have been created through emphasis on their differences, much of what has been written about the two disciplines indicates their similarities (Bachkirova and Cox, 2005; Bluckert, 2005; Kampa-Kokesch and Anderson, 2001; Popovic and Boniwell, 2007). Coaching has been termed an ally to counselling in the client's pursuit of well-being (Bachkirova and Cox, 2005), 'counselling in disguise' (Williams and Irving, 2001, p.3) or just another brand name for counselling work (Carroll, 2003). This seems particularly true for an existential approach to one-to-one work. Pearl (as cited in Jacob, 2011) calls existential coaching a 'therapy through the back door' in order to acknowledge the large overlap with the therapeutic realm and clients' desire to enter a helping relationship while avoiding the stigma attached to seeing a therapist. Similarly, existential practitioners have called coaching 'the acceptable face of counselling' (Spinelli, 2008; Summerfield, 2006). As existential psychotherapist and coach van Deurzen writes:

> Many people wish to tackle existential problems without running the risk of being considered mentally ill or suffering from some kind of personality problem … Where individuals seek to gain insight into their own possibilities and limitations without reference to mental health problems, a coaching model is often more appropriate and welcome. This is not to say that counselling and psychotherapy are not related to coaching, for there are many times when there will be a need to cross over from one realm into another.
>
> (van Deurzen, 2012, p.xvii).

Commonalities

The overlap and commonalities between existential coaching and existential counselling and therapy are not surprising considering that they all 'rely heavily on ideas and techniques derived from Western philosophical traditions such as

Socratic dialoguing, phenomenology, dialectics and logic as well as drawing on Eastern meditative practices' (van Deurzen and Hanaway, 2012, p.xix). Similarly, it is acknowledged that the actual methods of existential coaching 'match those of existential psychotherapy and counselling practice' (van Deurzen, 2012, p.11).

Philosophy and theory

Both approaches are grounded in existential philosophy and use philosophical methods of helping people to change, improve, cope, live more effectively or otherwise develop. Existential practitioners assume that people, even if they are able to manage their lives successfully, often long for a stronger sense of purpose. Existential practice allows them to explore the big questions of what it means to be human, how that relates to their reality and how to engage in life more fully through developing the courage to face its many challenges.

Phenomenology

Phenomenology is the playing field of existential work; the phenomenological method of inquiry (Husserl, 1977 [1925], 1986; Ihde, 1986; Merleau-Ponty, 1962) is its central method used to explore the client's reality. In contrast to many other methods of inquiry it does not make any assumptions about the client's experience. By being aware of and bracketing (putting aside) all personal biases and assumptions, the practitioner is able to fully listen to and explore what the client brings to the session, from their frame of reference as it presents itself (this is sometimes called 'tuning in'). The focus of the exploration is on description of the client's experience, rather than explanation thereof or reasons for it. Assumptions and interpretations are constantly verified (through summarising and clarifying) to check whether we understand the client's experience and meanings correctly and to enable the client to do the same. This happens within a spirit of active curiosity rather than critical questioning. The purpose is to help clients achieve clarity and increase their awareness so that they identify the range of possibilities that are available to them, realise their capacity for choice, discover their blind spots and distinguish true beliefs from false beliefs. If you find your attention wandering or searching for an explanation or theory, you are not attending to your client phenomenologically (van Deurzen and Adams, 2011). However, the other side of the coin is 'tuning out' of the client's experience, taking a step back and placing it into context. An encounter with 'the other' within the practitioner–client relationship provides the client with a new perspective on their presented issue and opens up new channels for learning and change.

Working with world-view and existential dimensions

In both coaching and therapy, the practitioner is exploring the client's world-view phenomenologically. World-view is a person's interpreted framework of making sense of the world, of others and oneself (see, e.g., Jaspers, 1971) and is based on the client's values, beliefs, purpose and meanings. Exploring a client's world-view provides great insight into their prevalent dilemmas on existential issues and vice versa. According to van Deurzen (1997), the practitioner may explore four existential domains of the client's world-view: the physical, the personal, the social and the spiritual. They can be related to existential givens of death, uncertainty, isolation and meaninglessness (Yalom, 1980). In whichever way approached, an exploration of the client's world-view frames the foundation from which learning and understanding can take place. What often naturally follows is a greater awareness of the client's freedom to choose active engagement with life as well as his or her possibilities to do so. In order to work with this method the practitioner requires a certain level of training and set of skills (see next section).

Spinelli, one of the first practitioners to write about existential coaching, summarises the work with world-views as follows:

> The creation of a secure and trustworthy 'life-space' encourages clients to get to know more accurately and to experience more honestly just what their worldview is, what it is like to experience oneself and others through that worldview, and how the current dilemmas, concerns and uncertainties that are presenting themselves may be challenges to, or outcomes of, that very same worldview.
>
> (Spinelli, 2005, p.1).

Skills

In addition to basic skills such as paraphrasing, summarising, questioning assumptions and bracketing one's own assumptions, both existential coaching and counselling require the same set of skills and attitudes, which are comprehensively outlined by van Deurzen and Adams (2011). Most importantly, the practitioner needs to be able to identify and reflect back features of the client's world-view and underlying existential themes in the client's discourse.

Supervision

Both existential therapists and coaches value supervision as an important source for exploration of one's own assumptions which gives way to valuable insights into the evolving relationship between practitioner and client and in turn improves the positive effect for the client (van Deurzen and Young, 2009).

Differences

Although there are many similarities between existential therapy and existential coaching, these practices can be differentiated in three aspects:

Temporality

Coaching is usually time-limited whereas therapy is typically open-ended. Existential practitioners are very aware of temporality and the impact of the client's perception of time on their reality. There is limited time to be spent on this earth and coaches and clients who chose coaching tend to prefer a more goal-focused approach. Therefore, coaches tend to explore the impact of the client's past on the present in relation to their future goals whereas therapists tend to explore in more depth the context of the client's past with regards to their current reality.

Degree of exploration (in the context of existential dimensions)

Following from the previous point, existential coaching and therapy usually differ in the extent of phenomenological exploration of what the client brings to the sessions. As coaching is usually time-limited, the degree of unpacking the client's issues against the backdrop of existential dimensions is more limited and the focus is more on what is really relevant to the contracted goals of the relationship.

Level of vulnerability of the client

Existential psychotherapists usually work with vulnerable clients, who come to therapy as a consequence of a crisis that they struggle to cope with (van Deurzen, 1997; Yalom, 1980). Practising within an existential framework seems to make sense for all clients as long as they express a wish to and are physically and mentally capable of exploring their life. Existential work offers a practical method for the direct discussion of the trials and tribulations of their human existence. That said, the coach will pay close attention to the client's level of vulnerability and engage in open discussion as to which aspects of their lives the client is willing or able to explore. Even though an existential coach may not be sufficiently trained to deal with an emotional breakdown in the face of an unpacked conflict, the applications of existential coaching are theoretically unlimited (van Deurzen and Hanaway, 2012) and therefore subject to the practitioner's judgement of his or her own skills and qualifications.

In conclusion, existential coaching on one hand and existential therapy and counselling on the other differ, but only at their extremes. A lot of overlap remains and, as discussed in the following section, clients – as they go through the change process – often fluctuate on the dimensions of temporality, degree of exploration and their level of vulnerability. Therefore, within an existential framework, it seems that coaching and therapy aspects are already naturally integrated.

Benefits of an integrative approach

Referring clients back and forth between a coach and a therapist, because of predefined domains of practice, is likely to disrupt the helping process severely and can be very frustrating to the client. Van Deurzen writes that

> clients want a [practitioner] who is trustworthy, understanding and capable. They imagine that it is possible to live rather more resourcefully than they are doing at present and they look for signs living in the professional they consult.
>
> (van Deurzen, 1997, p.189).

When a client has found such a person – a fellow traveller skilled at listening, interested in understanding, authentic, honest, direct, open, trustworthy and capable of providing a safe space in which to reflect, ponder and understand life better – they most likely do not want to be forced to find somebody else just because the practitioner's job description or adopted code of practice disallows a continuation of fruitful exploration outside the realm of their business card. While it is possible to find two such people, a coach and a therapist, the benefits of working with a single person are obvious.

I therefore believe that definitions that lead to arbitrary demarcations of disciplines can be unnecessarily restrictive. Without this burden the practitioners can focus on what is really important: the client's wants and needs at any given moment during the process of change.

Clients are changing quicker than you can ask 'How does that make you feel?'

As demonstrated, existential coaching and existential therapy overlap to a large degree. Even the areas where they differ are subject to change and fluctuation during the course of working with the client. The existential practitioner should be able to adapt to these changes that may involve the client's mood, cognitive capacities, and planning or making decisions.

Situations, memories, associations or other stimuli can trigger emotional responses that impact significantly on the dynamics of the relationship and require immediate attention. The practitioner will have to adjust their *being-with* the client on a moment-to-moment basis. Therefore I very much agree with Summerfield (2002, p.37), who noted that 'a good coach may be constantly switching between coaching and counselling during a single session' and I believe this is true for a good therapist also. The practitioner who is willing to adjust the initially contracted goals during the course of the relationship simply works with the client's human nature. As long as the practitioner adjusts their role in accordance with the client's needs and takes into consideration ethical issues such as dependency, personal boundaries or limits to their skills, this can only be beneficial to the client.

It will be worthwhile to investigate to what degree practitioners are already integrating aspects of counselling, therapy and coaching, respectively, into their work. Arguably, coaches have had more freedom to do so due to the non-regulation of their profession. In the face of upcoming regulations and with regard to the above mentioned arguments, an official formulation of models of integration has long been overdue and practitioners of both disciplines will benefit greatly from an open discussion about how to work in this way.

Need for psychotherapeutic training?

When working with existential themes, the practitioner is somewhat more likely to encounter 'living in bad faith' (the denial of existential givens) as an obstacle to growth, development or healing. Therefore, it may be necessary to bring these deep-seated and possibly long-denied existential issues to the foreground. Looking through case studies of existential practitioners, similar scenarios to the following are not uncommon: 'What began as a referral for panic [for which nowadays effective short-term CBT treatment exists] became a complete re-examination of the values by which she lived.' (Bretherton and Ørner 2004, p.424). The practitioner is at risk of 'pulling the rug' from underneath their client when his or her sedimented beliefs and world-view are being challenged, which may cause what Kierkegaard (1843) called 'fear and trembling'. The result may be heightened anxiety and possibly a need to help the client rebuild their world-view, which is clearly in the realm of psychotherapy. Brunning points to potential dangers by 'coaches who lack rigorous psychological training doing more harm than good' (Brunning, 2006, p.XXV). So, the question arises whether some degree of psychotherapy training should be mandatory for coaches when they work existentially (Bachkirova and Cox, 2005; Brunning, 2006).

What the existential perspective can bring into integration

Covering the whole spectrum of human experience

Linley and Harrington (2007, p.43) state that we should be 'striving to reclaim the study of people in their completeness'. I believe that, when working with people in a helping-by-talking relationship, we should similarly be striving to work with people in their completeness instead of focusing only on certain aspects of their existence.

Existential themes run underneath most issues that clients bring to therapy or coaching and all human beings will on occasion find themselves struggling with them. The dynamic interplay between positives and negatives is the main hallmark of Existential Positive Psychology, an integrational approach of positive psychology and existentialism (Wong, 2010). Wong proposes that 'positives cannot exist apart from negatives and that authentic happiness necessarily grows from pain and suffering' (Wong, 2010). Similarly, existential thinker and author Camus (1968) stated that '[t]here is no joy of life without despair'. This is to say that any form of one-to-one practice which does not address despair, hardship, adversity, pain or suffering in addition to positive aspects of existence cannot lead to growth and personal development. Authentic living therefore promotes facing the whole spectrum of one's experience including anxiety, death and meaninglessness, but also joy, happiness, purpose and direction, hope and faith, learning, creativity and positive change as well as more specific questions such as:

- Why do I procrastinate?
- Why do I feel depressed or anxious for no apparent reason?
- Why can't I decide between A or B?
- Why am I feeling alone even though I have good relations to others?

The existential practitioner is at an advantage having developed the skills and experience to identify the underlying teams in everyday situations.

Philosophical grounding

> Solid psychological science requires much more than an adequate acquaintance with quantitative methods and tools of investigation. It requires a refined analysis of assumptions that we, as researchers, make; an ability to see the context in which we are asking our questions; and acknowledge the implications of our hypotheses in relation to our assumptions and our context. In other words, we need a sound philosophical understanding of the ways in which we attempt to study ourselves.
>
> (Young-Eisendrath, 2003, p.170).

I strongly believe that this statement is valid not only for psychological science but also, if not even more so, for helping-by-talking practices that aim to generate long-term positive change. Only when our work is based on a coherent philosophical framework spanning the whole spectrum of human experience – which existentialism has been demonstrated to be – are we able to understand, notice, appreciate and acknowledge, if not manage or work across that very spectrum.

A different approach to each client

Since there is no unified school of existentialism (Moja-Strasser, 1996) an existential approach can be a fertile ground for facilitating the integration of many different psychotherapy traditions (Corey, 1996; Hubble and Miller, 2004). Cooper (2003) describes various forms of existential practice and similarly, van Deurzen and Hanaway (2012) have published a similar collection in the area of existential coaching. The mere fact that there are so many existential approaches, which incorporate methods, instruments, techniques and tools from a multitude of other disciplines, is in itself a good indicator that existentialism seems to provide a good ground for integration.

Existential philosophy is primarily a philosophy of human existence, not bound to one method. The only shared method is the phenomenological method of inquiry, which can be applied across the spectrum, from classic long-term existential psychotherapy (Yalom, 1980) to a structured, short-term and rather directive model such as LeBon and Arnaud's (2012) Existential Decision Coaching. As Cooper writes:

> At the heart of an existential standpoint is the rejection of grand, all-encompassing systems; and a preference for individual and autonomous practices. Hence, few existential therapists have been concerned with establishing one particular way of practising existential therapy. Indeed for most existential therapists, the idea that this approach can be systematised or even manualised is anathema to the very principles of the approach.
>
> (Cooper, 2003, p.2).

Hence, working existentially means to integrate its philosophy with one's personal style, background and ideological values. Furthermore, since the focus is on the client's lived experience, each client requires a slightly different approach which may need to be occasionally modified even with the same client. An existential framework not only allows the practitioner to do that, but encourages, or even requires, them to do so.

Existential practice and Personal Consultancy

Many aspects of the existential and the Personal Consultancy models seem to be similar: both are broad, open frameworks that allow integration of different modes of practice. Both explore their clients' experiences phenomenologically. Both embrace the complexity of human beings and hence stress the importance of developing an awareness of the client's individual values, assumptions, beliefs and any associated internal conflicts 'before we help them embark on any tangible change' (Chapter 4 in this volume). Both approaches therefore acknowledge that the helping process needs to be somewhat adjusted to fit the practitioner's own unique characteristics at the time, those of each client and, most importantly, the relationship between them at any given moment (non-linearity and diversity). Diagnosing clients is avoided and instead the person is approached as a whole. Furthermore, neither approach imposes top-down control or uniformity and both are unlikely to be prone to ideological bias.

The very definition of Personal Consultancy elements resonates well with an existential approach to integration:

> *consultancy* is defined as a meeting which is held to discuss something and to decide what should be done about it … *Personal* signifies that it is about

focusing on the person and personal matters that, of course, may include social and professional issues as well.

(Chapter 4, p.47)

Integration from an existential perspective includes elements of coaching (see Peltier, 2010). Existential practice, furthermore constitutes a philosophical exploration of the client's personal world (van Deurzen, 1997) and acknowledges that humans are complex, interconnected beings and that therefore workplace issues and personal issues can rarely be separated (van Deurzen, 2009).

This paragraph from an earlier chapter of this book signifies the link to existentialism particularly well with regards to uncertainty and the anxiety that is experienced as a result, as well as its whole approach to one-to-one practice:

> For many practitioners, however, being well versed in a particular approach gives them a sense of security and confidence. Adopting an open model can be anxiety-provoking. The Personal Consultant needs to be prepared to work *with* that anxiety rather than trying to get rid of it ... [W]e believe that a reasonable level of uncertainty and ensuing anxiety keeps practitioners alert and is conducive to the process ... [W]e need to embrace some uncertainty and the possibility that we may be frequently surprised, no matter how experienced we are.
>
> (Chapter 4, p.55).

The main difference that emerges between the two approaches is that in the PC model there seems to be a rather clear demarcation line between coaching and counselling (as well as other approaches to helping-by-talking) while existential coaching and therapy tend to be more of a fusion, using the same methods. Furthermore, existential practice, in contrast to the PC model, starts from a conceptualisation of the person (instead of the practice) and many of its advocates make some assumptions about human nature as being flexible and generally non-determined (van Deurzen, 1997; Yalom, 1980). However, existential philosophy allows for different assumptions in this respect, as it merely conceptualises the human *condition*, rather than deriving theories about human *nature* or *behaviour*. Other notable differences include PC's work with all time perspectives (past, present, future) to equal degrees, whereas existential approaches – though not ignoring or avoiding exploration of the past – generally prefer working with the here-and-now and its relevance to future goals. Also, while personal consultancy has no selection criteria for clients, existential therapy does (see below).

In summary, while a few differences emerge, many elements of existential practice may be useful to the Personal Consultancy framework. Existential philosophy may greatly enhance the practice of the Personal Consultant who feels attracted to its features. More importantly, Personal Consultancy clients who grapple with the issues that existential thinkers have investigated will undoubtedly benefit from their conceptualisations. The phenomenological way of working, as discussed in previous chapters, is also a great contribution of existential practice to the Personal Consultancy framework.

A brief example of working existentially

Marco

Marco stated that he approached me for coaching because of my background in positive psychology and science and that he wished to become happier and more satisfied in his life. During this initial conversation he was mainly concerned with whether I could provide a battery of psychometric assessments as to monitor his progress and ensure that his coaching worked and was worth his time and effort. However, throughout our relationship the themes of uncertainty and meaning re-emerged frequently in his narrative. Two changes that would lead to greater happiness were identified: spending more time with his family and changing his job. While his social world seemed important to Marco, his family usually entered the narrative as a stable and safe environment that provided certainty and meaning in his life. At this point it was challenging to bracket my own assumptions and values around family life.

A phenomenological exploration of the issues with Marco's job led to unpacking the same core values and revealing the extent of their importance. In the past three years his position had become increasingly unstable. Redundancy had become a very real possibility and felt like Damocles' sword dangling above his head. Not knowing if and when it would happen drove him 'absolutely and utterly mad'. At this point in the session Marco almost suffered a panic attack and the rest of the session was spent recovering from bringing this issue into the open. At the next session, Marco started with reflecting on the previous session. My feedback on his core values of meaning and certainty and a realisation that his family is a safe place from which he felt able to expose himself to what he called 'a realistic and bearable degree of uncertainty' led him to explore new job opportunities. The rest of the coaching focused mainly on his dilemma between time spent on a new meaningful and more stable job vs. time spent with his family. Two months later, Marco had left his job. His new one did require him to work more hours, but including his family in the discussions on what he planned to do had led to their full support and they decided to focus on the quality rather than quantity of their time together. Marco kept filing regular assessments of his mood and psychological well-being with a focus on dimensions of meaning as a reminder to engage in life and that a degree of uncertainty seems necessary to make a progress.

Conclusion

Existential philosophy has influenced many approaches to therapy and counselling and recently entered the realm of coaching. As a universal framework of human lived-existence it covers the whole spectrum of clients' experiences. Many practitioners who work existentially have already incorporated various aspects of other coaching and therapy approaches into their existential work and vice versa. In its own sphere, existential therapy and existential coaching share a great deal of commonalities and there is a large overlap between their characteristics and methods. Even the aspects in which they differ are subject to change during the one-to-one process, sometimes even within a single session. Therefore many practitioners need to be able to adjust to their clients' needs by adopting different roles. Both existential practice and the Personal Consultancy framework converge in this respect. However, a considerable degree of training and, more importantly, an active involvement in the exploration of existential themes in practitioners' own lives (e.g. through supervision) is a core aspect for good existential integrative practice. I therefore call for an active engagement in discussion and evaluation of integration so that practitioners can provide high standards of quality in their work and ensure ethical practice.

Chapter 15

A postcard from Down Under

An international perspective on practising as an integrative executive coach–therapist

Lesley Symons

Introduction

Coaching and psychotherapy in Australia are both unregulated professions. An 'integrative executive coach–therapist' is an unfamiliar term in Australia. However, I have been practising for seven years as an executive coach explicitly with training in psychotherapy and a background from business. I work with clients in the corporate world from a variety of cultural backgrounds and levels within organisations.

Overview

This chapter reflects on the experience of working as an executive coach–therapist in Australia. I discuss how training as a psychotherapist and having a background in business informs both the work with clients and my underlying coaching philosophy. I explore how certain principles apply when working with individuals and organisations, particularly when working across cultures in today's multi-cultural Australia. In addition, this chapter will discuss the 'grey area' of working in-between two modalities, the tension in holding them together and the responsibilities practitioners have when working in this way.

In order to develop my understanding of where Australia currently stands in the world of coach–therapy I started by researching the rules and regulations around the world for practising either as a psychotherapist or coach, or as a coach–therapist. Perhaps unsurprisingly, there was very little information available about the coach–therapy approach or practice around the world.

International regulations and rules for psychotherapy and coaching

This is not a definitive exploration of the topic but rather a dip into the murky waters of the many different regulations for practising and training in psychotherapy and coaching. My research concentrated on the regions of Australia, China, Europe, the USA and the United Kingdom. Coaching, being a younger and more emergent practice, seems to have greater global consistency in definition and training. The coaching psychology movement has developed the use of psychology-informed interventions for coaching, particularly in regions such as the UK, Australia, Europe and the USA, where coaching is well developed. However, psychotherapy practice and training are very variable. In some countries a medical or psychiatry degree is required whereas in others no regulation has been developed. Integrating coaching and therapy or a specific coach–therapy model seems largely unrecognised worldwide.

Psychotherapy practice around the world

The teaching and practice of psychotherapy seem to be relatively idiosyncratic to each country. In Europe, every country has different laws and levels of qualification necessary to be recognised and able to practise as a psychotherapist, although a Master's degree appears to be the benchmark overall (Warnecke, 2010). In Germany and Italy, however, psychotherapy can only be practised with a medical, psychology or psychiatry degree (Warnecke 2010). European Union member states are obliged to set up comparison systems for the qualifications of psychotherapists wanting to practise across borders.

A similarly variable picture exists across the USA, where legislation is different by state. In some states a psychology or psychiatry degree is sufficient to practise, whereas in other states an additional licence is also required. In some states a licence stipulating a minimum level of qualification alone is needed, whereas in other states a doctoral degree is a prerequisite. In Australia and the UK psychotherapy currently is an unregulated profession with anyone able to use the title and practise as a psychotherapist. However, both countries are attempting to put in some strict self-regulatory systems to counterbalance this. Professional bodies such as the Psychotherapists and Counsellors Federation of Australia (PACFA), the British Association for Counselling and Psychotherapy (BACP) and the UK Council for Psychotherapy (UKCP) are actively developing self-regulation schemes in their respective countries. In China psychotherapy is a relatively new phenomenon. In their survey, Qian et al. (2001) found that 84 per cent of practising psychotherapists had a medical or psychology degree or higher but of those less than 9 per cent had actual psychotherapy training.

Coaching practice around the world

The definitions of coaching and the competencies for practising as a coach are currently unregulated around the world. Coaching globally remains a growth industry. In the countries researched coaching is a self-regulated industry in varying stages of development with Australia, the USA, the UK and some parts of Europe being relatively well advanced. There is an emergence of global self-regulating bodies such as the International Coach Federation (ICF), The Association for Coaching (AC) and the European Mentoring and Coaching

Council (EMCC) which in 2013 agreed to form a working alliance. The ICF (2007) study found that the worldwide coaching industry was worth approximately 1.5 billion dollars and that there were an estimated 45 to 50 thousand business coaches worldwide (Bresser Consulting, 2009, p.10). Coaches tend to be highly educated with postgraduate degrees and predominantly female (ICF 2007). There is a proliferation of coach training available ranging from small independent providers to bachelor, masters and doctoral degrees from major recognised universities.

Coaching psychology and the integrative coach–therapist

There has been a growing influence on coaching from the psychology and psychotherapy professions (Stober and Grant, 2006a). There are coaching psychology units at Sydney University, City University (the first in the UK) and the University of East London. Certain modalities of psychotherapy have adapted their approaches to coaching, such as Brief coaching, Narrative coaching, Solution Focused and Humanistic coaching (ibid.).

The emergence of Coaching Psychology units at universities has encouraged the development of an evidence-based coaching psychology model for the coaching profession. Trained or registered psychologists deliver courses for students who may or may not have previous psychology training. This approach uses many underpinning counselling skills as well as a behavioural perspective when working with clients. Increasingly counsellors are working in the coaching arena whilst at the same time coaches are seeking a more psychological approach. The coaching psychology movement has therefore opened up the conversation around coaching from a psychological perspective. Within the coaching fraternity there are a number of differing attitudes to this way of working. Grant (2011b), in his presentation 'Developing an agenda for teaching coaching psychology', suggests that the future of coaching education, whilst maintaining the overarching agenda of goal attainment for clients, might include teaching those without psychology backgrounds the basic tenets of psychological theory. Coaches from all backgrounds might, for example, need to become more aware and knowledgeable about mental health issues so that they can refer clients on for specialist support when appropriate.

Globally, information and research is limited on an integrated coach–therapist model, and currently the UK seems to be leading the way in developing such an approach. The recently formed Association of Integrative Coach–Therapist Professionals (AICTP) aims to support and guide integrative coach–therapy practitioners and encourage discussion and research. In addition, The British Association for Counselling and Psychotherapy has a coaching division which specifically focuses on members who are counsellors or psychotherapists, but are also interested in coaching or are actively practising as coaches. Australia as yet has no recognised professional body; however, I am the international coordinator for AICTP based in Sydney so a new chapter has started there.

My experience of the integrative executive coach–therapist

In this section I will reflect on how I work as an integrative executive coach–therapist in Australia, looking at the skills I use and the tensions I experience when working in this way. My interest in psychotherapy and coaching arose after a long career in business. I drew upon my strengths and interests from my first career as a general manager (working in the retail and fast moving goods sector) in developing my second career. I have lived and worked across three continents and gathered a lot of experience. I wanted to understand the theory behind how best we can manage and motivate other people. These interests led me to the study of psychotherapy and counselling. From there, I went on to work with people from marginalised communities and volunteered as a face-to-face counsellor with Australia's pre-eminent helpline service Lifeline, and with Mission Australia's Court Support service for victims and witnesses of crime. For the past seven years I have worked as an executive coach using an integrated coach–therapist approach. The by-line on my business card is 'combining business know-how with a therapeutic foundation'. I use my training as a psychotherapist with my knowledge and experience in business to inform the coaching. I am a member of a number of counselling and psychotherapy associations in both Australia and the UK. I am also a member of the Association for Coaching, International division. I have worked with clients from varying cultures and in various countries.

Executive coaching and an integrative approach

Those that subscribe to a coach–therapist approach believe that appropriate therapeutic training is required as a basis for working in this way. When practising as a coach–therapist my training in psychotherapy underpins my work and my effectiveness as a coach. Kets de Vries (2007), Peltier (2010) and Kilburg (2009) state that, although one does not necessarily have to be a psychologist to provide executive coaching services, having psychotherapy knowledge (possessed by some but not all psychologists) greatly enhances the possible results from coaching. However, my training in psychotherapy does not determine the agenda. For example, using knowledge of family systems and attachment theories can underpin a way of coaching and help towards better outcomes, but does not become the driving force for the coaching. The definition of coaching as focusing on goal attainment and well-being for the client is not usurped or overridden by the coach becoming excessively focused on the therapeutic perspective. In my work I explicitly explain my approach to clients. Being clear about what issues a coach will or will not work with also seems crucial. I find it important to describe my methods of working and the approaches I use, including stating that coaching can sometimes involve working with unconscious motivators, past events and the emotional fallout from these events. Kilburg (2009) states that clients must be told about and agree to therapeutic methods being used and that the coach using them must be suitably trained in these methods. Finally, I believe that coaching from a coach–therapist approach is about developing self-awareness and self-analytical skills in the client so that over time they can learn to employ them for themselves when required (Kets De Vries, 2007).

The client perspective on an integrative coach–therapist approach

Clients who purchase this kind of coaching also have different perspectives. Because I am explicit about how I work as a coach–therapist I have come across clients with a range of views and beliefs about this model of coaching: from not wanting a coach with a therapy background to wanting *only* a coach with a therapeutic background. Both of these positions can, I believe, arise from misunderstandings about the role of a coach–therapist. I have heard many comments along the following lines from clients: 'will I analyse them?'; 'take them on a long journey?'; 'not be outcome focused?' or, 'might I counsel rather than coach them?' However, I am also asked if I can work with clients with underlying mental health issues, managers with difficult interpersonal relationships or those whom the company has not found a way to performance manage. I have found that I need to be alert to these preconceptions and clarify that my primary role is as a *coach first*. I use psychotherapy principles and teachings to assist the process for the client to attain their goals.

There are also clients who believe that coaching directed at behaviour is not always enough. They want a coach who will build a relationship of trust and work with the unconscious and conscious factors that drive motivation and behaviour. These clients understand how a therapeutic base to the coaching can help coachees to see for themselves, can create self-awareness which in turn can assist in goal attainment and creating change. Kets de Vries et al. (2007) state that a clinically informed coach, trained to see and explore not only the surface issues but also issues below the surface, will be more effective.

A client's perspective

Knowing that coaching is underpinned with a therapeutic approach gives comfort to me as the CEO of the company. I know that the coaching is not simply conducted on a one dimensional level. Working together with the coach we are exploring the depths of the individual to unearth what is really going on underneath the surface. We are dealing with essential cause of the behaviour and operating style, not simply commenting on the manifestation of the behaviour.

More profoundly, I as the CEO know that my team have the greatest opportunity to actually get to the bottom of this causal effect and deal with the real issues.

In doing so, our team has every chance of succeeding in the organization.

I'm convinced that this approach, as opposed to one that is more superficial, rational and one-dimensional, sets us up for success. I also believe that employees are anxious about seeking therapeutic support on their own initiative. Hence, without misleading them in any way, they have the opportunity to experience something they would otherwise never expose themselves to. We are talking here about 'real' work and an approach that sets them up for true success. Most importantly I have seen the follow on benefits to our employee's personal lives. The profound affect this work has had on the relationships in the home environment is a bonus that no one would have expected.

A well balanced home and work environment is obviously the ultimate goal for all.

G. Perlstein (CEO Specialty Fashion Group Australia, 2013)

How does therapeutic knowledge and skill inform the work as an integrative executive coach–therapist?

Overarching all is the important point that I remain in the primary role of an executive coach. Psychotherapy principles, however, underpin how I practise as a coach. I use psychotherapy skills such as deep listening and unconditional positive regard to build a trusting relationship. I work with and educate clients on family systems dynamics and potential transference and counter-transference issues in the workplace. My knowledge of business also assists in building relationships, as clients quickly recognise that I have an intimate understanding of the drivers for business success and the implications for individuals at work. Underpinning all this is a reflective practice approach to my work which is particularly important when coaching across cultures.

Coaching is predominantly about change, as stated by Stober and Grant (2006a) who also include the term human development. Executive coaching from an integrative coach–therapist perspective is like any other coaching modality in this respect. The aim of the coaching is to work on change and to assist clients to attain *their* goals however they combine the personal with business and the organisation (Kets de Vries, 2007; Stober and Grant, 2006a; Kilburg, 2009). Using an integrative coach–therapy approach to my practice is about developing awareness of conscious and unconscious patterns, past events and past relationships that are impacting on the client, and may be hindering the attainment of their identified goals (Kets de Vries, 2007; Kilburg, 2009; Brunning, 2007). It then means working with clients to manage or help shift behaviour, underlying beliefs and possible transference issues to best ensure change into the future.

Listening, unconditional positive regard and the relationship

Underpinning my executive coach–therapist work are the principles of listening, unconditional positive regard and most importantly building a trusting and respectful relationship between the coach and coachee. Listening in this way can be used across cultural backgrounds, gender and age groups. Listening to truly understand allows the client both to hear themselves and to experience a relationship that is truly accepting of *their* story. This is the basis for trust and building a deep coach–client relationship. Van de Loo (2007) in 'Coach on the Couch' states that listening is one of the most important factors that determine the quality of our relationships. Listening, for a coach–therapist, is also keeping the context and the outcome of the coaching carefully in mind. Listening is used to build a picture of all the inter-related components around the desired outcome. Van de Loo (2007) describes listening with the 'third ear' and explains that this is listening not only to what is presented but also what is *not* presented, listening for the unconscious meanings. The coach is listening to the client and at the same time listening to themselves listening to the client. The coach is present with the client and at the same time reflecting on the process. As Kets de Vries (2007) states, it is like us being an actor on the stage and also being on the balcony observing the actor on the stage. It is giving all information equal validity. A relationship of unconditional positive regard takes on an added dimension when coaching, because it is not just about believing in the client's ability to learn but also building a relationship based on mutual dialogue in which acceptance and understanding is integral (Passmore, 2007). Self-reflection by the client then becomes a by-product of this listening.

Being 'clean' in questions and thoughts

The Clean Language questions developed by David Grove (1991) help my coaching to be as free of my own biases, values and beliefs as possible. David Grove was a New Zealand-born psychotherapist who worked with victims of trauma. He developed a set of questions which, when used with the client's *own words*, attempts to decontaminate the question from the counsellor's biases. I use the questions to explore and clarify the client's story as well as to 'check in' on my biases or assumptions. For example, a client may state that they want 'clarity on where their career is heading'. I may then ask, 'and clarity on where your career is heading, what kind of clarity is that?' I find this particularly important when working across cultures or areas of business that I am either very familiar with, or have no knowledge of at all. Clean Language questions used during a coaching session can avoid assumptions present in our own language, beliefs and values. Using Clean Language enables me to *listen accurately* to the client and to keep my own biases from contaminating my questions (and thus potentially my client's story).

Transference-counter transference

For me, understanding of the principles of transference in a business setting is critical for a coach–therapist. Being able to reflect on and then introduce the principles of transference to the client can be important for developing the client's self-awareness. Kets de Vries (2008) speaks of how, when working from a therapeutic paradigm, there is a continuum between the past and present, in that the past often plays out in the present. Clients will often transfer emotions from past relationships onto present-day relationships in the workplace. Naming this, and helping the client develop awareness, enables them to exercise more choice and gives them options for the future. Counter-transference can also be used by the experienced coach–therapist as a way of understanding the client. The coach uses their own experience of the client as information about what may be going on outside of the client's awareness. Kets de Vries (2007) states that, while listening to the client's words and content, the coach should observe how they themselves are 'feeling' about their client's story. The coach is monitoring what is happening for them in relation to this client. All incoming information is useful and the coach's self-observation is weighed alongside the client's content. This information can then be carefully fed back to the client and used for developing awareness or as the basis for further exploration. For example, 'I'm aware I'm feeling a bit anxious as I hear you talk about your plans for your department so forcefully. I wonder if you've noticed others reacting in that way?'

Informing reflective practice

Therapy principles can support and inform reflection on the practice and the delivery of coaching. Being aware of my own journey and continuing to reflect on my biases, values, beliefs and transference underpins my practice. Striving for increased levels of self-awareness and continuous self-development, through on-going education (in coaching skills and psychotherapy models), regular therapy and supervision is critical for practising as a coach–therapist (Summerfield, 2006). I reflect with my supervisor on my biases, values and beliefs, which enables me to update my perspective on self, my perspective on my clients and the coach–client relationship. If, as coach–therapists, we do not reflect regularly on these topics, there could be a danger of us becoming intertwined in our clients' stories and/or transference issues. I continually learn more about myself through my clients and therefore need to be reflecting regularly on my own issues – updating my knowledge base so that I remain as open to my client as possible. This is critical when using myself and my responses when working with clients. Reflective practice is also important because it can enhance the authenticity of the coach. Carl Rogers discovered that he was most effective as a therapist when he could listen acceptingly to himself and 'be himself', including accepting his own imperfections (Rogers, 2004, p.17). The more I know and accept myself, the more real and genuine I can be with others in the coaching relationship. I know it would be hard for me to ask clients to reflect and become more aware if I was not doing this for myself.

Integrating business knowledge into an integrative coach–therapist model

When working in an integrative way, I believe it is also important to know the drivers for success in business. Peltier (2010) states that the skills psychotherapists possess can add greatly to today's managers and organisations, but having knowledge of the working and culture of business is also necessary. This can of course vary depending on the organisation that the client belongs to. As an executive coach–therapist I work with clients who manage staff, large sales and large budgets, infrastructure projects, shareholders and boards (to name but a few). Familiarity with the pressures, tensions, successes and expectations of a coachee's role is, in my experience, a valuable part of the integrative executive coach–therapist stance. Being able to speak and understand the language of business also assists the client and the organisation to be open to an integrative coach–therapist approach.

What does this mean when working across cultures and countries?

Australia is a multi-cultural society with 30 per cent of its 22 million population having been born outside of Australia. The top five nations for immigration to Australia are the United Kingdom, New Zealand (10 per cent of New Zealanders live in Australia), China, India and Italy (Australian Census, 2011). Coaching in Australia inevitably involves working with clients from diverse backgrounds and with different cultural norms from those of the coach. I myself am an immigrant from an English background. I have also lived in Switzerland and in South Africa and these experiences have informed my world-view, beliefs and norms.

The core coaching–therapy skills and principles become even more important when practising across cultures and borders. First, there is a heightened and continual 'check-in' with self during the coaching session; observing one's own cultural knowledge, understanding one's own biases, values, expertise and (at times) lack of expertise. This internal listening, to self, needs to be interconnected with listening to the client's content and monitoring the interactions between the two. It is about continuously updating one's own information with any new information that may be presented.

Second, there is a need to be aware of, reflect on and at times name *with the client* what the coach's cultural perspective may or may not be bringing to the coaching process. This process can be a different way of working for some coaches because it is about sometimes bringing who you are into the forefront of the coaching relationship. It is acknowledging for the client what your biases and cultural norms are and what meaning or implications they may have for the client and the coaching process. This might include identifying for the client what you, as the coach, may have heightened awareness of and more importantly what you may miss in the process. This creates a dialogue for naming in the 'here and now' differences and similarities and what this may mean for the client, their work and the process. Passmore and Law (2009) state that, when working with diversity, or different cultural perspectives, the role of the coach is to challenge and bring to the fore the client's beliefs, values and cultural perspectives.

Two examples of this follow.

Sylvie

Sylvie is a doctor of Indian descent, married through an arranged marriage. She was struggling with living and working in a 'western' culture like Australia's whilst adhering to strong traditional values and beliefs in her family of origin and at home.

In this example I openly disclosed that I was from a culture with different norms and values and had little knowledge of the details of her traditional culture. We then discussed what I may miss or misunderstand of her story, coming from my cultural perspective. Sylvie wanted to hear herself. She also wanted someone to listen to her reflect out loud on her beliefs, values and norms without fear of judgement. By openly discussing our differences, I discovered that she also wanted and needed to hear my perspective on her beliefs and values. This assisted Sylvie to navigate through the complex situation of living with two cultures. Instead of having a conversation with herself she could have that conversation with me. This process alone helped her achieve clarity.

Peter

Peter is a Chinese-born financial manager who works for a large building society. Peter wanted to develop his influencing skills, as he was finding it hard to manage and influence his peers. This was in turn impacting on his ability to push through changes to other departments.

I started out by coaching Peter on some specific influencing skills for engaging his peers. I soon realised, however, that there was more to the situation. Through listening to Peter's story and questioning his experiences at work, I heard Peter's beliefs about 'how Australians work' versus 'how Chinese work'. We then explored the meaning of work from the perspectives of the two different cultures. During this process I challenged Peter's beliefs but also was careful to validate them and their cultural origins. We explored what meaning holding onto his beliefs had – Peter's Chinese origins are part of his identity and therefore his relationship with work was part of his identity. He believed that by accepting the 'Australian way' of working his Chinese identity would be further eroded. However, he also knew that, if he did not adjust to the environment, he would fail in his role. Through working with Peter's beliefs and enabling him to explore ways he could become flexible to the 'Australian way' without compromising his own beliefs, Peter began to see how he could adjust his style. We also explored how Peter could educate his peers on his culture and his experience of the workplace.

Throughout this process I used my coach–therapist skills of listening in an environment of unconditional positive regard. Peter experienced what it was like for someone from a different culture (the culture of the majority) to really understand his world-view. I also was explicit about my own values on work and

I hypothesised with Peter about how he could be perceived by his colleagues. Gradually Peter began to enjoy some 'wins' at work and this then changed his approach and his behaviour with his peers.

Peter came to coaching reluctantly because he saw it as a loss of face. I found it hard to connect with him initially. However, over time we forged a strong professional bond of mutual respect. At the conclusion of our coaching, Peter was truly grateful for the experience and the support he had been given, not least because of the progress he was making at work.

Psychotherapy principles in coaching or the 'grey area'

Having a therapeutic training has enhanced my coaching and working as a coach enhances my counselling practice. Yet how do we work in this way with clients and ensure that we are respectful and do no harm? We need to be aware of and draw on the client's ability for reflection, as well as our own ability to judge when it is appropriate to use which modality. Above all, I am an executive coach and this is the mandate I have with the client. As this is an area which is continuously evolving we need to remain attentive to the nuances of it, to our client's feedback and to the complexities of choosing which intervention to use when, knowing we may not get it right all of the time. We therefore need to be able to sit with the tension of holding the dual process of learning in the moment and being in a state of not knowing. In some ways this is exactly what we ask of our clients.

Conclusion

As an executive coach–therapist professional, psychotherapy principles and practices heavily influence how I work with clients. They also influence my coaching philosophy and a reflective practice stance. I am explicit with my clients about how I work. Knowing that in Australia, like the rest of the world, coaching is unregulated and encompasses a wide variety of practice means that we have a long way to go in educating our clients (and other coaches) about the nature of an integrative coach–therapist model. There are many opportunities for development and research in this modality.

Chapter 16

Listening to the practitioners about integration

Sarah Baker

Introduction

Within both counselling and coaching fields recurring themes of similarities and differences between approaches are frequently discussed. Discrete differences in theoretical boundaries and approaches have been proposed in literature (Bluckert, 2005; Grant, 2003). However, in practice, the theoretical boundaries are often disputed (Bachkirova, 2007) and concerns about applying boundaries in practice have been illustrated in recent research. Studies have indicated that, rather than observe theoretical boundaries, many coaches rely on personal experience and understanding to define boundaries idiosyncratically (Maxwell, 2009a). As a result explanations of where the boundaries lie are inconsistent and fuzzy (Jopling, 2007; Price, 2009).

For instance, a recent survey has shown that the majority of coaches and counsellors (70 per cent) believe that they have learnt where the boundaries are from their experience (with 60 per cent of practitioners reporting they intuitively feel when the dynamic has changed). However, the strength of this conviction does not seem to reflect practice fully, as 43 per cent of participants admit they find it hard to identify the boundary when working with clients (Baker, 2013).

Whilst these figures give an overview of practitioners' experience, they don't adequately reflect the nuances of unique perspectives and dilemmas. In order to develop a deeper understanding of how counsellors and coaches work with the boundaries, the practitioners needed to be heard.

This chapter will explore the thoughts and feelings of counsellors and coaches who volunteered to share their views on the similarities of the approaches and working with boundaries in practice. The practitioners identified themselves as counsellors, coaches, therapist–coaches or Personal Consultants. Some practitioners clearly stated that they worked as coaches and counsellors, but did not combine their approaches with the same client. All the practitioners felt their training, experience, personal beliefs and values underpinned their views about segregation or integration of approaches. Pseudonyms have been used throughout to protect anonymity.

Identifying clear boundaries

One coach, Diana, highlighted the need for differentiation between the helping by talking approaches and was emphatic about drawing very specific boundaries between coaching and counselling: 'Ethically, I believe it's a professionally more sound decision [to keep them separate].'

Diana was ardent in emphasising that she had clear boundaries with her client and wanted to ensure that her point was made about ensuring the boundaries were maintained between coaching and counselling. She felt strongly that blurring the boundaries would diminish the rigour of the individual approaches. 'I wouldn't choose to. I think it's extremely messy. I'm a pragmatist. So I'm not saying it's wrong. For me it's extremely messy.'

Although Diana had both counselling and coaching skills, she was clear she would only provide help that had been agreed in advance and clearly specified in the contract. In a coaching context, if the client appears to be needing counselling, as a coach she would remind the client that they had agreed to work on specific issues. They would not be investigating emotional difficulties or personal history in-depth in the coaching relationship. Instead Diana stated she would suggest to the client to visit a counsellor. This is what she said:

> I would personally prefer not to be a coach and counsellor to the same person, as different dynamics may arise which makes the whole thing tougher … there's a slight difference in the relationship, although I say this cautiously … If I'm going to coach you, then I'm really going to toe in the water … I'm going to understand your emotion enough to match you, to actually demonstrate I've understood you enough to make an intervention … With counselling that might be different, so how the client sees me may or may not be different in each instance.

The concept of integrating counselling and coaching practice appeared to concern Diana (and some other participants) on many levels. Primarily they stressed unease about client safety: 'For me, adding boundaries adds safety for the client. I don't trust the safety of the client in the changeover activity.'

After further consideration, she questioned the rigour of using intuition or gut feeling to identify the shift between counselling and coaching: '[When I am coaching a client and they talk about a sensitive topic] how do I decide this is for counselling? I mean what criteria to use? I don't really think they exist.'

There was also discomfort with what was shared within the coach/counsellor in the helping relationship and how this could be managed appropriately in an integrated approach: 'It's about the level of disclosure that I might share with you. It's about the kind of feelings that I might express towards/with you … whether or not I will be receiving feedback from you.'

Maintaining clear boundaries, setting expectations and clear contracting were highlighted as ethical consideration by Diana: 'It's ethics and clarity – If I'm a paying client, I have a perspective. I want to know what you're going to give me.'

Managing the process

Contracting was seen as fundamental by all participants. Coaching contracts were seen to be more rigid and defined whereas counselling contracts were more fluid. The need for contracting and being very clear with clients about what was being offered was made by several participants. This seemed to be particularly pertinent if the contract was commissioned by a third party. Contracting needs to make competencies apparent, to corporate customers and clients. The coach should then work within the specified skill set (Price, 2009). All practitioners expressed awareness of the need for open and clear contracting for their services.

The coach without counselling training

Within the coaching literature there appears to be an assumption that all coaching clients are mentally healthy, fully functioning and not inhibited by underlying psychological issues. Whilst coaching clients may appear to be robust and able to manage their emotions, in reality they could be just as vulnerable as counselling clients, but attempt to conceal their psychological problems (Maxwell, 2009a). Concerns have been compounded by recent research which revealed that many coaches rely on personal experience and understanding to idiosyncratically define boundaries rather than observe theoretical boundaries (Maxwell, 2009a; Baker, 2013). There is therefore a risk that coaches may not be aware of the potential to cause harm and may not exercise sufficient duty of care when working with vulnerable clients.

These issues were discussed by many of the practitioners in the study. Sonya expressed worries about coaches who state that no harm can be done simply by talking. Sonya felt that moving away from 'clean language' (using the client's own words) and interpreting when reflecting back could be very powerful; the very process of talking and expressing fears could potentially unlock many emotions and memories. Consequently, practitioners who don't have the appropriate skills or training could find themselves in a very difficult position and ill equipped to adequately manage.

Some therapist–coaches and counsellors expressed apprehension about the rigour and validity of brief training programmes and whether coaches were aware of working within their competencies. Counsellors in particular discussed whether coaches who didn't have counselling or psychological backgrounds had sufficient awareness of how their self could impact on the relationship with the client.

The coach with counselling training

Coaching literature often emphasises the dynamic nature of the process. Coaching is portrayed as focusing on achieving goals and improving performance. Indeed, Bluckert (2005) has suggested relationship and personal life issues are better addressed in therapy. However, research has shown that the idea that coaching only addresses professional issues is unsubstantiated. Coaches reported that, far from being clearly separated, professional and personal matters are tightly interwoven. Coaches are often required to work with 'the whole messy human' with their emotions and past histories as well as their performance targets (Maxwell, 2009a). One participant (Shirley) stated: 'What I also think is emerging from the coaching work that I do is major issues with mental health. And that often it is the first time that anybody has had a legitimate opportunity to speak about an issue.'

Amanda and Shirley stated that specific contracts with employers for performance coaching could feel uncomfortable as they could identify distress, but were unable to help the client.

> You know the organisation requires a certain set of behaviours and you know you kind of get on with that. And I think in a world where there's a recession and people are fearful about their jobs there are more and more people just zipping up ... and I suppose it made me quite sad really. To think of how many people are just zipping themselves up and carrying on. Where actually they're not, on the inside, they're really not coping.

Therefore if any deep personal issues arose during coaching, they would be obliged to highlight the problem and suggest that the matter would be better addressed with a counsellor. Amanda makes this point: 'I think one of the reasons I trained as a counsellor was that a lot of people would come to talk to me about different things and they'd end up in tears very early on and I had not really said anything.'

Although they had the skills to work in-depth with their client, they felt that they were bound by their contract and obliged to refer the client onto alternative professional services. However, there was some apprehension as to whether counselling skills had inadvertently been used to assist on occasions and concerns for the ethical implications of integrating practice. Shirley stated:

> And I think where I feel I'm in a tricky position in that I can see that I could help and my tendency is to, but is that OK? And I think what I feel is that, I know my attention is good but what I sometimes feel is am I putting myself in danger, would I be criticised for that if it ever, if it didn't go well? Would I ever be putting myself in a position of danger ethically?

This is a very interesting point indicating that practitioners want clear boundaries not only for the sake of clients, but also to protect themselves. We will come back to this issue later in the chapter.

Blurring the edges

Conversely, some companies may actively seek professionals who are able to manage and support clients with in-depth issues. Rather than distinct and rigid, the boundary was often felt to be blurry and flexible. Indeed the edge of coaching was defined according to clients and coaches' expectations of what would be appropriate to discuss within the working relationship (Maxwell, 2009a).

Georgia, Annie and Sonya all mentioned long-term consultancy relationships with companies who valued their counselling skills and coaching abilities. The organisations were aware that they would utilise their counselling skills to work in-depth with their clients, to explore underlying issues from the past and use coaching strategies help the client develop in the present.

Integrating skills and approaches

It is widely acknowledged that coaching and counselling draw on similar skill sets when working with clients (Bachkirova, 2007; Bachkirova and Cox, 2005). When asked to define similarities in approaches many counsellors glided over the comparison implying the integration of skills was implicit. Martha, for example, asserts: 'In terms of the values and the skills there are huge amounts of overlap between the two.'

When considering differences between coaching and counselling, some practitioners referred to commonly proposed boundaries such as focusing on the past in counselling whereas coaching is seen to emphasise the present and future. Some also discussed working at depth and exploring issues in counselling compared to focus on goal achievement in coaching. However, many acknowledged that these aspects weren't specifically confined to one approach or the other. For instance, clients may explore their emotions or refer to their past history to understand their current behaviour. Additionally, in some counselling approaches there may be homework and a focus on moving forward. This may be disconcerting for some. Shirley stated: 'I think we're in transition on this whole subject ... It's extremely confusing.'

Moreover, Sean and Martha felt that there are probably more differences between some counselling/therapy approaches than between coaching and counselling, As Martha pointed out:

It depends on which approach you have in mind when you're talking about coaching and counselling. So, for example, I don't think solution focused coaching and solution focused counselling have many differences at all. Whereas if you are talking about psychoanalytic psychotherapy and CBT the differences may be greater.

From discussions with practitioners, it would appear that the model or approach adopted by the practitioner may be a key factor in whether they choose to separate coaching and counselling or integrate the approaches. Practitioners who specifically applied one modality when working with clients seemed to favour segregation of approaches, either clearly identifying with coaching or counselling or valuing the boundaries between the approaches. On the other hand, practitioners who had developed their own integrative or transpersonal approach explained how working integratively with coaching and counselling felt authentic, as it drew on all their skills, knowledge and experience. Heather, for instance, stated: 'It's like a zigzag sometimes. When you're coaching you're inevitably going to be using aspects of counselling and I'm guessing that counsellors are inevitably going to be using some aspects of Coaching.'

The holistic approach of working with the whole person, using psychological or counselling training to explore underlying issues and help improve work performance, appealed to integrative counsellors (Maxwell, 2009a). A recent survey indicated that 30 per cent of counsellors and coaches think that the counselling and coaching should be integrated (Baker, 2013). This was illustrated by the integrative practitioners' enthusiastic discussion of blurring the boundaries and working with their skills and abilities to help the client. Shirley made this point: 'I feel that if I was to follow the absolute letter of the boundaries, the client would get less value.'

However, when describing her stance and tentative integration of coaching and counselling, Shirley appeared to feel vulnerable and lack confidence in whether it was the right thing to do. Shirley was concerned that by integrating both approaches with clients she could in some way breach the ethical guidelines of their professional bodies. Her discomfort was tangible in her body language and expression. Shirley articulated a need for either a collection of case studies that could illustrate how others had navigated integration effectively or a framework that would enable her to work ethically, by allowing them to hold the client in a safe place and work within their competencies:

> I know nobody will ever be able to go 'this is the absolute truth, this is the way', but I think to have more understanding of the ethical aspects of your decision would be really helpful. Because I feel like if you box yourself in and go that's coaching, that's counselling you lose something about that whole kind of, that holistic view.

Annie drew on a breadth of experience and knowledge to define their way of working. She described how, when integrating coaching and counselling, she felt the service she offered was seamless and bridged the divide. She felt that clients valued being able to work in a holistic and transpersonal way. Her approach was actively sought by people who wanted to have an approach which combined both counselling and coaching.

Julie spoke of her belief that most people's problems can be mitigated by providing them with skills so that they can reflect and move forward by themselves.

Having undertaken some research on effectiveness of her model, Julie felt that the development of her own strategies would be of benefit to health care providers and practitioners who wanted to combine brief counselling and coaching approaches. She has subsequently developed a training framework which has been validated by an education accreditation body.

Christina emphasised that her integrative approach allowed her the depth and breadth that she needed to work with her clients whether they needed some therapeutic help or personal development. All stressed that integration felt very authentic and the right thing to do for them and the client.

Personal Consultancy in practice

Practitioners who had adopted the Personal Consultancy model (Popovic and Boniwell, 2007) also felt the framework fitted their working style and met the client's needs. Personal Consultancy aims to help practitioners to work with the depth normally associated with counselling and also to facilitate goal-focused actions normally aligned with coaching. Janet, who had recently adopted the Personal Consultancy model, explained that clients appeared to engage with working holistically within the framework:

> I've never had anyone say 'I don't really want to do that', people say 'Okay'. And it just happens ... and they just come every session with whatever they're bringing to the session and it just seems to work.

As the Personal Consultancy model supports exploration of depth and personal growth, the relationship between client and consultant is fundamental. The existential philosophy 'I-thou' emphasises the importance of the coach fully engaging in the relationship and identifying what is happening in their self and with the client. Janet explained how much the relationship means to her:

> I think the relationship is very important. I think in both relationships it has to be quite a high element of trust. There has to be an environment where people feel that they're held and cared for.

From the dynamics and interaction in the relationship, something can emerge in the space between the practitioner and the client which enhances self-awareness and self-reflection for both parties (Jopling, 2007). As Amanda put it: 'I feel that I've been evolving too, I understand myself much more and ... how I influence the relationship.'

Janet made a similar point: 'And using that relationship too ... what might be happening with me, as well as what's happening to them in the relationship to give me clues as to what might go on outside the room.'

Shirley also suggested that the practitioner demonstrating that they were willing to take the risk and make the leap could encourage the client to reciprocate:

> [You] take all that you are into the room, you know and for them to bring all that they are into the room, 'cause how can you ask them to take risks if you're not prepared to risk yourself in it as well?

Janet felt that by engaging with the client and helping them resolve underlying issues the Personal Consultant becomes the client's facilitator, helping them to negotiate their process of change: 'but then I find there's always the stage, you know during psychotherapy, when people have dealt with a lot and they're thinking "what now, what do I do with it now?"'

Both Janet and Martha discussed how they felt the Personal Consultancy model provided a framework that reflected how they wished to work. It provided guidance of how to effectively integrate the depth of counselling and the surface goal achievement of coaching. They believed that the title 'personal consultant' was an accurate description of how they worked. Janet stated:

> I call myself a personal consultant now ... which sits more comfortably you know? I had to think about it for awhile, but the therapist-coach still sounded as if you were separating the two things, so personal consultancy ... it feels better to me.

Martha seems to concur:

> Well it's very much a work in progress still. For me it's a framework that really enables me to integrate ... and offer ... coaching and therapy. ... It's a useful model to share with clients.

However, there was a sense of learning how to work with the model and equally how to make the model work with them. As Martha put it: 'I'm still in that process of sorting that out. Exploring it, rather than sorting out probably.'

Supervision

When working with clients in supportive relationship, practitioners may encounter personal challenges in practice that are difficult to understand or manage. Support from supervision was seen as essential by counsellors and has been adopted by many coaches. However, some coaches appeared to be resistant to the concept of supervision. They had reservations that supervision was the right word to describe a supportive relationship. Whilst they understood the term had originated in counselling, they felt the power dynamic inferred by the title would be off-putting to professional coaches. Further on the coach felt that regular supervision was unnecessary for coaches as contracts were more specific and coaches were less likely to encounter emotional or challenging situations. The practitioner suggested that support could be provided when required. In a recent survey, many practitioners (67 per cent) reported discussing the boundary between counselling and coaching in supervision (Baker, 2013). Heather, one of the participants, admits that 'just about every session I have with my supervisor is about boundaries.'

Ironically, practitioners who worked integratively highlighted difficulties locating appropriate supervision. They describe frustrating experiences with supervisors who were able to provide supervision for either counselling or coaching issues, but did not have sufficient knowledge or understanding to fully support an integrative approach.

Understanding practitioners

Listening to counsellors, coaches, therapist–coaches and Personal Consultants has highlighted concerns and confidences about negotiating boundaries in practice. These issues have been apparent in previous research (Jinks, 2010; Jopling, 2007; Maxwell, 2009a). Recent studies have indicated that, rather than looking for clear boundaries between approaches, many practitioners are either undecided about the issue (17 per cent) or believe that counselling and coaching should be integrated (30 per cent) in practice (Baker, 2013). These findings do not seem to represent the desire for clear boundaries indicated in coaching literature. Undoubtedly, there will be some practitioners who wish to differentiate between the two approaches. Interestingly, the practitioners that argue for boundaries 'shouted loudest and longest' (Jinks, 2010) and may reflect the wishes of those against integration to protect discrete professions.

In practice, many practitioners have found the boundaries indistinct and blurry (Maxwell, 2009a). The majority of practitioners who volunteered to share their views and experiences appeared to want to embrace the integration of approaches. They developed authentic ways of working, which allowed them to effectively utilise their skills, knowledge and experience. Some had created their own models to structure their work, whilst other have adopted established models which facilitate the integration of counselling and coaching approaches.

Practitioners expressed their concerns about coaches without psychological or counselling training working beyond their competencies at the boundary (Jinks, 2010). Further, the potential to cause harm to vulnerable clients was also considered (Jopling, 2007). Clear contracting was seen as essential by counsellors, therapist–coaches, Personal Consultants and coaches. However, some therapist–coaches questioned their integrity and felt vulnerable when encountering psychological difficulties in practice, as they felt they may be breaching the ethical guidelines of their professional bodies if they integrated approaches.

Overall it was felt that practitioners wished to work with their skills and abilities to help clients in a way that felt authentic. To be able to practise confidently, many would appreciate some support and guidance from their professional bodies about appropriate practice and how much they could integrate approaches ethically.

Part III

Critique and future developments

Chapter 17

Some reflections on Personal Consultancy

Gordon Jinks

This chapter is an attempt to develop a critique of the Personal Consultancy model in its current state of development. Given that the model is relatively new, and that the only available literature on the subject originates from the authors themselves, it seemed useful to include some other voices in this, the first book on the subject. To that end, there are a number of chapters included here from colleagues who have pioneered the approach (or some aspects of it) in a variety of contexts. My brief is to offer some ideas about what might be the strengths and limitations of the model and to raise some questions from the perspective of a 'critical friend'. I certainly feel well qualified for the 'friend' aspect in that one of the authors is a much valued colleague at the University of East London and I am married to the other. In terms of being 'critical' I also feel well placed. I have had many interesting conversations, discussions and some disagreements with both authors. I think they are onto something with this model and I think there is a momentum around at this time related to the kind of practice it addresses. But, at the same time, no model is perfect. I hope that what I have to offer will be helpful to the authors – I am confident that both see the model as something which will continue to be developed and refined.

However, there would be little point in including this chapter in the book if it wasn't also helpful to the reader. Practitioners or trainees need to approach all models from a critical perspective, and of course they don't need to be perfect to be useful. What I aim to do here is to give my perspective on the strengths and limitations (or areas for development) of the model in the hope that this will both inform readers and encourage them to reflect on the model in a critical way for themselves. In that way they will be more likely to use it wisely and to integrate it effectively with the rest of what they know at the service of their clients.

The case for personal consultancy and the case for Personal Consultancy

- How strong is the case for an integrated approach to one-to-one talking practices which might be described by the term 'personal consultancy'?
- Is there a need for a formal model to describe such practice?

* * * *

I am starting this discussion by making a distinction between the *concept* of personal consultancy as an integrated approach to one-to-one talking practices, and the more specific Personal Consultancy model laid out in this book as a framework for such practice. If the case for the former is not clear, then there is a danger that the latter is subject to the criticism that it is just another model in a field that certainly does not suffer from a shortage of models. It may still have some merit – indeed I am confident it does and will explore it below – but the authors are making bigger claims for its relevance, so this first critical question seems important.

Counselling and psychotherapy are relatively established practices, but it is interesting to explore the different ways in which they have developed and are practised around the globe. McLeod (2009) gives an outline of the differences between counselling and psychotherapy in the UK in terms of their historical roots, rather than what actually happens when the activity takes place, and that seems relevant here. Coaching has emerged as an energetic presence in recent years, and its roots are different again. It draws on counselling skills, theory and to some extent research, but it also draws on attitudes and processes from sports coaching and the corporate world.

There was a relatively brief upsurge of interest in 'counselling in the workplace' in the latter part of the twentieth century, which went beyond counselling services for employees as part of occupational health provision or employee assistance programmes. For a while there was some enthusiasm about how counselling and counselling skills could contribute to a more general development of well-being and productivity within organisations, to culture change and to bringing together the goals of a successful organisation with happy, fulfilled and productive employees. Counselling skills were being promoted as part of the core skill set for managers and the hope was that by embedding empathy, acceptance and openness in the culture of an organisation, things could be better all round (see e.g. Carroll and Walton, 1997.) In the intervening years coaching seems to have annexed that particular arena of work, probably because it has been free from the potentially negative connotations of counselling. It is explicitly more focused on goals and performance, it doesn't have the association with remedial work or the potential stigma of mental health problems, and it probably seems a lot less 'fluffy' to most CEOs or managers. However, as the authors have illustrated both in this book and previously (Jinks and Popovic, 2011) the situation becomes much less clear when one examines what actually happens in practice. They refer to a number of findings suggesting that differentiating between coaching and counselling is problematic – that many coaches do engage in 'therapeutic' work with their clients, that the boundary is frequently unclear or unrecognised, and that a significant number of practitioners are actively engaged in practice which combines aspects of both.

They also make a point of principle, that the activities of 'counselling' and 'coaching' are actually inextricably linked, because it is potentially futile to focus exclusively on goals and performance without addressing underlying issues, and because it is potentially futile to only address underlying issues without working in a proactive way to enable 'internal' shifts in insight, thinking or feeling to have an impact on the client's life in the broadest possible sense.

This reflects my own experience both as a practitioner and an educator. As a counsellor I have had a relatively small though consistent proportion of clients who have come without a clear 'problem' or even 'issue', but rather a more general sense that they might not be getting the most out of themselves and their lives. These clients usually say they hope to benefit by developing greater self-awareness; exploring their potential and the opportunities available to them; and getting more in touch with what is important to them – hopes, dreams, aspirations – so that they can better achieve ... whatever it turns out to be. In other words they come to counselling for personal development. These days, some of them might find their way to a 'life coach' rather than a counsellor, but I very much agree with the authors that something important could be lost if the potential to work in a more 'depth' mode is not clearly a part of the process. As an HE lecturer in counselling and psychotherapy, I am aware that there has been a clear growth over the last five years or so in the number of students who come to us from a coaching background, with a desire to develop the therapeutic aspects of their work and offer a portfolio of services which might include coaching, counselling and some hybrid or integration of the two. Additionally, more and more of our students whose aspirations originally focused on therapy practice are becoming interested in developing more explicit coaching skills and integrating the two. The overlap area and the issues of differentiation and boundaries have also been the focus for some interesting research dissertations.

The approach taken by the authors – to focus less on the differences and similarities between coaching and therapy and rather to see coaching and the range of therapy approaches as all belonging to a continuum of one-to-one talking practices – seems in retrospect both obvious and wise. Feltham (2011) supports the point that on such a continuum Solution Focused therapy is much closer to coaching than it is to more insight-oriented therapy approaches – citing psychodynamic therapy as an example. This suggests that drawing a dividing line on the continuum based mostly on the historical development of a given practice, rather than what actually happens between practitioner and client, may not be the most helpful approach for us, our clients or for the development of our field.

This leads me to the last question I would like to raise in this section, which is around the scope of the concept of personal consultancy. Two contrasting possible futures seem to be visible from where we are now. The less radical sees the development of personal consultancy (or integrated coach–therapy practice) as a third option in the 'marketplace' of one-to-one talking practices, alongside coaching and therapy. Clients (whether individual or organisational) will develop an understanding of the similarities and differences and will make hopefully informed choices about what to engage with, depending on a range of contextual factors. This seems to be the future which the authors espouse explicitly (Jinks and Popovic, 2011). A more radical future is also possible though – Feltham (2011) refers to the phase shifts which happen from time to time in the development of practice – and I wonder if there is at least a hope that this might be one of them. In this scenario, an integrated approach would become the norm. I suspect the authors may be keeping relatively quiet about this possibility in order to avoid scaring people or seeming to claim too much. However, I would certainly value a situation in which proactive work focused on 'external' change, helping clients clarify and then achieve their aspirations and goals, becomes more generally integrated into our sense of what the practice of therapy encompasses, and in which coaches are more attuned and better equipped to deal with the underlying issues, traumas and blocks which impede performance improvement and fulfilment. Whether or not these aims are best served by the development of a more generic approach to integrated practice remains to be seen, but there is certainly some appeal in the notion of a wider range of needs being met within a single relationship. In other words I don't yet know if one day we will all be 'personal consultants', but one of the strengths of the Personal Consultancy framework seems to me to be a very clear acknowledgement that different practitioners will practise in different ways, depending on their experience, training, skills, preferences and perhaps most importantly their clients. This enables us to conceptualise ourselves as practising across different 'bands' of a spectrum, but recognise that it is indeed the same spectrum.

On the other hand, from the consumer – or potential client – perspective, this could seem confusing and there may be a need for greater clarity, unless we really are developing a 'one size fits all' profession. A small number of categories of practitioner may be more helpful than the idea of a continuum, so that clients are able to be clear that 'these people here are called x, they have such and such in common, and they are different from these other people, called y and z, in the following ways ... '.

We might then accept that there is a case for the integration proposed here, because at least to an extent it is already happening, and because if it is practised with appropriate attention to boundaries, ethics, client safety and well-being, supervision, training, competence, etc., it has the potential to be A Good Thing – enriching practice across the spectrum and enabling clients to benefit from a more rounded service where their needs for both therapeutic and coaching work are met within a single relationship and not artificially compartmentalised.

The next question would be: do we need a new model (or models) in order to work in this way? The authors suggest that at present two classes of alternative exist. The first is to turn to existing models which can be applied across the spectrum (or in the simplest case to both coaching and therapy) and the examples given are Solution Focused therapy/coaching and Person-Centred therapy/ coaching. In both the cases the argument from practitioners with those orientations seems essentially that the existing 'therapy' model can be transferred 'whole' into a coaching approach. The differences are differences of context, but the underlying principles and techniques apply more or less unchanged. Accepting this, one is still left with the core argument for integrative approaches – that no one approach has all the answers or is likely to be the best fit for all clients given the complexity and diversity of human beings – which is made convincingly in earlier chapters.

The second alternative would be to turn to an existing 'open' model for integration and Egan's Skilled Helper model (Egan, 2013) is cited as the most likely candidate. The Skilled Helper model is established and successful. The tenth edition of the book has recently been published and the model has been going through a gradual process of refinement since the mid 1970s. It has been influential across a wide range of 'helping' contexts. I first encountered the model while training as a nurse, and it is used in education, social work, health, organisational development, youth work, mentoring and coaching as well as counselling and psychotherapy. At my present institution it forms the core conceptual framework for the postgraduate diploma in counselling and psychotherapy, but is also a central element of the educational psychology programme and a key part of others.

The authors state that the Personal Consultancy model starts from a different place in its attempt to develop an integrating framework, and I think it might be illuminating to look a little more closely at that. My view is that the Skilled Helper model starts from Egan's assumption that it is possible and desirable to develop a generic 'helping' model which will apply across a range of contexts. He suggests that the model can be useful to a very wide range of formal and informal 'helpers' – from bar staff and hairdressers to counsellors and psychotherapists – and he focuses from there on the commonalities of the helping process (including the relationship, core skills and the process). He does not focus to any great extent on challenging that assumption or exploring what might be *different* across the range of helping contexts and modalities. The success and influence of the model would suggest that this is not a major shortcoming or limitation.

The Personal Consultancy model on the other hand is less focused on the widest possible generic applicability and what is common to different contexts. Instead it concentrates on what it describes as 'one-to-one talking practices' (which seems to mean essentially the integrative therapy–coaching continuum) but does pay specific attention to how aspects of the relationship and process vary and change when working in different modes or stages. So (and I would have to admit that I am over-simplifying here to make a point) Personal Consultancy provides a framework for how 'therapeutic' and 'coaching' work are *different* in terms of the practitioner, the client and the relationship, rather than what they have in common. It rests on the assumptions that they *can* be combined into an integrated approach and they *do* have a lot in common, but those assumptions have been explored in some depth in the preceding chapters and I think largely justified.

Returning then, to the question of whether there is a need for a new model in order to work in this way, my view is essentially a qualified 'yes'. The therapy and coaching arenas probably suffer from an excess rather than a shortage of models, so it would be difficult to make a case for an absolute *need*. However, a model specifically aimed at this kind of integrative one-to-one talking practice, which offers a sufficiently coherent framework, and most importantly is *useful*, could have considerable value. Such a model would need to provide a recognisable and accurate representation of practice; it would need to be sophisticated enough to provide meaningful insights and guidance to practitioners, but simple enough to assimilate, retain and apply in practice; and it would need to be based on values, assumptions and principles that a sufficiently wide range of practitioners could agree on, without these being reduced to platitudes or truisms.

The underlying philosophy and assumptions of the Personal Consultancy model

How well are the underlying assumptions and philosophy of the model expressed? How valid and useful are they? What contribution do they make to understanding and guiding practice?

A few years ago I was reading an internet discussion in which a number of references to the Personal Consultancy model had been made. One of the participants in the discussion, who had not previously encountered the model, took some time out to read the original article (Popovic and Boniwell, 2007) and returned to the fray with some fairly scathing criticism. Essentially, disappointment was expressed: that there was 'nothing new here' and instead just another example of setting up and then knocking down 'straw men' while recycling ideas that are familiar. Of course, everyone is entitled to their opinion, and I would always encourage critical evaluation, but I am referring to this here because I want to spend a little time exploring what models are, and what we might want from them (clearly the individual referred to above wanted novelty and originality and was disappointed).

Models, whether they are model trains or conceptual models for practice such as Personal Consultancy, are representations. They attempt to represent something real but at the same time they are not that thing. Hopefully they represent enough aspects of the thing to be seen as pleasing or useful. A model train is not a train, but will represent some aspects of a train: sometimes just the appearance, but somewhat reduced in size; sometimes movement will be a feature of the model; sometimes it will include noise or produce steam. Similarly, *transference* is a model for a process that can occur within human relationships. It is not the phenomenon itself, but a representation of the phenomenon, which is in itself inevitably more complex than the model. Nevertheless, sometimes, transference is a useful model for understanding a process or interaction, and its value is largely determined by questions of how useful and how often? Ultimately that is how models tend to be judged, rather than on questions of novelty. In fact I think there are some new ideas in the Personal Consultancy model, but more importantly I think it puts together a number of ideas in a new configuration and attempts to represent aspects of reality in a different way to other models I am familiar with. Mostly I'm interested in how well it does that, and how useful it might be, rather than how exciting and new it might be.

There are many things to commend about the underlying principles and assumptions of the Personal Consultancy model, and my view is that they are expressed clearly and coherently in the preceding chapters. The authors begin from an inclusive and pragmatic position and attempt to create a framework which can allow for 'whatever works and is ethical'. The approach to theory is clearly thought through, recognising its value (in contrast with some eclectic approaches) but not over-valuing it. The model does what an open model of this type needs to do in that it provides a structure and a container for theory but keeps it relatively in the background. It is recognised that we do not have an all-encompassing theory of everything, and no attempt is made to provide one. Instead, the authors suggest that many different theories can have value, but that value is determined by their applicability within the specific and unique relationship with the client. Any theories, approaches or techniques used should be demonstrably relevant and applicable within that relationship. This seems to me to represent genuine commitment, visible across many aspects of the model, to being 'client centred' in the deepest sense and to working in a collaborative way not just in terms of addressing the client's issues, but involving them in the process – in Bordin's (1979) terms genuinely involving the client in negotiating the goals and tasks of the working alliance. In Chapter 4 they state: 'We find that the experience of being human and interacting with other human beings (which by default we all have and do) is a richer source of understanding than a theory.' This sounds like a description of what narrative psychologists would term 'narrative knowing' in contrast with the 'paradigmatic knowing' associated with theory. I wonder if there is scope for drawing on more of the narrative perspective in developing a clearer account of the place of such knowing in the model.

The model takes account of and incorporates much of what can be gleaned from the available research into what works in therapy (see e.g. Duncan et al., 2009) – which it assumes can be applied across a spectrum to include coaching. It sees the relationship as central, and pays appropriate attention to the client's perception of the relationship, hopefully maximising the probability that they will feel listened to, understood and accepted. It also recognises the importance of what the client brings to the relationship and the process. It is possible to read the Duncan et al. distillation of research findings and potentially feel disempowered as a practitioner. The evidence strongly suggests the importance of what the client brings to the table in terms of the likelihood of positive outcomes. There can seem relatively little room left for the practitioner to influence the outcome, and there is a temptation to revert to the often heard refrain 'it's all about the relationship' when considering the practitioner's role. This seems to me an over-simplification and fortunately not one the Personal Consultancy model subscribes to. In fact, although this issue is not addressed explicitly, the Personal Consultancy model provides opportunities to help the client play their part to the full by doing things which are known to be associated with positive outcomes (Duncan et al., 2004). Examples are:

- it recognises the importance of their existing strengths, resources and insights;
- it provides an opportunity to identify and work with a focal issue or problem, but also to see such a focus clearly in the context of the 'big picture' of the client's life;
- it works with and attempts to develop their existing frameworks for understanding themselves, their experiences and the process of change;
- it balances the importance of internal change with the value of recognising, owning and building on success in external change; and
- it sees personal consultancy as part of a process of personal development but recognises that such development can be facilitated by many other factors.

I suspect this – helping the client to be the most effective client they can be – is a fruitful area for further exploration for all of us and it something I am thinking about in relation to my own work. It may also be an area for the authors to build on in future, making their ideas for doing so more explicit and developing their thinking around the client axis of the model.

The authors have clearly thought carefully about various ways 'integration' can happen, both in providing examples of how techniques and frameworks from other approaches can be integrated into the structure of Personal Consultancy (Chapter 9) and in clarifying the principle of integrating prudently. The 'tequila' analogy from Chapter 4 seems to me to encompass similar principles to those espoused by Cooper and McLeod (2010) in relation to 'pluralistic' therapy.

There is a recognition and to an extent I think a celebration of *complexity* both in the model and in the way the authors write about it. I think they are generally successful in avoiding the simplistic and the reductionist, and instead communicate a sense that personal consultancy is complicated, it is subtle, and you'll need to keep your wits about you. On the other hand the model itself is not over-elaborate in a way that might render it difficult to hold in mind as a guiding framework. A toe is dipped into the potentially murky water of chaos theory in identifying the client-consultant relationship as a 'non-linear system' (Chapter 4). Again I would in time like to see this thinking developed further. The tension present in non-linear systems between the 'butterfly effect' wherein small changes in one area can precipitate large effects on the system as a whole, and the existence of 'strange attractors' – relatively stable states which non-linear systems seem to gravitate towards and move between – seems relevant. The *stages* of the Personal Consultancy model might perhaps usefully be seen as such islands of stability between which the client–consultant system moves.

Finally in this section I would like to raise a question about inclusivity. The Personal Consultancy model goes a long way in this regard in recognising the value of a range of approaches and enabling practitioners to integrate their own approaches within the model. It explicitly encompasses the spectrum of counselling/psychotherapy approaches and coaching, yet seems to stop short of welcoming mentoring into the fold. An argument could certainly be developed that similar commonalities and difficulties in differentiation exist between mentoring and coaching as between coaching and therapy. Mentoring has a longer history than either coaching or therapy, and its exclusion leaves us with an historical overview in Chapter 1 that begins with Freud and feels fairly 'conventional' to me in a book which is otherwise refreshing in its challenges to convention.

The dimensions

What is the structure of the model? What is it intended to represent and how effectively does it do that?

In terms of structure, the Personal Consultancy model starts from the proposition that there are three elements essential to the process: the client, the consultant and the relationship. This seems a reasonable starting point for the reasons stated by the authors, though of course it is open to argument. If one wanted to start with the bare minimum of components, then the relationship could be seen as the interaction between client and consultant and therefore not a core element in its own right. However, the authors present a case which is essentially a variation of the whole being greater than the sum of its parts for considering the relationship as a separate entity, and that seems consistent with the weight of evidence in support of its importance in terms of positive outcomes.

These three elements then are assigned as the horizontal, vertical and depth axes of a three-dimensional 'graph'. Each axis is further defined by a chosen 'property' of the element it relates to: 'being with' versus 'doing with' in the case of the consultant; 'existing patterns' versus 'emerging patterns' in the case of the client; and 'depth' versus 'surface' for the relationship. Clearly some choices have been made here. It is acknowledged that these chosen bi-polar constructs only represent certain aspects of the elements they relate to. For example, it is clear that the consultant–client relationship is complex and multi-faceted. The research suggests that the client's *perception* of the relationship is a key variable in terms of positive outcomes, and that success is associated with a relationship perceived as one of acceptance and mutual understanding. One might therefore question whether the choice of depth versus surface is sufficient to model the importance of the relationship in the consultancy process.

However, at this point it is important to be clear about what the authors are trying to achieve with this aspect of the model. The intention is to describe the 'space' within which consultancy takes place. The process of consultancy will then essentially be represented by a 'journey' through this space. It is unlikely to be a straightforward or linear journey, but will involve moving into and out of the various sectors described by the axes. For this to be useful I would suggest it needs to provide both a meaningful description – enabling us to have some better understanding of where we are and what we are doing – and it needs to be capable of offering some guidance as to how to proceed, which should probably include how to do what we are engaged with right now as effectively as possible, plus some sense of what we might do next.

Having spent some time thinking about this model, applying it to my own practice, and trying it out as a way of keeping track of things in supervision, I have come to the conclusion that it is at the very least 'fit for purpose'. I have found it illuminating to reflect on where a particular piece of work is located in terms of being with/doing with, existing/emerging patterns and depth/surface. Often this provides a useful insight into what is happening, but perhaps more importantly it also often provides useful insight into whether it is useful to remain in that place or to develop the work in a particular direction.

I don't feel qualified to judge at this stage whether the authors have arrived at the *best possible* descriptions for the axes. I know that considerable thought has gone into the model and the choices made, and they seem to work, in that they reflect the kinds of things that happen in the real life situation, and they seem to be helpful. I would encourage readers to reflect on these questions in terms of their own work.

A three-dimensional model such as this has both advantages and disadvantages, when compared for example to a two-dimensional model such as Egan's 3 x 3 grid representing the stages and tasks of the Skilled Helper model process (Egan, 2013). Three dimensions offer the possibility of a more sophisticated representation – there are more dimensions! So for example the relationship axis can be integrated into the core structure of the model and be seen as part of the dynamic process of moving around the consultancy 'space'. In Egan's model the grid essentially represents the steps or tasks of the process and the way the relationship might change or be differently emphasised in different tasks is not represented. Rather the relationship is dealt with as an underpinning foundation of the process. On the other hand, a three-dimensional model is harder to represent on paper, and for most of us I think harder to conceptualise quickly and hold in mind while engaged in the foreground activity of working with a client.

Of course the model is more than just the basic structure. In the preceding chapters, the authors have shared a lot of their accumulated experience and wisdom about how to put it into practice. In particular this includes their ideas about how to work in the various sectors and how best to manage the process as a whole in moving between the sectors. I have (unsurprisingly) found much to agree with in these chapters, the essence of which I hope will be clear from the comments above. One further question remains for me in this regard, however, and it does in fact link to a structural question about the model as well, which is the extent to which the axes are to be seen as representing a continuum or scale between the chosen polarities; or to what extent they represent an either/or choice. In respect of the depth versus surface (relationship) axis, it seems fairly clear that we are dealing with a continuum, and that tracking where we are along that continuum will be a useful part of the process. In relation to the existing vs. emerging patterns (client axis) it also seems clear in that sometimes we will be working purely on what *is,* sometimes on what *might be* or is desired, and sometimes we will be comparing and contrasting aspects of both. My question relates more to the consultant axis, where my sense sometimes is that the authors are presenting this more as an either/or choice between the 'being with' and 'doing with' modes. For example, in Chapter 6, the impression is that the *being-with mode* is very much about a 'pure listening'. I think this is useful in order to make the point, but practitioners coming from different orientations may have different views, and I wonder if the value (or otherwise) of different *shades* of 'being with' vs. 'doing with' might be explored more fully.

The stages

How does the model work in practice? How effectively does it help the practitioner (and client) to make the most of the opportunity of working together?

In some ways, it is in arriving at the 'stages' (Chapter 6) that the Personal Consultancy model comes into its own as a model for practice. The hard work of getting to grips with the underlying assumptions and principles and developing an understanding of the space delineated by the three axes should hopefully pay off, as four useful stages or modes of working with the client emerge. These are described clearly, the differences are apparent and make sense in terms of the axes of the model, and I suspect most practitioners will recognise them as representing the useful things that can happen in the consultancy room. I think they model quite effectively the islands of stability (or periods of dynamic equilibrium) which can occur within the sea of potential chaos which is the complex and non-linear system of the Personal Consultancy process.

The importance of the Authentic Listening stage is particularly emphasised, and in terms of guiding the practitioner on moving between stages, there is a clear expectation that in most cases this stage will essentially be like 'base camp' and we will return to it between each of the other stages of our 'journey'. If done well, this should ensure that the critically important relationship is held carefully in mind, that the client really does feel accepted and understood, and that the relationship doesn't get 'lost' in the potential energy and enthusiasm of the more 'doing with' stages of Rebalancing and Generating.

For some practitioners, and in some cases, the necessity of frequently returning to Authentic Listening in the sense in which it is described here may not be seen as essential. I am thinking particularly of the Solution Focused approach as an example here, where there is an emphasis on using the time spent together in the most efficient way possible. The starting point is what the client wants, and if attempting to integrate Solution Focused working with the Personal Consultancy model, the Generating phase might be seen as more central, and the process would possibly be characterised by movement between Rebalancing and Generating. (What are the existing patterns, and in particular what is already working? How can we build on that in order to move towards the desired new or emerging patterns?) In such a conceptualisation authentic listening would need to be present and underpin the process, but the Authentic Listening stage might rarely be explicitly visible.

Rebalancing and Generating could be seen (perhaps crudely) as delineating the therapeutic and coaching aspects of the model but as the authors point out in several places, that differentiation is seen as less meaningful than the differentiation between existing and emerging patterns, which could, depending on context, be applied to both therapeutic and coaching work, or an integration of the two. Rebalancing and Generating seem to me conceptually useful in analysing and applying other approaches. For example, the exploratory work of CBT or REBT (teasing out and challenging the existing causal relationships between experiences, cognitive appraisal in terms of thoughts and beliefs, emotions and behavioural responses) is followed by a period of experimentation to find new ways of thinking or behaving or new beliefs that result in new patterns of perceiving, thinking, feeling and behaving. In other words there is a pretty good 'fit' here with the Personal Consultancy model. With other approaches it may become clear that the conceptual framework offered is mostly located in a particular stage of the Personal Consultancy model – I am thinking of the Psychodynamic approach as mostly intersecting with the rebalancing stage here – so the Personal Consultancy model can provide some useful guidance as to what else might need to be done with the client in order to round out the process.

The Supporting stage also seems useful to me in emphasising, perhaps more than many other models, the need to 'be with' the client as they engage with an 'implementation' phase in relation to emerging patterns. The consultant is supporting the client as they work on integrating any changes to themselves, their circumstances, behaviour, relationships etc. In some ways I wonder if this is the least developed stage of the model, in terms of clarity around what it involves and how it is best approached, but it seems highly useful that it is explicitly identified as a stage.

The identification of the stages and the guidance offered on working within and between them involves collapsing the three-dimensional diagram used earlier into two dimensions – the client and consultant axes – so that the relationship axis to an extent fades from view. Inevitably something is lost as a result. The authors note that the relationship underpins and is central to each of the stages. There are useful examples at the end of each section in Chapter 6 about how the stages might operate in relation to 'depth' and 'surface', but I wonder if the possible subtleties of further exploring the interactions of the relationship axis with each of the identified stages might remain an area for future development?

On the other hand, the reduction to two dimensions does make the model more manageable in practice. In essence I suppose the 2-D map of the stages is what we take into a session with us and is relatively foreground in keeping track of where we are. (It would probably be useful to share it with the client whenever possible.) The model can be expanded into 3-D when needed to look a bit deeper into the process – at times perhaps during sessions, but probably more usually on reflection afterwards or during supervision.

Finally, I would like to note that the model doesn't *structurally* incorporate the collaborative nature of the client–consultant relationship. I am certainly not suggesting this is not addressed. It is clear throughout that the authors see collaboration as vitally important and that decisions to be made about the process of the work are consistently seen as joint decisions which involve the client and consultant working together and arise from the relationship. This is something I have been thinking about a lot of late. I am increasingly convinced that issues of informed consent, collaborative planning (including determining the 'best fit' approaches and strategies to use in the sessions), joint reflection on process issues and evaluation of the work are a vital aspect of therapy and coaching; that few approaches explicitly give them enough attention; and that much of the 'common factors' research points towards the value of making all this as explicit as possible (see e.g. Duncan et al., 2004). I don't have an answer for how to really build this into a model, but I would be interested in how much scope there is within the Personal Consultancy model for such development.

Conclusion

I have really valued the opportunity to get to know this model in more detail. I think it is an interesting way to conceptualise one-to-one talking practices and I find its values and assumptions generally easy to agree with. I think it borrows ideas prudently from a wide range of other perspectives, but it combines them in interesting new ways. I also think that there is enough here that is new and challenging to make it a worthwhile addition to the field, and in particular I think it opens up a way of thinking about open integration of therapy approaches and coaching which is in tune with the times.

I don't think it is perfect, but most of the questions I have raised are less about what I would see as flaws in the model and more about areas where I think there is room for development, or where I would like the authors to think a bit more about something because I would be interested in what they might come up with! In an ideal world I will be able to read about some interesting developments in the next edition. I hope that readers will by now be engaged in their own critique of this model and I hope that what I have had to offer has been useful both in terms of the perspectives I have shared and the questions I have suggested for exploration at the beginning of each section.

Chapter 18

Areas for development

Introduction

Since its creation the Personal Consultancy model has developed somewhat organically from being a seed of an idea into a tangible working framework ready for practice. It has been examined and dissected through a number of different lenses and discussed, appraised and discussed again. This process and those involved in it (colleagues, students, supervisees, clients and readers) have helped us to nurture, shape and develop the seed into hopefully the robust and healthy young plant that is presented in this volume. It reflects the excitement of new possibilities and embodies a sense of adventure, but we recognise that it will need continued nurture, challenge and guidance if it is to develop into full maturity. We also understand that we need to further challenge and develop our own thinking, learning and understanding if we are going to be responsible caregivers. For this we need continued input and feedback from a variety of sources because we believe true learning does not usually happen in isolation.

Responses to the critique

In light of the above, we much appreciate the thorough and constructive critique in the previous chapter as it has given us yet another lens through which to examine the Personal Consultancy model. It has almost seemed like looking at the framework and the book in 'high definition' with the bonus of being able to zoom in, zoom out and consider them from other angles. This has provided a fresh perspective stimulating our thinking about strengths and limitations, areas for future development, as well as applications and possibilities for the future. We find the opportunity to do this before the book even goes to print extremely valuable. We don't seek to respond in great detail here to what we think is a balanced and fair review of both the Personal Consultancy model and this book. This is because we agree in the main with the arguments that have been presented.

Dimensions

As we have demonstrated, some models are often criticised for being too mechanistic and for overriding the client's agenda (see Chapter 9). We also think that frameworks which are presented and taught in a linear format can often result in a 'one-dimensional' type of practice that may be easy to follow, but might be missing something important. In our view, the three-dimensional model reflects the nature of human interaction in all its complexity better. Keeping in mind all three dimensions results in richer, fuller and more authentic interactions between consultant and client. However, we take the point that representing a three-dimensional model in two dimensions presents some difficulties. We had many ideas and discussions about how best this might be done and the diagrams throughout this book are the result of these discussions. We still see this as 'a work in progress' though. We welcome any thoughts about how the three-dimensional model may be represented more clearly.

Other disciplines and approaches?

We agree with the point raised about the possible merits of including mentoring in the Personal Consultancy model. We are sympathetic to Garvey et al.'s (2009) description of the 'tribal' tensions that exist between the mentoring and coaching fraternity for example. Perhaps this is because it resonates plainly with our own experience(s) of what have sometimes seemed like territorial disputes between coaches and counsellors. Garvey et al. do hint that they come down more favourably on the side of the 'similarities' (as opposed to focusing on the differences) argument between coaching and mentoring. This might suggest that there is a case to be made for extending the scope of the Personal Consultancy model to explicitly encompass mentoring. Mentoring is a closely related area of one-to-one talking practices and shares a lot of ground in terms of core skills and processes.

Indeed, the decision we have made in this respect was influenced by the fact that, for the time being, our knowledge and experience of this discipline is fairly limited. We therefore felt restricted in our ability to present a balanced rationale for including mentoring into the model and in practical terms *how* it might be done. With hindsight, we think having a contributor who could have effectively explored this for us would have been an asset and we are disappointed we didn't think of it. That said, as the Personal Consultancy framework emphasises restorative and proactive rather than counselling and coaching, much in this book could be relevant to mentoring too. We really hope to examine this more fully in the future and encourage the reader (especially those with knowledge and experience of mentoring) to think about the model and the ways that it could be relevant to mentors who are also coaches or counsellors.

Supervision

Supervision has been a 'hot topic' for coaches for a number of years. From the many discussions about this subject on social networking sites such as LinkedIn it is clear that individual practitioners recognise the merits of supervision in order to ensure best practice. Professional coaching bodies are also taking the issue of supervision for coaches seriously. The Association for Coaching (AC) noted, in their second survey into coaching supervision (AC, 2008), that members who had regular supervision had risen from 48 per cent in 2005 to 71 per cent in 2008. The AC encourages all coaches to undertake supervision as a continuous process. They state that supervision is *essential* for applicants seeking accreditation and have recently made the process more rigorous. In addition, they state on their website that they have joined with a number of professional coaching bodies in order to establish the principles of best practice in supervision.

Being engaged in regular supervision is nothing new for those with a counselling background. Most of us have been in a regular supervision relationship since our training. We are clear about the amount of supervision we need to meet the requirements and standards set by whatever therapeutic body we belong to. Most of us, we think, appreciate the opportunity to share with our supervisor(s) concerns and dilemmas around our clients (or anything that might impact or compromise the quality of our practice). In addition we benefit from, at different times, being supported, guided, encouraged, challenged and/or stretched as practitioners by our supervisors. It is a way of sharing the burden of responsibility that can sometimes seem very heavy when working with clients in isolation, and it is a place for continued learning and professional development.

Finding a suitable supervisor

Even without the added complexities that the Personal Consultancy way of working may bring, it can sometimes be challenging for a practitioner to locate a supervisor who best fits their needs. Supervisors vary in relation to a number of factors such as:

- focus on client work;
- broader approach to incorporate issues that impact on practice (restorative);
- educational component;
- expertise in a particular context;
- supervision training and experience.

In addition, supervisors occupy a range of positions on the 'directiveness–non-directiveness' continuum. Having a supervisor with appropriate experience relevant to the type of work undertaken and who provides a suitable mix of challenge and support is essential to safeguard clients, maintain best practice and facilitate the practitioner's growth and development.

Supervision for Personal Consultants

We propose the same standards of supervision for Personal Consultants as we do for counsellors. It is even more important that the supervisor is familiar and sympathetic to the implications of working in an integrative coach–therapy way. This requires the supervisor to understand the nuances of Personal Consultancy and the shifts in boundaries that can occur when moving between stages so that they can support and challenge the practitioner appropriately. This presented something of an obvious challenge when Personal Consultancy was in its infancy. We know practitioners who have engaged in group or peer supervision because they have been unable to find someone who could supervise their Personal Consultancy work in a one-to-one setting. Whilst we appreciate the virtues of group and peer supervision, we think that this style of supervision is best used to complement one-to-one supervision, especially for inexperienced consultants. We have recently noticed a surge in the number of practitioners specifically offering integrative coach–therapy supervision. This perhaps reflects practitioners' growing confidence in using the Personal Consultancy framework. It also suggests that a high number of Personal Consultants and integrative coach–therapists are also clinical supervisors and are now starting to incorporate an integrated coach–therapy approach to their own supervision offerings. We suggest therefore that availability and choice for Personal Consultancy supervision will continue to increase.

Personal Consultancy as a model for supervision

One of the areas in which we would like to develop the Personal Consultancy model is its application to supervision. For several years we have both included supervision as part of what we offer. We work with coaches, counsellors, trainees and, inevitably, more and more integrative coach–therapists and Personal Consultants. We work with groups and on a one-to-one basis and we are both passionate about this area of our work, because we see it as a way of ensuring that clients get the best service possible. Furthermore, it is rewarding and fulfilling to see practitioners grow and develop and to experience some vicarious sense of satisfaction in hearing about clients overcoming obstacles and achieving their goals.

In the past we have both found many of the existing supervision concepts and models to be somewhat lacking. Our own experience led us to select what we thought were the best aspects of particular models so that they matched our values and provided a framework we could work with. For example, we both agree that supervision should be client-centred, focused (clear about what the supervisee wants to get from a session and how it can inform their practice and/or client) and relational (the relationship between supervisor and supervisee, supervisee and client, and client and significant others are all taken into account).

The Personal Consultancy model can be used in two ways or at two levels in supervision. First, it provides a framework for exploring the work the supervisee is doing with their clients. Attention is thereby focused on to the relationship, the being/doing with axis for the consultant and the existing/emerging patterns for the client, as well as the stages of the model. However, the model can also be applied to the process of supervision itself, with the axes relabelled as supervisor, supervisee and relationship. Here also the stages of the model provide a useful structure as supervision can also be seen as moving between Authentic Listening, Rebalancing, Generating and Supporting as exemplified in this excerpt:

One of us was working with a supervisee who had strongly stated that he wanted practical support in planning a training session for his client (a third sector organisation). However, he was exhibiting some anxiety, which he indicated had been holding him back from being able to engage with his strengths and resources and make progress with his planning. The supervisor felt pressure from the supervisee who seemed to have a very clear goal for the session and she was aware of some anxiety in herself about to what extent she could meet those demands. Despite some initial resistance (and perhaps irritation) the supervisee agreed to talk about the anxieties and what might be associated with them. Spending some time in Authentic Listening allowed the supervisee to unload his thoughts and feelings in an uninhibited way. He described how the manager of the project he was working with, although appearing seemingly appreciative of his input, also communicated resistance, scepticism and even fear. The supervisee wondered if the manager was frightened that he might discover his perceived shortcomings. When thinking about it he admitted that he too felt insecure. He felt pressure (self-imposed) in having to deliver a training package that would 'do what it said on the tin'. He communicated doubts about his own ability and wondered if he would be revealed as a 'fake'.

The time spent in the Authentic Listening stage meant he had been able to talk unchecked, ask questions and answer some of them with minimal input from the supervisor. Moving into the Rebalancing stage he was ready to explore what his doubts meant. He realised that he had experienced the 'dread' that he might be exposed as a fake many times. He recalled his experiences as student nurse, working with a particularly difficult ward sister who, he feared on a daily basis, would discover him as being incapable. Some time was spent exploring these thoughts, beliefs and feelings; the extent to which they were true at the time; and what place they held in his life currently.

'No wonder when I was eighteen I was so frightened of the ward sister – she was a bitch!' he said with certainty, adding, 'I know I'm more than capable of planning and delivering this training.'

He also recognised that his feelings of insecurity mirrored those of the manager whose project was receiving the training and wondered if the two were linked. Looking at it this way helped the supervisee to consider what might be driving the manager's fears and how best he could respond to them.

Addressing these issues in the Authentic Listening and Rebalancing stages meant that the supervisee could easily move into Generating to plan the practical aspects of the training. He felt confident, knowing that he had tackled other more difficult tasks in the past, was a skilled and experienced trainer and was able to connect with beliefs in his abilities to do it well.

Applying the same model at the same time to both the consultant/client- and supervisor/supervisee-relationships can be useful in picking up a variety of different types of parallel process. In the above case, the recognition that the client had similar feelings as the supervisee and that both were responding to these feelings in a similar way was significant. In addition, the supervisor had also felt similar feelings in the face of the supervisee's anxiety and expectations for the session. It is unlikely the feelings experienced by client, supervisee and supervisor were completely unconnected. Although the supervisee had been most insistent initially to spend the supervision session devising a plan for the training, this wouldn't have had raised insight into the parallel process between himself and the client or himself and the supervisor. He also wouldn't have had the opportunity to bring to awareness times in the past when he had felt disempowered in the way he described. Addressing these underlying issues (in depth) gave him confidence and freedom to plan the more practical aspects of the training (surface) without undue anxiety.

It was only when we were discussing what we wanted to include in this last chapter that we realised that we were each using the Personal Consultancy model with our supervisees. We have only had a few brief conversations about the relevance of the model for this purpose with a handful of other consultants. So there is still work to do in exploring its applicability for supervision and if and/or how we might adapt it. Hence, further development of the Personal Consultancy model as a framework for supervision is an area that will no doubt involve many more creative conversations and discussions and we invite thoughts and suggestions from interested parties.

Training and education in Personal Consultancy and coach–therapy integration

As one of us has argued elsewhere (Russell and Jinks, 2011), there is an important distinction to be made between training and education. Training can sometimes be mechanistic and repetitive if the focus is only on how to do something without fully understanding why. On the other hand, education is interested in developing both ability and a spirit of enquiry and wisdom. We believe that in order to develop fully rounded, capable, perceptive and ethical Personal Consultants, *both* training *and* education need to occur.

Training for coaches who are also counsellors?

As things stand, there are few courses available for those interested in Personal Consultancy or integrative coach–therapy training and education although some are beginning to appear at postgraduate level. In the private sector courses can range from one-day introductory workshops to certificate level. We expect growth in this area. The current picture typically sees coaches and therapists being trained, educated and experienced in both disciplines and then looking for something that can help them integrate the two effectively. Practitioners want to know how much training and education they might need to safely and ethically be a Personal Consultant. This is a difficult question to answer and probably needs further exploration. We are concerned that short courses can perhaps provide sufficient training but may sometimes lack enough of the educational element. A day workshop can provide a 'taster' of what might follow but can't possibly cover the amount of breadth, depth and critical thinking we would see as necessary or even desirable. Ideally, such education should include theory of integration, training in Personal Consultancy (and/or other models), integration of other concepts and approaches, managing the boundaries, ethics, supervision, modelling, discussion in small and large groups, skills practice and robust assessment. A suitable recruitment process should be established that would address existing skills and experience, self-awareness and personal development, ability to manage ethical and professional issues, resilience and ideally access to a client base. We prefer to see courses that span several months because the student then has the opportunity to apply new ways of working whilst still being supported by the education/training institution.

Training requirements for practitioners trained and experienced in one discipline?

Interestingly, we also talk to practitioners who are trained and experienced in only one of the disciplines. They are typically counsellors who recognise the benefit of being able to work more proactively and practically with their existing clients or who want to develop their practice to include coaching and an approach that integrates the two. In addition, we have had many conversations with coaches from a variety of backgrounds (e.g. business, education, positive psychology) who ask us what their route might be to becoming a Personal Consultant. These questions probably need further discussion and exploration. One view is that practitioners get adequate training in the discipline they are lacking but this begs the question: what is adequate? Price (2009) presents a convincing argument that practitioners should work in line with their competencies. If we agree with his line of reasoning this might negate the need for a clear answer. However, as highlighted in Chapter 11, some consumers and practitioners like to know exactly what it is they are buying or engaging in. To be able to do this they appreciate categories and often demand clarity about what requirements and criteria exist in order to belong to a particular category. We don't have a definitive answer for to these questions. We promote safe and ethical working and we value inclusivity but we also understand the need for a degree of clarity. These issues create a tension that will form the basis of many discussions for some time to come as integrative coach–therapy practice continues to evolve.

Personal Consultancy training from scratch?

We see more and more trainees entering both counselling and coaching with training and experience of the other discipline. It would seem, from anecdotal evidence at least that potential trainees are also much more discerning than they were in the past about the courses they select. This may be a response to the economic climate in that potential students think carefully about whether their chosen career path will be able to sustain them financially as well as fulfil their ambitions. It may also be due to the fact that because information is so readily available in this age of technology they can research a career, possible training/ education routes and potential employment more easily than ever before. In any case, attitudes do seem to have changed. We have both had many conversations with experienced practitioners who describe their initial choice of approach in the past as 'having fallen into it', 'it was what was available at my local college or university' or 'I simply had no idea about the range of counselling/coaching approaches out there.' Potential students taking a more assertive and focused approach to their career path can only be a good thing. For the evolution of Personal Consultancy and coach–therapy integration it means that potential students and trainees are becoming more and more aware of working in this way and an increasing number are asking how they might go about it at the outset.

If the demand is high enough, then training institutions may have to consider developing a more direct pathway to becoming a Personal Consultant or integrative coach–therapist. It could be modular in format with some modules focused on therapeutic, restorative work, others on proactive, practical ways of working and then an element that covers integration. They could achieve qualifications in counselling, coaching and Personal Consultancy if the content of the courses satisfied guidelines from the professional bodies that offer accreditation and endorsement to the course.

Professional bodies and ethics

At the moment in the UK many coaches who are also therapists belong to a professional body for counselling and another for coaching. BACP introduced their coaching division in 2009, which was the first attempt to provide therapists who were also coaches an option to get all their professional needs met under one roof. This was an innovative and brave move. Although sympathetic to the concept and practice of integrative coach–therapy (as evidenced by publishing articles in *Coaching Today* and *Therapy Today* on the subject), at the time of writing they have stopped short of issuing a formal statement about their stance. In addition, their ethical framework doesn't adequately take into account issues that may arise (and how to deal with them) for the practitioner who is working across the boundary.

In March 2011 the Association of Integrative Coach–Therapist Professionals (AICTP) was established, whose main focus is integrative coach–therapy practice.

The authors were both instrumental in AICTP's creation and subsequent development. The association began as a special interest group to provide guidance and support to those practising in an integrative way or interested in doing so, and at the time of writing AICTP is not yet a standard setting body. However, interest has been high and Associate membership has been introduced as a first level of membership. It is probably inevitable that the association will develop other levels and criteria for membership. There is no doubt that this will involve the development of a suitable ethical framework for this kind of practice.

Practitioners need an appropriate ethical framework (based on clear values, principles and aims) to be able to feel safe, supported and guided in their practice. At present integrative coach–therapy practitioners are faced with the prospect of also integrating ethical frameworks and codes from both disciplines. We have heard many testimonies from practitioners who describe working in a way that combined both disciplines but felt 'beneath the radar'. As a result they felt a degree of anxiety about the implications of doing so. This is unlikely to be helpful to anyone, least of all clients. If the consultant doesn't feel safe, then how can the client? So it is desirable that an integrated ethical framework be developed and sooner rather than later. On the other hand, all these things take time and an ethical framework for integrative coach–therapy practice needs careful consideration and should not be rushed. It probably requires input from a range of interested parties. At the time of writing this tension remains unresolved, but interested readers might wish to check the AICTP website for the latest news.

Conclusion

This book represents a first attempt at giving a comprehensive description of the Personal Consultancy framework, the issues that face integrative coach–therapy practitioners and guidance in how to address these. As we see it at the time of writing, the main areas of development will be around supervision, training and education and the development of an ethical framework. We are also very interested to see if and how mentoring might be included in the Personal Consultancy framework.

We recognise that this is a work in progress. We will continue to develop and adapt the model and we hope other people will join us in this process. We genuinely hope that the reader will process what they have read, evaluate and create their own critique. One of our main aims has been to engage and interest practitioners in what we have had to say and encourage them to respond. We feel proud that the young plant we have raised is reaching maturity but we are aware that many hands will be needed to enable it to reach its true potential.

References

AC (2008) 'Increasing number of coaches are using supervision as part of their practice'. Association for Coaching, 2nd survey into coaching supervision. Available at http://www.associationforcoaching.com/pages/resources/press-releases/increasing-number-coaches-are-using-coach-supervision-part-their/ (accessed 15 March 2013).

Alexander, G. (2010) 'Behavioural coaching: the GROW model'. In Passmore, J. (ed.) *Excellence in coaching: the industry guide*. London: Kogan, pp. 83–93.

Allen, Woody (1977) *Annie Hall*. MGM. Producer: Charles H. Joffe.

Aspey, L. (2010) 'The art of coaching: seeing the potential'. *Therapy Today* 21(2) (March), 27.

——(2012) 'Why we need to stop asking so many questions – and what to do instead'. *AICTP Journal* (Summer).

——(2013) 'The spectrum of independence'. Available at http://www.coachingforleaders.co.uk/2013/02/the-spectrum-of-independence-in-coaching/ (accessed 15 March 2013).

Atkinson, R. L., Atkinson, R. C., Smith, E. E., Bem, D. J. and Hilgard, E. R. (1990) *Introduction to psychology* (10th edn). San Diego, CA: Harcourt Brace Jovanovich.

Australian Census (2011) 'Census 2011'. Available at http://blog.id.com.au/2012/australian-census-2011/2011-census-australias-changing-multicultural-mix/ (accessed 23 May 2013).

Bachkirova, T. (2007) 'Role of coaching psychology in defining boundaries between counselling and coaching'. In S. Palmer and A. Whybrow (eds) *Handbook of coaching psychology: a guide for practitioners*. Hove: Routledge, pp. 351–66.

Bachkirova, T. and Cox, E. (2005) 'A bridge over troubled water, bringing together coaching and counselling'. *Counselling at Work* 2(9) Spring.

BACP (2008) 'What is counselling?'. Information sheet C2, British Association for Counselling and Psychotherapy, BACP House, Lutterworth.

——(2010) 'Attitudes to counselling and psychotherapy: key findings'. British Association for Counselling and Psychotherapy. Available at http://www.itsgoodtotalk.org.uk/assets/docs/Attitudes-to-Counselling-Psychotherapy-Key-Findings-BACP-June-2010_1331121114.pdf (accessed 22 May 2013).

——(2013a) 'Ethical framework for good practice in counselling and psychotherapy'. British Association for Counselling and Psychotherapy. Available at http://www.bacp.co.uk/ethical_framework/ (accessed 22 May 2013).

——(2013b) 'Policy and position statements'. British Association for Counselling and Psychotherapy, BACP House, Lutterworth.

Baker, S. (2013) 'Study to examine experienced practitioners' perceptions of the boundaries between Counselling and Coaching'. Unpublished research, University of Bedfordshire, Bedford.

Bambling, M. and King, R. (2000) 'The effect of clinical supervision on the development of counsellor competency'. *Psychotherapy in Australia* 6(4), 58–63.

Batmanghelidjh, C. (2009) 'How teenagers become violent'. *BACP Children and Young People Journal*, December 2009, 13–15.

Bayne, R., Jinks, G., Collard, P. and Horton, I. (2008) *The counsellor's handbook: a practical A–Z guide to integrative counselling and psychotherapy* (3rd edn). Cheltenham: Nelson Thornes.

Biswas-Diener, R. and Dean, B. (2007) *Positive psychology coaching: putting the science of happiness to work for your clients*. Hoboken, NJ: John Wiley & Sons.

Bluckert, P. (2005) 'The similarities and differences between coaching and therapy'. *Industrial and Commercial Training*, 37(2), 91–6.

——(2006) *Psychological dimensions of executive coaching*. Maidenhead: Open University Press and McGraw-Hill.

Bollas, C. (1987) *The shadow of the object: psychoanalysis of the unthought known*. New York: Columbia University Press.

Bordin, E. S. (1979) 'The generalizability of the psychoanalytic concept of the working alliance'. *Psychotherapy: Theory, Research & Practice.* 16(3), 252–60.

Bresser Consulting (2009) 'Global Coaching Survey 2008/2009: the state of coaching across the world'. Available at http://www.frank-bresser-consulting.com/globalcoachingsurvey.html (accessed 12 June 2013).

Bretherton, R. and Ørner, R: (2004) 'Positive psychology and psychotherapy: an existential approach'. In P.A Linley and S. Joseph (eds) *Positive psychology in practice* (pp.165–78). New Jersey: John Wiley & Sons.

Brown, P. (2013) 'The limbic leader'. *Coaching at Work Magazine* 8(2).

Brunning, H. (2006) *Executive coaching-systems-psychodynamic perspective* (2nd edn) London: Karnac Books.

Buber, M. (1937) *I and thou*. London: Continuum.

Buckley, A. (2007) 'The mental health boundary in relationship to coaching and other activities'. *International Journal of Evidence-based Coaching and Mentoring*, Special issue (summer) 17–23.

Bugenthal, J. (1978) *Psychotherapy and process: the fundamentals of an existential-humanist approach*. New York: McGraw Hill.

Burnett, R. (2009) 'Mindfulness in schools'. The Mindfulness in Schools project. Available at http://mindfulnessinschools.org/ (accessed 13 June 2013).

Camus, A. (1968) *Lyrical and critical essays*, trans. E. C. Kennedy. New York: Knopf.

Carroll, M. (2003) 'The new kid on the block'. *Counselling Psychology Journal* 14(10), 28–31.

Carroll, M. and Walton, M. (1997) *Handbook of counselling in organisations*. London, Sage.

Clance, P. R. and Imes, S. A. (1978) 'The impostor phenomenon among high achieving women: dynamics and therapeutic intervention'. *Psychotherapy Theory, Research and Practice* 15(3) 241–7.

Clutterbuck, D. (2010) 'Coaching reflection: the liberated coach'. *Coaching: An International Journal of Theory, Research and Practice* 3(1), 73–81.

——(2012) 'The liberated coach'. Available at http://www.davidclutterbuckpartnership. com (accessed 6 March 2013).

Coleman, J. and Hagell, A. (2007) *Adolescence, risk and resilience: against the odds.* Chichester: Wiley.

Cooper, M. (2003) *Existential therapies*. London: Sage.

Cooper, M. and McLeod, J. (2010) *Pluralistic counselling and psychotherapy*. London, Sage.

Corey, G. (1996) *Theory and practice of counselling and psychotherapy*. Albany, NY: Brooks/Cole.

Coutu, D. and Kauffman, K. (2009) 'What can coaches do for you?'. *Harvard Business Review, Research Report.* January.

Cox, E. (2011) 'Coaching philosophy, eclecticism and positivism, a commentary'. Annual Review of High Performance Coaching, special supplement of *The International Journal of Sports Science and Coaching* (January), 59–63.

——de Haan, E. (2008) *Relational coaching: journeys towards mastering one-to-one learning*. Chichester: John Wiley & Sons.

——(2008) 'I struggle and emerge: critical moments of experienced coaches'. American Psychological Association. *Consulting Psychology Journal: Practice and Research* 60(1), 106–31.

de Haan, E. and Blass, E. (2007) 'Using critical moments to learn about coaching'. *Training Journal* (April), 54–8.

de Shazer, S. and Berg, I. K. (1988) *Clues: investigating solutions in brief therapy*. London: W. W. Norton & Co.

Dexter, G. and Russel, J. (2008) *Challenging blank minds and sticky moments in counselling*. Preston: Winckley Press.

Dexter, J., Dexter, G. and Irving, J. (2011) *An introduction to coaching*. London: Sage.

Dryden, W. (2006) *Counselling in a nutshell*. London: Sage.

——(2007) *Dryden's handbook of individual therapy*. London: Sage.

DSM-IV-TR (2000) *Diagnostic and statistical manual of mental disorders* (4th edn). Arlington, VA: American Psychiatric Press.

Duncan, B., Miller, S. and Sparks, J. (2004) *The heroic client: a revolutionary way to improve effectiveness through client directed, outcome informed therapy* (2nd edn). New York: John Wiley & Sons.

Duncan, B., Miller, S., Wampold, B. and Hubble, M. (2009) *The heart and soul of change: delivering what works in therapy*. Washington, DC: American Psychological Association.

Duncan, B. L., Miller, S. D., Wampold, B. E. and Hubble, M. A. (2010) *The heart and soul of change: delivering what works* (2nd edn). Washington, DC: American Psychological Association.

Edgerton, N. and Palmer, S. (2005) 'SPACE: a psychological model for use within cognitive behavioural coaching, therapy and stress management'. *The Coaching Psychologist* 1(2), 25–31.

Egan, G. (1994) *The skilled helper: a problem management and opportunity-development approach to helping* (5th edn). Belmont, CA: Brookes/Cole.

——(2010) *The skilled helper: a problem management and opportunity-development approach to helping* (9th edn). Belmont, CA: Brooks/Cole.

——(2013) *The skilled helper: a problem management and opportunity-development approach to helping* (10th edn). International Edition, Belmont, CA: Brooks/Cole.

Erikson, E. (1950) *Childhood and society.* London: Norton.

——(1968) *Identity, youth and crisis.* New York: W. W. Norton.

Fairley, S. and Stout, C. (2003) *Getting started in personal and executive coaching.* New York: John Wiley & Sons.

Feltham, C. (1997) *What is counselling?* London: Sage.

——(2011) 'In conversation'. *TherapyToday.net* (online edition), 22(10). Available at http://www.therapytoday.net/article/show/2833/.

——(2011) 'What are counselling and psychotherapy?'. In C. Feltham and J. Horton (eds) *The Sage handbook of counselling and psychotherapy.* London: Sage.

Frankl, V. (1967) *Psychotherapy and existentialism.* New York: Washington Square Press.

——(1984) *Man's search for meaning.* New York: Washington Square Press.

Garcia, I., Vasiliou, C. and Penketh, K. (2007) 'Listen up: person-centred approaches to young people's mental health'. Mental Health Foundation. Available at http://www.righthere.org.uk/home/assets/pdf/Listen_Up.pdf (accessed 13 June 2013).

Garvey, B. (2004) 'The mentoring/counselling/coaching debate: call a rose by any other name and perhaps it's a bramble?' *Development and Learning in Organisations* 18(2), 6–8.

Garvey, B., Stokes, P. and Megginson, D. (2009) *Coaching and mentoring: theory and practice.* London: Sage.

Geldard, G. and Geldard, K. (2010) *Counselling adolescents: the proactive approach for young people* (3rd edn). London: Sage.

Gendlin, E. (1981) *Focusing.* New York: Bantam Books.

Grant, A. (2001) 'Towards a psychology of coaching'. Available at http://psychd.edu.au/psychcoach/Coaching_review_AMG2001.pdf (accessed 26 July 2010).

——(2003) 'The impact of life coaching on goal attainment, metacognition and mental health'. *Social Behavior and Personality,* 31(3) 253–64.

——(2006) 'A personal perspective on professional coaching and the development of coaching psychology'. *International Coaching Psychology Review* 1(1) (April).

——(2009) 'Coach or couch?' In D. Coutu and K. Kauffman (eds) *The realities of executive coaching* (HBR Research Report).

——(2011a) 'Coaching philosophy, eclecticism and positivism: a commentary'. Annual review of high performance coaching, special supplement of *The International Journal of Sports Science and Coaching* (January), 33–8.

——(2011b) 'Developing an agenda for teaching coaching psychology'. *International Coaching Psychology Review* 6(1) (March).

Grove, D. (1991) *Resolving traumatic memories.* New York: Irvington Publishers.

Hanaway, M. (2012) 'Conflict coaching using an existential approach'. In E. van Deurzen and M. Hanaway (eds) *Existential perspectives on coaching.* Basingstoke: Palgrave Macmillan.

Hart, V. (2001) 'Coaching versus therapy: a perspective'. *Consulting Psychology Journal: Practice and Research* 53(4) (Fall) 229.

Hayes, S. C., Villate, M., Levin, M. and Hildebrandt, M. (2011) 'Open, aware and active: contextual approaches as an emerging trend in the behavioural and cognitive therapies'. *Annual Review of Clinical Psychology* 7, 141–68.

Heidegger, M. (1962) *Being and time,* trans. J. Macquarie and E. Robinson. New York: Basic Books.

Hoffmann, S. G. (2011) *An introduction to modern cbt: psychological solutions to mental health problems.* Oxford: Wiley-Blackwell.

Horne, A. (2001) 'Sexuality in childhood and adolescence'. In C. Harding (ed.) *Sexuality: Psychoanalytic Perspectives*. Hove: Brunner-Routledge.

Horton, I. (2012) 'Integration'. In C. Feltham and I. Horton (eds) *The Sage handbook of counselling and psychotherapy*. London: Sage.

Hubble, M. A. and Miller, S. D. (2004) 'The client: psychotherapy's missing link for promoting a positive psychology'. In P. A. Linley and S. Joseph *Positive psychology in practice*. Hoboken, NJ: Wiley.

Hubble, M. A., Duncan, B. L. and Miller, S. D. (1999) 'Directing attention to what works'. In M. A. Hubble, B. D. Duncan and S. D. Miller (eds) *The heart and soul of change*. Washington, DC: American Psychological Association, pp. 407–47.

Husserl, E. (1977 [1925]) *Phenomenological psychology*. The Hague: Martinus Nijhoff.

——(1986) *Phänomenologie der Lebenswelt*. Stuttgart: Reclam.

Ihde, D. (1986) *Experimental phenomenology: an introduction*. Albany, NY: State University of New York Press.

ICF (2007) 'ICF global coaching study'. International Coach federation. Available at http://www.coachfederation.org/articles/index.cfm?action=view&articleID=50&menu ID=24 (accessed 15 February 2013).

Jacob, Y. U. (2011) 'Therapy through the back-door: the call for integrative approaches to one-to-one talking practices and existential coaching as a possible framework'. Unpublished manuscript. Available at http://www.existentialcoaching.net/resources/ Jacob2011-Therapy_through_the_Backdoor.doc (accessed 4 March 2013).

——(2012) 'Covering the whole spectrum of human experience: positive psychology meets existentialism in the coaching room'. Unpublished manuscript. Available at http://www.existentialcoaching.net/resources/Jacob2012-Positive_Existential_ Coaching.doc (accessed 4 March 2013).

Jacobs, Y. (2012) 'Solution focused coaching and solution focused therapy'. *AICTP Journal* 1 (autumn), 31–2.

Jarvis, J., Lane, D. A. and Fillery-Travis, A. (2006) *The case for coaching: making evidenced-based decisions on coaching*. London: CIPD.

Jaspers, K. (1971) *Philosophy of existence*, trans. R. F. Grabau. Oxford: Blackwell.

Jinks, D. (2010) 'An exploration into the thoughts and perceptions of four coaches around the concept of "personal consultancy"'. Unpublished MSc dissertation, University of Hull.

Jinks, D. and Dexter, J. (2012) 'What do you really want: an examination of the pursuit of goal setting in coaching'. *International Journal of Evidence-based Coaching and Mentoring* 10(2) 100–110.

Jinks, D. and Popovic, N. (2011) 'Personal consultancy'. *Therapy Today* 22(10) 17–20.

Jopling, A. (2007) 'The fuzzy space: exploring the experience of the space between psychotherapy and executive coaching'. Unpublished MSc dissertation, New School of Psychotherapy and Counselling, London. Available at http://de.scribd.com/ doc/17168879/Research-Thesis-The-Fuzzy-Space-Between-Psychotherapy-and-Executive-Coaching (accessed 4 March 2013).

——(2012) 'Coaching leaders from an existential perspective'. In E. van Deurzen and M. Hanaway (eds) *Existential perspectives on coaching*. Basingstoke: Palgrave Macmillan.

Joseph, S. (2006) 'Person-centred coaching psychology: a meta-theoretical perspective'. *International Coaching Psychology Review* 1(1) (April) 47–54.

Kabat-Zinn, J. (2004) *Wherever you go, there you are: mindfulness meditation for everyday life*, London: Piatkus.

——(2012) *Mindfulness for beginners*. Boulder, CO: Sounds True inc.

Kampa-Kokesch, S. and Anderson, M. Z. (2001) 'Executive coaching: a comprehensive review of the literature'. *Consulting Psychology Journal* 53, 205–28.

Kellaway, L. (2005) *Who moved my Blackberry?* London: Penguin.

Kenrick, J. and Lee, S. (2010) *A proven early intervention model: the evidence for the effectiveness of Youth Information Advice Counselling and Support Services (YIACS)*. London: Youth Access.

Kets de Vries, M. F. R (2007) 'Are you feeling mad, bad, sad or glad?'. INSEAD Faculty and Research Working Paper. Available at http://www.insead.edu/facultyresearch/ research/doc.cfm?did=18768 (accessed 22 May 2013).

——(2008) 'Leadership coaching and organizational transformation: effectiveness in a world of paradox?'. INSEAD Faculty and Research Working Paper. Available at http:// www.insead.edu/facultyresearch/research/doc.cfm?did=38545 (accessed 22 May 2013).

Kets de Vries, M. F. R., Korotov, K. and Florent-Treacy, E. (2007) *Coach and couch: the psychology of making better leaders*. London: Basingstoke: Palgrave Macmillan.

Kierkegaard, S. (1843) *Fear and trembling*, trans. Alastair Hannay. New York: Penguin.

Kilburg, R. R.(2009) *Executive coaching: developing managerial wisdom in a world of chaos* (5th edn) Washington DC: American Psychological Association.

Kline, N. (1998) *Time to think: listening to ignite the human mind*. London: Cassell Illustrated.

LeBon, T. and Arnaud, D. (2012) 'Existential coaching and major life decisions'. In E. van Deurzen and M. Hanaway (eds) *Existential perspectives on coaching*. Basingstoke: Palgrave Macmillan.

Leonard, L. (2011) *The relationship between Navajo adolescents' knowledge and attitude of Navajo culture and their self-esteem and resilience*. Ann Arbour, MI: Proquest UMI.

Lewis, J. (2012) 'Using existential integrated coaching in the workplace'. In E. van Deurzen and M. Hanaway (eds) *Existential perspectives on coaching*. Basingstoke: Palgrave Macmillan.

Lewis, T., Amini, F. and Lannon, R. (2001) *A general theory of love*. New York: Vintage Books.

Linley, P. A. and Harrington, S. (2007) 'Playing to your strengths'. *Psychologist*, 19, 86–9.

McLeod, J. (1998) *An introduction to counselling* (2nd edn). Buckingham: Open University Press.

——(2009) *An introduction to counselling* (4th edn). Milton Keynes: Open University Press.

McMahon, G. and Wilson, C. (2006) 'What's the difference?'. *Training Journal*, September, 54–7.

Malan, D. H. (1979) *Individual psychotherapy and the science of psychodynamics*. New York, Butterworth.

Martin, C. (2001) *The life coaching handbook*. Carmarthen: Crown House.

Maxwell, A. (2009a) 'How do business coaches experience the boundary between coaching and therapy/counselling?'. *Coaching: An International Journal of Theory, Research and Practice*, 2(2) 149–62.

——(2009b) 'The co-created boundary: negotiating the limits of coaching', *International Journal of Evidenced-based Coaching and Mentoring*, Special issue no. 3 (November), 82–94.

Merleau-Ponty, M. (1962) *The phenomenology of perception*. London: Routledge.

Miller, S. D., Duncan, B. L. and Hubble, M. A. (2004) 'Beyond integration: triumph of outcome over process in clinical practice'. *Psychotherapy in Australia*, 10(2) 2–19.

Milner, J. and Bateman, J. (2011) *Working with children and teenagers using solution-focused approaches: enabling children to overcome challenges and achieve their potential*. London: Jessica Kingsley.

Mirea, D. (2012) 'Cognitive behavioural coaching: friend or foe for the existential coach?'. In E. van Deurzen and M. Hanaway (eds) *Existential perspectives on coaching*. Basingstoke: Palgrave Macmillan.

Moja-Strasser, L. (1996) 'The phenomenology of listening and the importance of silence'. *Journal of the Society for Existential Analysis* 7(1), 90–102.

Mumby, C. (2011) 'Working at the boundary'. *BACP Children and Young People Journal* (December).

Nanda, J. (2012) 'Why mindfulness-based existential coaching?'. In E. van Deurzen and M. Hanaway (eds) *Existential perspectives on coaching*. Basingstoke: Palgrave Macmillan.

Neenan, M. and Dryden, W. (2000) *Essential rational emotive behaviour therapy*. London: Whurr.

Nurco, D. N., Hanlon, T. E., O'Grady, K. E. and Kinlock, T. W. (1997) 'The association of early risk factors to opiate addiction and psychological adjustment'. *Criminal Behaviour and Mental Health* 7, 213–28.

O'Connell, B. (1998) *Solution-focused therapy*. London: Sage Publications.

Palmer, S. (2011) 'Coaching philosophy, eclecticism and positivisim: a commentary'. Annual Review of High Performance Coaching, special supplement of *The International Journal of Sports Science and Coaching* (January), 29–32.

——(2012) 'Multimodal therapy'. In C. Feltham and I. Horton (eds) *The Sage handbook of counselling and psychotherapy* (3rd edn). London: Sage, pp. 361–7.

Palmer, S. and Whybrow, A. (2006) 'The proposal to establish a special group in coaching psychology'. *The Coaching Psychologist* 1, 5–12.

Passmore, J. (2009) *Diversity in coaching: working with gender, culture, race and age*. London: Kogan Page.

——(2007) 'An Integrative model for executive coaching'. *Consulting Psychology Journal: Practice and Research* (March), 68–78. Available at http://www.langleygroup. com.au/images/Passmore---2007---An-integrative-model-for-executive-coaching.pdf (accessed 22 May 2013).

Passmore, J. and Law, H. (2009) 'Cross-cultural and diversity coaching'. In Passmore, J. (ed) (2009) *Diversity in coaching: working with gender, culture, race and age*. London: Kogan Page.

Peltier, B. (2001) *The psychology of executive coaching*. Hove and New York: Routledge.

——(2010) *The psychology of executive coaching* (2nd edn). Hove and New York: Routledge.

Popovic, N. (2005) *Personal synthesis*. London: PWBC.

Popovic, N. and Boniwell, I. (2007) 'Personal consultancy: an integrative approach to one-to-one talking practices'. *International Journal of Evidence-based Coaching and Mentoring* 5 (Special issue), 24–9.

Price, J. (2009) 'The coaching/therapy boundary in organisational coaching'. *Coaching: An International Journal of Theory, Research and Practice*, 2(2) (September) 135–48.

Pringle, D. (2012) 'Existential coaching using the MBTI® and FIRO-B® psychometric assessments'. In E. van Deurzen and M. Hanaway (eds) *Existential perspectives on coaching*. Basingstoke: Palgrave Macmillan.

Prochaska, J, O. (2004) 'How do people change and how can we change to help many more people?'. In Hubble, M. A., Duncan, B. L. and Miller, S. D. (eds) *The heart and soul of change: what works in therapy*. Washington, DC: American Psychological Association, pp. 227–55.

Pullinger, D. (2012) 'Career development as a life changing event'. In E. van Deurzen and M. Hanaway (eds) *Existential perspectives on coaching*. Basingstoke: Palgrave Macmillan.

Qian, M., Smith, C. W., Chen, Z. and Xia, G. (2001) 'Psychotherapy in China: a review of its history and contemporary directions'. *International Journal of Mental Health* 30(4) 49–68.

Reed, J. (2012) 'Existential coaching first, neuro-linguistic programming second'. In E. van Deurzen and M. Hanaway (eds) *Existential perspectives on coaching*. Basingstoke: Palgrave Macmillan.

Rock, D. and Page, L. J. (2009) *Coaching with the brain in mind: foundations for practice*. Hoboken, NJ: Wiley.

Rogers, C. R. R. (1999) *A therapist's view of psychotherapy: on becoming a person*. London: Constable.

——(2003) *Client-centred therapy*. London: Constable.

——(2004) *A therapist's view of psychotherapy: on becoming a person*. London: Constable.

Rogers, J. (2008) *Coaching skills: a handbook*. Milton Keynes: Open University Press.

Russell, J. and Dexter, G. (2008) 'Differentiation of coaching'. PGDip/MSc Personal and Corporate Coaching handout, University of Hull.

Russell, J. and Jinks, D. (2011) 'Training and the road to professionalisation: some introductory questions'. Available at http://ac.somcom.co.uk/media/uploads/publications/ACB1104.pdf (accessed 15 March 2013).

Ryan, R. M. and Deci, E. L. (2000) 'Self-determination theory and the facilitation of intrinsic motivation, and well-being'. *American Psychologist*, 55(1) 68–78.

Sanderson, C. (2008) *Counselling adult survivors of child sexual abuse* (3rd edn). London: Jessica Kingsley.

Sartre, J.-P. (1956 [1943]) *Being and nothingness: an essay on phenomenological ontology*, trans. H. Barnes. New York: Philosophical Library.

——(1973 [1944]). *No Exit*. New York: Vintage Books.

Seligman, M. E. P. and Csikszentmihalyi, M. (2000) 'Positive psychology: an introduction'. *American Psychologist*, 55, 5–14.

Sercombe, H. (2010) 'Teenage brains'. *BACP Children and Young People Journal* (March).

Siegel, D. J. and Bryson, T. P. (2012) *The whole-brain child: 12 proven strategies to nurture your child's developing mind*. London: Robinson.

Smith, V. J. (2011) 'It's the relationship that matters: a qualitative analysis of the role of the student/tutor relationship in counselling training'. (Unpublished) Health, Wellness and Society Inaugural International Conference, 20–22 January, University of California, Berkeley, CA.

Social Exclusion Unit (2005) 'Transitions: young adults with complex needs'. A Social Exclusion Unit final report, London: Office of the Deputy Prime Minister.

Spinelli, E. (1997) *Tales of un-knowing: therapeutic encounters from an existential perspective.* London: Duckworth.

——(2005) 'Existential coaching'. Available at http://www.plexworld.com/exist01.html (accessed 4 March 2013).

——(2008) 'Coaching and therapy: similarities and divergences'. *International Coaching Psychology Review* 3(3) 241–9.

——(2010) 'Coaching and therapy: similarities and divergences'. *Psychotherapy in Australia* [online] 17(1) (November) 52–8.

Stober, D. R. and Grant, A. M. (2006a) *Evidence-based coaching handbook: putting best practices to work for your client.* Hoboken, NJ: John Wiley & Sons.

Stober, D. and Grant, A. M. (2006b) 'Toward a contextual approach to coaching models'. In D. Stober and A. M. Grant (eds) *Evidence-based coaching handbook,* New York: Wiley.

Strasser, F. and Strasser, A. (1997) *Existential time-limited therapy: the wheel of existence.* London: Wiley.

Summerfield, J. (2002) 'Walking the thin line: coaching or counselling?' *Training Journal* (November) 36–9.

——(2006) 'Do we coach or do we counsel? Thoughts on the "emotional life" of a coaching session'. *The Coaching Psychologist* 2(1) May.

Taylor, C. (2007) 'Counsellor: job description and activities'. Available at http://www.prospects.ac.uk/cms/ShowPage/Home_page/Explore_types_of_jobs/Types_of_Job/p!e ipaL?state=showocc&idno=77&pageno=1 (accessed 5 February 2008).

Tillich, P. (1952) *The courage to be.* Newhaven, CT: Yale University Press.

Toates, F. (2004) 'Motivation'. In Open University (eds) *Emotions and mind,* Course SD226 Biological Psychology: exploring the brain, Science Level 2, Book 6. Milton Keynes: Open University, p. 21.

Townsend-Handscomb, D. (2013) 'How often do coaches encounter coachees with mental health issues?'. *The UK Bulletin of the Association for Coaching,* 11 (Winter) 21–5.

van de Loo, E. (2007) 'The art of listening'. In Kets de Vries, M. F. R., Korotov, K. and Florent-Treacy, E. (eds) *Coach and couch: the psychology of making better leaders.* Basingstoke: Palgrave Macmillan

van Deurzen, E. (1997) *Existential dimensions of psychotherapy.* London: Routledge.

——(2009) *Psychotherapy and the quest for happiness.* London: Sage.

——(2012) 'The existential ideology and framework for coaching'. In E. van Deurzen and M. Hanaway (eds) *Existential perspectives on coaching.* Basingstoke: Palgrave Macmillan.

van Deurzen, E. and Adams, M. (2011) *Skills in existential counselling and psychotherapy,* Sage.

van Deurzen, E. and Hanaway, M. (2012) *Existential perspectives on coaching.* Basingstoke: Palgrave Macmillan.

van Deurzen, E. and Young, S. (2009) *Existential perspectives on supervision: Widening the horizon of psychotherapy and counselling.* Basingstoke and New York: Palgrave Macmillan.

Vaughan Smith, J. (2007) *Therapist into coach.* Maidenhead: Open University Press and McGraw-Hill Education.

Walker, Y. (1993) 'Aboriginal family issues', Australian Institute of Family Studies. Available at http://www.aifs.gov.au/institute/pubs/fm1/fm35yw.html (accessed 20 November 2012).

Warnecke, T. (2010) 'Working as a psychotherapist in Europe: the psychotherapist'. *The Journal of the UK Council of Psychotherapists* 47 (winter), 39–40.

Weare, K. (2012) 'Evidence for the impact of mindfulness on children and young people'. The Mindfulness in Schools Project in association with Mood Disorders Centre. Available at http://mindfulnessinschools.org/ (accessed 13 June 2013).

Westen, D., Novotny, C. M. and Thompson-Brenner, H. (2004) 'The empirical status of empirically supported psychotherapies: assumptions, findings, and reporting in controlled clinical trials'. *Psychological Bulletin*, 130, 631–63.

White, N. (2008) *A brief history of happiness.* Oxford: Blackwell.

White, M. and Epston, D. (1990) *Narrative means to therapeutic ends.* London: W. W. Norton & Co.

Whitmore, J. (1997) *Need, greed and freedom.* Shaftsbury: Element Books.

Williams, D. I. and Irving, J. A. (2001) 'Coaching: an unregulated, unstructured and (potentially) unethical process'. *The Occupational Psychologist* 42.

Williams, P. (2003) 'The potential perils of personal issues in coaching – the continuing debate: therapy or coaching? What every coach should know'. *International Journal of Coaching in Organisations* 2(2) 21–30.

Wingfield, R. (2008) *Teenage killings: loss, trauma and abandonment in the histories of young people in trouble.* London: The Bowlby Centre.

Wong, P. T. P. (2009) 'Positive existential psychology'. In S. Lopez (ed.) *Encyclopedia.* Oxford: Blackwell.

——(2010) 'What is existential positive psychology?'. *International Journal of Existential Psychology and Psychotherapy* 3, 1–10.

Yalom, I. (1980) *Existential psychotherapy.* New York: Basic Books.

Yalom, I. D. (2009) *The gift of therapy: An open letter to a new generation of therapists and their patients.* New York: Harper Perennial.

Young, S. (2000) 'Existential counselling and psychotherapy'. In S. Palmer (ed.) *Introduction to counselling and psychotherapy.* London: Sage.

Young-Eisendrath, P. (2003) 'Response to Lazarus'. *Psychological Inquiry*, 14(2) 110–72.

Index

Note: 'f' after a page number indicates a figure.

Printed in Great Britain
by Amazon

49504599R00147